KOREA'S OLYMPIC ICON

Kim Un-yong's Resolute Odyssey

Korea's Olympic Icon
Kim Un-yong's Resolute Odyssey

Copyright © 2019 by David Miller
All Rights Reserved.

No part of this book may be reproduced or utilized in any form or by any means without the written permission of the publisher.

Published in 2019 by Seoul Selection U.S.A., Inc.
4199 Campus Drive, Suite 550, Irvine, CA 92612

Phone: 949-509-6584 / Seoul office: 82-2-734-9567
Fax: 949-509-6599 / Seoul office: 82-2-734-9562
E-mail: hankinseoul@gmail.com
Website: www.seoulselection.com

ISBN: 978-1-62412-124-1 52500
Library of Congress Control Number: 2019942452

Printed in the Republic of Korea

KOREA'S OLYMPIC ICON

Kim Un-yong's Resolute Odyssey

BY DAVID MILLER

Seoul Selection

Innovative Partnership. IOC president Samaranch (left) regards Kim Un-yong as strategic successor.

In pursuit of truth surrounding the dramatic, often exhilarating life of Kim Un-yong (although knowing him personally through four decades), I am immensely indebted for much background, both documentary and personal, to Dr. Kim's elder daughter Helen, a solicitor resident in London. Helen's quest to uphold her father's honour, in homeland South Korea and across the sporting world, has itself been privately epic and emotionally profound, while at the same time attentively scrupulous in relation to fact: to the indelible gifts and impact of his energy and intuition upon contemporary Korean history and the Olympic Movement. While I am familiar first-hand with much of Dr. Kim's career, Helen has granted deeper insight. Yet there remain undeclared details, of actions and words by those closely implicated in Dr. Kim's switchback odyssey, which she might come to expose if and when she recounts her own involvement alongside her father's exceptional, ultimately persecuted journey: she being restrained by her sensitivity to Christian convictions yet simultaneously motivated by unappeased filial loyalty and quest for justice. It is to Helen, in part, that this book is dedicated, her commitment to upholding her father's reputation as resolute as his in promoting his nation's prestige.

There are many other significant contributors, beginning with IOC Members, and especially Ser Miang Ng and Vitaly Smirnov, respective contributors of the Foreword and Preface, with their affectionate and grateful recollections of a remarkable colleague. Alongside with anecdotal appreciation are Philip Coles (Australia), Francisco Elizalde (Philippines), Alex Gilady (Israel), Kevan Gosper (Australia), Gerhard Heiberg (Norway), Paul Henderson (Canada), Nat Indrapana (Indonesia), Arne Ljungqvist (Sweden), Craig Reedie (UK), Ryu Seung-min (South

Korea), Walter Troeger (Germany) and Ching Kuo Wu (Taipei).

Perceptive officials recognising Dr. Kim's many talents and contributions have included Francois Carrard (Switzerland), IOC Director-General; Francoise Zweifel (Switzerland), IOC Secretary-General; Fekrou Kidane (Ethiopia), Samaranch's aide-de-camp; Richard Palmer (UK), NOC consultant; Manolo Romero (Spain), president, International Sports Broadcasting; Jean-Claude Schupp (France), GAISF secretary-general; John Boulter (UK) and Jon Tibbs (UK), commercial agents; and Karl-Heinz Huba (Germany) and Morley Myers (UK), international journalists for *Sport Intern* and *UPI*, respectively. I am grateful for the inclusion of extracts from Christopher Hill's *Olympic Politics*; for an abridged reproduction of Dr. Kim's interview with Italy's taekwondo journal; and for analysis from Professor Arne Ljungqvist's *Doping Nemesis*.

Specialists aware of Dr. Kim's creative administration in the establishment of taekwondo as Olympic sport have included Michal Buchel, CEO, International Sambo Federation; General Ahmed Fouly, vice-president, African Taekwondo Union; Lisa Lents, Danish referee, WTF; Shinsuke Sano, *Sankei Shimbun*, Japan; Yosuke Fujiwara, Japanese Olympic Committee; Ana Lopez, Spanish referee, World Taekwondo; Piao Meizi, Shanghai University of Sport; Jurapas Pitaksethakarn, Pinco World Group; Seyed Mohammad Pouledgar, president, Iran Taekwondo Federation; Nadia Sobhi, secretary-general, African Taekwondo Union; Grandmaster Yonten Tharchen, secretary-general, Bhutan Taekwondo Federation; and Dr. George Vitale, Original Taekwondo Club, Brooklyn, USA.

A host of Koreans around the world have collaborated in their recognition of Dr. Kim's tireless contributions to South Korea's international prestige: Haley Cha, anchor, YTN; Choi Jae-keun, secretary-general, World Martial Arts; Grandmaster Hong Sung-chon, chairman of the board, Kukkiwon; Kim Jung-heun, secretary-general, Korea Taekwondo Promotion Foundation (TPF); Kim Seong-jo, president, Korea National Sports University; Lee Dong-sup, president, National Assembly Taekwondo Federation; Lee Kee-heung, president, Korean Sport and Olympic Committee (KSOC); Lee Kyu-seok, president, Asian Taekwondo Union; Lee Seung-hyung, world taekwondo champion; Lee Si-jong, president, World Martial Arts; Dr. Ken Min, martial arts director, Hearst Gymnasium, University of Berkeley, CA, USA; Oh Hyun-deuk, president, Kukkiwon; Professor Cindy Park of Youngsan University, Yangsan, Gyeongsangnam-do; Park Young-ok, president, Korea Institute of Sports Science; Seo Hyun-suk, secretary-general, Kimunyong Sport Committee (KUYSC); Seo Jung-jin, CEO, Celltrion, Incheon; and Song Chun-wang, International Sports Relations Foundation.

My late wife Marita supportively endured my travelling absences, entertaining IOC officials in London and occasionally attending Asian conferences. My two typists, Susan Buck and Karen Game, have patiently delivered over two protracted years.

My Friend and Colleague Dr. Kim Un-yong

Ng Ser Miang, IOC Executive Board Member
Honorary Chairman, Kukkiwon

Sometime in early 2008, Dr. Kim Un-yong spoke to me about a series of articles he would be contributing to the Korean media, recounting his 30 years of service to the Olympic Movement and 40 years of service to taekwondo. These articles capture important moments of his rich and fulfilling life and will now serve as important documents for those who are interested in his life's work.

Without a doubt, Dr. Kim was the most influential and innovative world sports leader from Asia during his time.

For sports in South Korea, his vision and strategy to develop a driven and focused sports policy and strategy became the cornerstone for the rapid rise of Korean sports. His push for the national sports institute and national training centres for Korean athletes have made South Korea a world sport powerhouse. South Korean athletes have consistently done well at the Summer and Winter Olympic Games, Asian Games and world championships – a testament to his vision and prominent part of his legacy.

When I was appointed Chairman of the Singapore Sports Council in 1991, I went to visit Dr. Kim to learn about South Korea's sporting success. He was open, generous and frank with his advice. He personally took me around to see the developments and shared with me his future plans. That was the beginning of our friendship, continuing to be close colleagues ever since, exchanging ideas at Olympic and international sports events in Seoul and in Singapore. Our East Asian culture and values were our bond and our mutual respect and shared passion for the Olympic Movement the foundation of our friendship.

Dr. Kim's vision gave birth to the Kukkiwon in 1972 and the World Taekwondo Federation in 1973. Through his uniting of the fragmented taekwondo federations in South Korea and transformation of ancient taekwondo into a competitive sport with spectator appeal and internationalising the sport, taekwondo became his gift to the world. With his influence at the IOC and his strong lobbying, taekwondo became an Olympic Sport as of the 2000 Sydney Olympic Games. The values, the discipline and the respect continue to distinguish Taekwondo as a sport with a difference.

Many have justly credited Dr. Kim with the success of the Seoul Olympic Games and with bringing taekwondo to the world. They have recognised his contributions to the Olympic Movement through his many years of service. There are also those who discredit him and emphasise the charges brought against him by his own government in 2003. Dr. Kim always maintained his innocence and blamed the politics of the day for bringing about his predicaments.

In the fateful IOC Session in Prague in July 2003, he made a comeback to the IOC Executive Board, winning the election to serve as Vice-president. In the same Session, Pyeongchang had lost to Vancouver two days earlier by 53 votes to 56 in its bid for the 2010 Winter Olympic Games. Dr. Kim was accused by his opponents of putting self-interest ahead of his nation and was subsequently accused of 'corruption' and jailed in Seoul. He, however, believed that without his return to the IOC Executive Board, Pyeongchang – which was relatively unknown at the time – could not have won on its own.

Even in his old age, he continued to protest his innocence and fought to clear his name. I could see that when we were out together in Seoul, he received the attention and respect of the common people – something he was always very proud of. At the age of 85, he continued contributing to the promotion of taekwondo with the establishment of an international competition in his name. Mere weeks ahead of the launch of his final

Ng Ser Miang, IOC Executive Board Member (Singapore), Kukkiwon Honourary Chairman, and intimate link in Kim Un-yong's Asian expansion

project, he suddenly passed away. The Kimunyong Cup International Open Taekwondo Championship was launched shortly after his unexpected death in October 2017 and has been a huge success.

Dr. Kim treasured and cherished friendship. I heard many stories from his friends from all over the world of his loyalty and generosity. I have also heard from several sources that he spent huge amounts of his personal fortune to found the Kukkiwon and World Taekwondo Federation and to support sports. He could be tough and was no pushover, but no one could fault him for his patriotism and his passion and devotion to taekwondo and the Olympic Movement. He was also a family man who loved his wife and children dearly and continued to worry over them until his last days.

His lifelong contributions and experiences should be taken in context with the time and the world that he lived in. In all aspects, he lived a remarkable life during a time when the East was just beginning to emerge. I am sure that David Miller's book will be an exciting story of the man and his memorable life.

Kim Un-yong: Exceptional Vision, Priceless Legacy

Vitaly Smirnov, IOC Member, USSR/Russia, 1971–2018

We may list numerous positions that Dr. Kim Un-yong held within the international sports community and also in his native country, yet this is insufficient for acknowledgement of the magnitude of his personality and character.

Organising and hosting the Olympic Games in Seoul in 1988 was his idea of a lifetime. This was a momentous challenge. One need only recall the previous Olympic Games on the way to Seoul '88: two boycotts in a row at Moscow '80 and Los Angeles '84; Montreal '76 taking place without Africa; and, of course, the infamous tragedy at Munich '72. Staging successful Olympics at a full scale in 1988 was vitally important for the Olympic Movement. And this came to pass, thanks to the main initiative and creator of the spirit of the Games: Kim Un-yong.

As for the Soviet Union, our athletes on the one hand eagerly awaited the Games in Seoul after the boycott of Los Angeles. On the other hand, the political situation was exceedingly difficult. Our country did not have diplomatic relations with South Korea. It was even considered an enemy country, with almost no contact existing between us. We had to rely on mediators from third countries to discuss many matters with the Games' administrators. Remarkably, Kim Un-yong managed to make even this fraught process effective.

Kim Un-yong had an exceptional vision for 1988. Apart from sports competitions, he considered it vitally important to have a prominent cultural festival. IOC President Juan Antonio Samaranch used to say, "Real Olympism is sports and culture together." The history and art of South Korea were powerfully presented at both the Opening and Closing Cer-

Kim Un-yong in Red Square with Soviet IOC Member Vitaly Smirnov in 1985, consolidating the Cold War bridge for the Seoul Games collaboration.

emonies, and also during the Games as a whole. Numerous guests of the country enjoyed the chance to appreciate the unique cultural heritage of Koreans; the cultural legacy of the Seoul Olympics was truly priceless.

Kim Un-yong was also the head of the General Assembly of International Sports Federations. In this capacity he managed to make the Asian Games equally important alongside the Games of African and American continents. All taekwondo lovers should also take note of the extended efforts that Kim Un-yong made to introduce this sport to the Olympic Programme.

Thanks to all of this, he earned the right to launch his candidature at the IOC Presidential election in Moscow in 2001 – a challenge in breach of the tradition of almost every IOC President before then having come from Europe.

Personally, I consider Kim Un-yong to have been my friend. We were truly close and many times visited each other together with our families. I feel warmth and happiness remembering those times. Kim was extraordinary both in the professional field and as a person.

Coincidentally, his daughter Hae-jung is a celebrated concert pianist, a graduate of the Juilliard School of Music in New York. I remember the time that she first came to Moscow to take part in the Tchaikovsky Piano Competition. There were no Korean missions or diplomats in Russia at the time, and she was a very young teenaged girl alone in the huge city. Because of that, we suggested that during her preparation time and the contest itself, she could live with our family. For several weeks we were privileged to enjoy her engaging company and beautiful music.

My admiration endures for the lasting legacy that Kim Un-yong created for the development of sports in his own country and for the Olympic Movement worldwide. He will be long remembered. I welcome this biography by David Miller, a close observer of Korean sport and experienced author who is widely respected for his official history of the IOC and the Olympic Games.

CHAPTER 1

—

EMERGENT PHENOMENON

There is no limit to what a man can do or where he can go
if he doesn't mind who gets the credit.

Ronald Reagan

Global consciousness of the Korean Peninsula, long an ancient and lit-tle-known Asian home of civilisation, emerged only in the second half of the twentieth century. The Koreans are proud, introspective people. Neolithic archaeological evidence indicates that during the third millennium BC, nomadic Mongoloid invaders moved into the peninsula from central Asia and were originators of the Korean language. The top-down, authoritarian belief system of Confucianism, introduced by the Chinese in the first century BC – alongside Buddhism, over which it had become dominant by the fourth century AD – remains a conspicuous national characterisation, notwithstanding the advent of Christian Catholicism during the 17th century. In the 20th century, this fundamental element of formal discipline has – following an occupation by Japan that terminated at the end of World War II – generated a nation of exceptional social, cultural and industrial organisation, within which Kim Un-yong was to become an iconic global leader of Olympic sport. Yet arrival onto the world stage as a powerhouse of Eastern Asia has been accompanied by a regime of rare, total judicial extremity which contravenes most aspects of morality and human rights; leaving aside the peninsula's traumatic political division into North and South, with a ferocious dictatorship arbitrarily established north of the 38th parallel in the Democratic People's Republic of Korea at the conclusion of the Korean War of 1950–53.

In South Korea there now exists a life of bizarre contradictions: in-toxicating geophysical and cultural beauty (the proverbial magic of the Orient), of lyrical artistic creativity, of dominant and expanding commerce and technological enterprise and, not least, of sporting excellence, all alongside subliminal emotions of jealousy and rampant political vindictiveness. Perplexed foreigners view Korea as a nation where success is likely to be ultimately penalised within a judicial convention in which the emperor (president) is a benevolent patriarch, assisted by officials ranked in descending order – a flawed principle of officialdom always believing itself to be correct irrespective of facts.

The mainspring for my story is the remarkable, ultimately tortured yet resilient career of Kim Un-yong, a far-sighted, innovative and adroit administrator whose inspiration helped raise South Korea suddenly from comparative obscurity to international prominence, seated on level terms in a triangular East Asian power bloc alongside China and Japan – though admittedly in its early days as a developing economy ruled by semi-democratic military government riding pillion on American nuclear capability.

Fully to appreciate the exceptional, multiple achievements of Kim Un-yong, both national and global, it is necessary to understand the idiosyncrasies of the International Olympic Committee, that self-electing organisation responsible for conducting mankind's largest social, would-be humanitarian biennial festival. This Lausanne-based, intendedly benevolent, wishfully ideological non-profit body, governed by a Charter extolling its exclusion of any prejudice, has two faces. Foremost, it gathers nations across the globe, devoid of their often contentious political affiliations, in sporting friendship and competition within an ethic of taking part, as opposed simply to winning.

One of the most heart-warming anecdotes of my six decades' association with the Olympic Movement involved Mikhail Bobrov, modern pentathlon coach of the Soviet Union at Rome's Olympic Games in 1960. Twenty years earlier, as a 17-year-old accomplished skier and mountaineer, Bobrov had performed the perilous job of volunteer steeplejack, camouflaging golden church roofs which German artillery exploited as range-finders in the 900-day siege of Saint Petersburg (then Leningrad).

Several of his colleagues died of hunger during this tortuous manoeuvre, during which they were often strafed by fighter planes. While attending a gathering in St. Peter's Square in Rome to listen to an address by the Pope, Bobrov's eye caught in recognition that of someone close by, of whose identity he was yet uncertain. Days later, they met coincidentally again as spectators at the football final. They wept in silent joy and embraced as they walked back to the Village. Lt. Otto Bauer, coach to the combined East-West Germany team, was the lone survivor of a mountain rifle conflict between Bobrov's Soviet platoon and German ski troops in the Caucusus, whom Bobrov had taken wounded by sled for medical aid and recovery. It was an epic reunion, the epitome of Baron de Coubertin's revived, historic Olympic spirit.

Yet within the IOC's ideological context – speaking of administrators as opposed to participant athletes – there exist among the 100 or so IOC Members, as Kim was to discover, not merely enduring goodwill and harmony but other reflections of life's inevitable emotions: elements of personal ambition, envy, nationalism, bureaucratic or continental bias and, increasingly in the 21st century, financial priorities. A notable principle of current IOC President Thomas Bach – an Olympic fencing champion and German lawyer sensitive to egalitarian regulations – has been to distinguish between honourable Olympian competitors and any suspect doping offenders. But that is to run ahead of the story. Symptomatic of the self-interest which can pervert the IOC's best intentions was, for instance, an aberration by Keba M'Baye of Senegal, an international judge at The Hague. Amid IOC negotiations in the 1990s to establish an 'African Fund' charity to promote sport among impecunious children and led by M'Baye and Kim Un-yong, a letter arrived from M'Baye requesting Kim 'to arrange a loan of four million dollars from major Korean sponsor Samsung' to enable M'Baye's elder son to launch a new bank in Senegal. Kim recognised the impropriety, discussed the issue with

Africa Olympic Foundation meeting, Senegal 1994, with Keba M'Baye (far left), subsequently IOC Ethics Commission chairman and an attempted evader.

then President Samaranch – and ignored it. The incident would have implications in events much later on when M'Baye became head of the IOC's Ethics Commission – Kim confirming the incident in his memoirs published in *JoongAng Ilbo* in 2008.

Human nature can do its best to impede ideology. Kim Un-yong, recipient of three bravery awards from the Korean War of 1950–53, was to prove equal, indeed challenging, to the demands. Though the IOC strives to maintain a clear conscience in all its thousands of decisions in controlling more than two hundred National Olympic Committees and in excess of forty affiliated International Federations – each of the latter administering simultaneous parallel world championships at either Olympic Summer or Winter Games – the task is accompanied at times with near-impossible deliberation. It is in this maelstrom of often confusing priorities that Kim Un-yong, in harmony with then IOC President Juan Antonio Samaranch, would make an impact that helped change sporting history – literally, within his own country, in governmental diplomatic relationships, underscoring what Dutch socialist Ruud Stokvis long-ago observed:

> There is no other organisation that has such a strong relationship with the population of the whole world as does the IOC, nor one that has proved so enduring – a majority attach more importance to the Olympic Games than to meetings of the UN General Assembly.... A more democratic organisation would have failed long before.

Kim Un-yong lived and campaigned for democratic expansion and modernisation of the IOC, which current IOC President Thomas Bach energetically pursues, intent on protecting virtue as much as suppressing cheats. Despite Kim Un-yong's epic achievements in the Olympic field, he was ultimately and reprehensibly to be brutally betrayed by both the Korean judiciary and a later IOC Ethics Commission, headed by Keba M'Baye, which failed to uphold the principle of 'innocent until proved guilty'. Here is a tale of someone whose strategic vision led his government through the metaphoric eye of a needle: gaining the capital city of Seoul election against all odds to host the Olympic Games of 1988, and thereby opening the corridor to senior diplomatic doorways hitherto closed (see Chapter 2, 'Seoul Spectacular'). Furthermore, from that springboard – the most spectacular of four-yearly Olympic festivals that had thus far ever been witnessed – Kim proceeded to establish taekwondo, an esoteric Korean leisure activity, as a global and expanding competitive sport of eighty million participants, elevated through his networking to the Olympic Programme schedule (see Chapter 3, 'Asian Leadership'). On a mounting tide of prestige, Kim – although peripherally damaged by an inaccurately imposed IOC Commission warning arising from scandal surrounding the host city election of Salt Lake (see Chapter 4, 'Salt Lake Subterfuge') – became the second most influential figure in the International Olympic Committee. Viewed privately by

Juan Antonio Samaranch as the prime candidate to succeed him as President – and thereby potentially to break the historical near-monopoly of this self-elected body by Europeans – amid controversial circumstances in the 2001 election he was runner-up (see Chapter 5, 'Presidential Turmoil').

His reward? Two years later, with a summary prison conviction of two-and-a-half-years driven by strands of envy of his reputation among politicians, media and colleagues, a tsunami of character assassination overwhelmed both Kim and his family – an act of simultaneous revenge and largely uncontested testimony by former colleagues, exploiting accusations of ambitious self-advancement placed ahead of national interests (see Chapter 6, 'Pyeongchang Reversal'). The provocation? A host-city bid defeat for what was then an obscure Korean winter sports venue: provincial Pyeongchang, as yet undeveloped and untested though buoyantly riding on the back of Kim's personal generation of global goodwill. Only marginally was Pyeongchang's first of three bids outvoted by Vancouver. Condemnation focused on Kim's near simultaneous successful campaign to be elected IOC Vice-president – a venture lodged *after* Pyeongchang already lost, and only because of an Asian rival candidate withdrawing, yet this opened the gate to Kim's crucifixion for alleged 'division' of his country's collective objective.

During my six decades involved in the affairs of international sport, the treatment of Kim, a benign individual noted for his generosity of spirit, was abusive beyond comprehension: the wilful destruction of not merely a national icon but a respected global figurehead. It would not be an exaggeration of his diplomatic and cultural impact upon the fortunes of South Korea to suggest that exposure to the hosting of the Seoul Olympic Games was strategically, politically and economically comparable to, say, British Premier Benjamin Disraeli's 19th century transfer of the East India Company trade emporium to control of the Crown, and the acquisition of the Suez Canal – a landmark empire builder. The

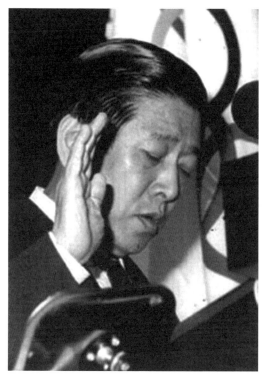

Kim Un-yong takes the Olympic Oath upon election as IOC Member, 1986.

wilful refusal by the Korean judiciary to contemplate the truth and their upholding of false allegations were a measure of their own intellectual myopia, not to mention an abuse of human rights.

Victimisation of Kim was, at least in the short term, damaging to the reputation of the Korea Sports Council and Korean Olympic Committee, for both of which Kim had served as both president and inspiration, the KOC having been formed at the IOC Session in Stockholm in 1947 after Korea's liberation from Japanese occupation. He was, moreover, president of the General Association of International Sports Federations (GAISF), the body through which he had accumulated far-reaching influence across the whole Olympic Movement, his wisdom embraced additionally in Korea's joint hosting of FIFA's World Cup in 2002. Most significant of all was his promotion of taekwondo, more of which will be shared on the following pages. It was on account of the magnitude of his friendships and trust established across many sports that Samaranch had ensured Kim's election to the IOC in the autumn of 1986, at the time of Seoul hosting the Asian Games; Samaranch was already so aware of Kim's competence that he contrived an immediate swearing-in on the day of election rather than at the next Session as normal. So comprehensive did Kim's grasp of the Olympic arena become that it can be claimed that, as a sports administrator in the 20th century, he stands alongside only Siegfried Edstrom of Sweden – the fourth IOC President – as having had the farthest-reaching impact upon his own nation's sporting evolution.

Fundamental for Kim's qualification as a benevolent administrator was his exceptional memory and his talent as a linguist and as fluent speaker and writer in five languages besides his own: French, Spanish, German, Japanese and English – plus Russian, which he learned specifically to conduct negotiations pre-'88. He also possessed first-rate ability in martial arts, including judo and boxing, as well as track and field, not to mention his potential as a concert pianist. His educational breadth was a platform for inevitable leadership in whatever field he might choose – yet he would later admit that his agreement in 2000 to become a member of the National Assembly at the insistence of President Kim Dae-jung from the Millennium Democratic Party was his most ill-advised move, one that ultimately exposed him to political revenge on the national stage. He reluctantly recalled, 'It would have been offensive to have pulled out; all might have been different had I not joined the National Assembly.'

In South Korea's novice democracy, one climbing nervously out of military dictatorship, any position in public life lacked certainty. To possess the spontaneous fluency of Kim Un-yong in his perception of national identity, in foreign languages and in international culture, was thus simultaneously to breed both admiration and envy among contemporaries. Even Kim's uninhibited magnanimity was to become in

Korean President Kim Young-sam (1993–98) appoints Kim Un-yong as Ambassador for International Sports Relations – a status that would rebound adversely.

due course his own damnation. There were so many tell-tale moments. Attending a Presidential Blue House celebration for Millennium 2000 members, Kim was introduced as 'someone famous around the world'. President Kim Dae-jung responded, 'When we go outside, he's more famous than me.' It was a recurring theme – which Kim Un-yong no doubt privately enjoyed. Attending the Montreal Olympics way back in 1976, Kim had watched Korea's volleyball teams. Accredited with a Korean Olympic Committee 'B' identity card, he was seated *in front* of Korea's volleyball and shooting presidents, lacking his 'seniority'; they were visibly offended and left cursing. Arriving at the airport for China's Harbin Winter Asian Games in 1996 as an IOC Member and recipient of President Kim Young-sam's International Relations Ambassador title, Kim was ushered through a VIP exit to an awaiting limousine, while

Kim Un-yong, reluctant politician, introduces a South Korean National Assembly-US Forum at the invitation of the US Ambassador, 2001.

South Korea's team leaders departed by a rear entrance. In 1997, Kim Dae-jung was campaigning for the presidency in the south-eastern city of Busan, accompanied by Kim Un-yong for tangible political allegiance. Visiting the East Asia Winter Games taking place in Busan at the time, Kim Dae-jung found himself uncomfortably seated in the second row of the main tribune *behind* organiser Kim Un-yong. Thus can fame become defamatory.

Much of the formal record of Kim Un-yong's academic career would be destroyed during the Korean War. He graduated from Kyungdong High School in Seoul in 1949 and entered Yonhi (now Yonsei) University before subsequently moving to Texas Western College in Fort Worth, Texas, in 1952. Graduating four years later, he returned to Yonsei University for a degree in Political Science and Diplomacy in 1960. Before completing his dissertation, he had been appointed assistant to the minister of defence. He served three prime ministers between 1961 and '63 – one of whom, Park Chung-hee, had a powerful interest in tae-

kwondo and deemed it to be the national sport, embracing Kim in its national development. Appointed counsellor at the Korean embassy in the
US in 1963, Kim was transferred to the United Nations as representative
in 1965 and from there to the Korean embassy in Great Britain, where
he served until being called to Seoul in 1968. He was subsequently appointed as deputy director-general of the Presidential Protective Service,
making him responsible for US relations that included the US army stationed in Korea. It was a position he held until 1974, during which time
he also spearheaded the formation of taekwondo's competitive and organisational structure by founding the Kukkiwon in 1972 and was elected president of the sport's first world federation, which he also founded
in 1973. By 1979 he was presiding over the inaugural World Games; a
year later, he was elected to the Executive Council of GAISF.

It was coincidental that Kim's steady emergence and mounting authority across the Olympic Movement should coincide with the deeply
controversial shift, across front-rank Olympic sport, from the traditional
amateur ethic to an increasingly rampant – and arguably unavoidable –
professionalism. As an old-fashioned amateur myself who grew up with
the Corinthian attitudes of Britain (to which the modern Games' founder Pierre de Coubertin had, to his own late admission, been misguidedly dedicated), I was only too conscious, as I reached senior competitive
level in the 1950s, that for a competitor to attain the highest level of performance, somebody has to pay for his or her preparation: his or her
parents (if they are affluent), a school, a university, a sponsor, the government, a national federation, an Olympic committee or lottery funding, as
in the UK today. There is no alternative to training, and training requires
finance. I gave a presentation regarding this principle at the height of the
amateur-professional controversy in the late 1980s at the IOC Academy
in Olympia.

Kim Un-yong, with his unfailing instinct in the psychology of human endeavour, was himself alert to the mounting conflict enveloping

Olympic sport. It was his foresight that enabled Korea to advance as rapidly and spectacularly as the nation did in an era of transformation when de Coubertin's code was terminally threatened. As Olympic historian David Young described it in reflection of a 19th century English tradition, it was 'an ideological means to justify an elitist athletics system that sought to bar the working class from competition.' Young recorded the comment of de Coubertin to a French journalist in 1936: 'How stupid has been this Olympic history of amateurism.' The raging debate engaged philosophical comment from intellectuals lacking direct contact with the practicalities of elite sport. Christopher Hill, in his *Olympic Politics,* quotes the neo-Marxist message of French philosophers Michel Caillat and Jean-Marie Brohm in *Les Dessous de l'Olympisme* ("the hidden underside of Olympics"): 'Olympic philosophy continues to be a cruel deception, just another of the world's illusions, . . . the substitution of sport as the new religion.' In *The Times* of London, editor William Rees-Mogg, distant from any playing field, pronounced: 'I have fifteen reasons why I shall not go to Seoul, . . . a grotesque jamboree of international hypocrisy, ultra-nationalism and vulgar bureaucracy.' In London's *Observer,* renowned commentator Hugh McIlvanney wryly reflected, 'After discussing rampant commercialism, crude nationalism, subservience to the arrogant power of television, the abandonment of ethics and pervasive drug abuse, what more could we ask (of sport) to make us feel at home?' Kim was indeed engaged within an arena of multiple controversies, yet himself possessed the wit and appreciation to perceive and value the elegiac emotions that can exist within sport.

One of the complexities confronting Kim, in his ambition to elevate the sporting status not only of Korea but of Asia, was a prolonged dominance of the Western world, with the West's embedded suspicion of all practices Asian. Working parallel to Kim in a sense was John Boulter, the British former middle-distance Olympian, who was busily sustaining the multiple business affairs of sportswear manufacturer Adidas. Sensitive and a fluent linguist himself, Boulter has always been aware of inter-racial tensions – starting with mutual reservations between the French and English, he being resident in France. 'There were always IOC members (in the West) who were suspicious of Kim – not that they didn't like him, but he wasn't one of those you would sit down with to have a beer, sensing he was a wily oriental,' he recalled. 'His arrival had followed the era in which Latin influence had overtaken traditional Anglo-Saxon monopoly – the new world of Havelange in football, Nebiolo in athletics, Acosta in volleyball, Samaranch in the IOC. There was still a mood in Europe, and America, of "foreigners" taking control. This sensitivity continues to exist in the 21st century with muted discomfort, say, about successive current Games today going to Beijing, Pyeongchang, Tokyo – three Asian hosts in a row.'

Jean-Claude Schupp, who worked hand-in-glove with Kim for many years as secretary-general of GAISF, echoes this view: 'There have always been intercontinental rivalries – Asians led by Kuwaiti sheikhs or by Africans, with European resistance. It's there, but nobody will admit it, though it's the way of nature.' Dick Palmer, the former long-time general-secretary of the British Olympic Association, acknowledges that Mary Glen-Haig, an Olympian fencer and the first woman IOC member, 'could not abide Kim's elevation', she being a relic of the pre-War era of Lord Exeter and Stanley Rous, Anglo pillars of world athletics and football International Federations respectively. 'Kim's rise from middle-office management was outstanding,' Palmer recalls. Walter Troeger, mastermind of Munich '72 and sports director for IOC, is fulsome in his appreciation of Kim: 'Whenever I was in Korea he was always on hand with advice. He worked with everyone, collaborated on every issue, though sometimes his tactics were admittedly borderline. Yet how could you survive in the IOC arena without accepting some practices in that vein? Kim's pragmatism was everything, especially in his own country, more particularly in the unification and globalisation of taekwondo both at home and abroad.'

That was not easy. International expansion was a basic obstacle in any field for this emerging democracy which lacked not only funds but the experience in negotiating diplomacy and linguistic fluency. The fact that Kim Un-yong surmounted communication obstacles, while remarkable on the one hand, would at the same time separate him from the herd and inevitably arouse the envy which would ultimately undermine him. As he wrote in *Challenge to the World*: 'Nurturing talented sports diplomats is not something that happens artificially in a short time. There is no manual or textbook for it. It is something you acquire through experience. The shortcut is through meeting lots of people, clashing with them at times, building relationships and trust. Just as education is a long-term investment, so the training of sports diplomats must proceed from the ground upwards. Building international knowledge and experience only comes through closeness and mutual friendship. Diplomacy is not a matter for the imagination or theories; it is based on information and pragmatic gains and requires researching and understanding the other side's culture.'

Aware throughout his administration of the inherent beauty of so much of sport, Kim's pragmatism enabled him to embrace commercialism without undermining the ethic. By the time of his personal crisis amid the first defeat of a Winter Olympics bid by Pyeongchang, commercial power in hosting the Olympics had itself become a contradiction – essential, yet increasingly unavailable as expenditures escalated. Pyeongchang would lose again in 2007 to Sochi's Kremlin autocracy, prompting the *Agence France Press* to allege that Russian President Vladimir Putin had 'bought the 2014 Olympics'. Vienna's daily *Österreich* mourned 'Salzburg's bid of hearts', and the legendary Franz Klammer, downhill hero of Innsbruck '76, admitted, 'Anything that has tradition doesn't matter anymore.'

The coincidental advantage for Kim in his perception of how sport

Kim Un-yong interprets at the unveiling ceremony for the statue of General Van Fleet at the Korea Military Academy, April 1960. President Rhee Syngman and First Lady Francesca Donner Rhee are seated at the centre.

could help energise South Korea's global status was the flourishing rate of GDP, which stoked the financial capacity to fund progressive cultural ideas. At the heart of a blossoming industrial power from Korea's post-war surge was Chung Ju-young, an innovative industrialist. His sixth son Chung Mong-joon succeeded his father as chairman of Hyundai Heavy Industries, the world's largest ship builder and subsequent auto manu-facturer, which cleverly emulated Japan's design-based development of mass production. The father's initial springboard – as Mong-joon relates in *I Say This to Japan,* a budding would-be politician's triumphant pub-lication in the wake of serving as co-chairman of the joint organising committee of World Cup 2002 – was to show Greek shipping magnate George Livanos a picture of *geobukseon,* the world's first iron-clad vessel, which had been invented by Admiral Yi Sun-sin (1545–98) to counter the Japanese invasion of 1592. An impressed Livanos was thus encouraged to order two massive crude oil carriers, and the rest, as they say, is history: the son's initiative galvanised Korean government ambition, which had hitherto languished due to the nation's lack of urgently needed industrial raw material imports. Chung also disputes the notion that Korea's supportive rail network was a legacy of the Japanese occupation from 1910; in fact, it was essentially built to facilitate ambitious plans for an invasion of China, and prior back-up for the Russo-Japanese war had begun in 1904. Yet most of the Japanese track was destroyed in the Korean War. 'As coloniser, Japan took from us; it did not give,' Chung recounts. In the miracle of Korean development, he points to the educational foundation, with eighty-five per cent of school graduates proceeding to university; to the nation being a monogamous culture; to an individual savings rate of 33.7%, compared with 18.8% for the United States and 16.2% for the UK. Thus, in Chung's view, a country that in the semi-democratic era of President Rhee Syngman (1948–60) had been less developed than the Philippines or Pakistan wholly created its own prosperity, giving the lie to predictions that 'a rose cannot flower in a dustbin.' President Park Chung-hee's five-year economic plan of 1961 was the starting point. The key to volcanic change two decades later would be Kim Un-yong's concept, which rode on the vehicle of astonishing GDP expansion along Seoul's Hangang River as Korea rose to become the world's 11th largest economy. Kim was confident that his foresight could be backed by vigorous finance.

Christopher Hill, in his *Olympic Politics*, quotes remarks by Lord Killanin (IOC President from 1972 to 1980) in relation to Moscow's election as host for 1980: 'The Olympic Games surpass all political and ideological barriers.... Thanks to the Olympic Movement countries which have very different political, religious and social views are able to come together.' When the IOC elected unheralded Seoul as host for 1988, there was every reason for it not to have done so. There had been the consecutive boycotts of 1976–80: of Montreal by African nations protesting

South Africa's apartheid regime, and of Moscow led demonstrably by the United States in response to the Soviet Union's invasion of Afghanistan. In the 1981 decision to elect a host for 1988, the Japanese city of Nagoya seemed the unavoidable nomination, whatever Killanin's philosophical mindset had been. The alternative to Nagoya was Korea's capital city of Seoul, located fifty kilometres from the demilitarised powder-keg border with the People's Democratic Republic of Korea, technically on a permanent twenty-four-hour trigger-finger setting. Howard Cosell, the domineering voice of America's ABC TV sports channel, trumpeted, 'You cannot stage an Olympics in a war zone.' Surely the Soviet Union, and all of its Eastern Bloc allies plus Cuba and others, would veto the choice of politically equivocal South Korea, whatever de Coubertin's idealistic 'universality' may have proposed?

Michael Payne, the former lynchpin of IOC's marketing strategy, observed the following in his authoritative financial analysis of the Olympic Movement, *Olympic Turnaround*: 'Although a nominal democracy, politically South Korea was precariously balanced. The president, Chun Doo-hwan, former army general, had assumed power in the latest military coup, shortly before the 1981 election.... It was more than likely there would be several more in the intervening seven years.'

There was some sympathy for Korea's viewpoint. Paul Henderson, a Canadian IOC Member during his leadership of World Sailing, recalls, 'The Olympic Movement at that time wanted to have another Games in Asia, following the marked success of Tokyo in 1964. There existed an unwritten rotation: Europe, America, Somewhere Else. In the aftermath of the vote, it was undoubtedly Kim Un-yong who eased President Samaranch's alarm at the likely prospect of another boycott.' Equally open-minded was Craig Reedie of Britain, a later IOC Member and chairman of the World Anti-doping Agency who was campaigning at the time for badminton's inclusion in the Games. 'Japan had a bigger language problem than Korea, and Kim, a fluent linguist, already had an

Kim Un-yong, Bibi Samaranch, Mme Park Dong-sook, and President Samaranch, during one of Samaranch's 17 coordination visits to Seoul.

international view of sport, having appeared from almost nowhere yet a seamless mover and shaker,' he noted. Kim, of course, was not alone in his motive-driven capability. At the time of election, South Korea did not have colour television; by the arrival of the Games, it had become in seven years one of the world's ten largest TV-trading countries. It was South Korea's immense good fortune that the careers of two exceptional sports administrators should coincide: Kim and Juan Antonio Samaranch. While Kim on the one hand was the unfailing conduit providing Samaranch with daily direct access to the country's political policy-brokers, Samaranch's extended trust in the artful Korean persuaded him that here might be an ideal eventual successor – a candidate to become the first Asian commander of the IOC.

That job is one of almost intolerable pressure, as Thomas Bach has discovered, and before him – with only mixed success – Jacques Rogge. Samaranch was a master strategist who swiftly detected in Kim a crucial lieutenant: first for the bureaucratic security of the Seoul Games, second as controller of GAISF (see Chapter 3, 'Asian Leadership'). Canadian Richard Pound, an Olympian swimmer and Montreal lawyer whom Samaranch also adroitly appointed for critical IOC responsibilities, was candid in his comments about Samaranch in *Five Rings over Korea*, the first of his two comprehensive studies of the Olympic Movement. 'Hardly a day went by when I did not learn something from watching Samaranch, even though it might have been something I did not want to learn or something I would never want to do myself,' he wrote. 'He had a highly developed cynicism regarding the motives of others, which were more than matched by his own. He knew, as do all leaders, that those who came to him generally wanted either to attain advantage for themselves or to bring damning commentary down upon others.... His Presidency was by far the most important of any to date.' To this, Paul Henderson adds, 'In the late 1970s and early 1980s, the IOC was dominated totally by Europeans and a few from the USA. Samaranch wanted to broaden the focus. Kim filled that void. This was especially acute after the Korean and Vietnam Wars. Samaranch was sensitive to the needs of International Federations, and saw in Kim a powerful possibility from which to operate within GAISF.' Walter Troeger was equally impressed. 'Un-yong was highly efficient, a fluent linguist, always in contact with all IFs, creating a very stable Olympic platform in Seoul, arranged an invitation to the Blue House (government HQ) whenever I was in Seoul as IOC sports director,' he recalled. 'Un-yong's replacement of Thomas Keller as head of GAISF, an enemy of Samaranch, was important. I knew both sides. Keller's first impression of Samaranch had been "Napoleon has returned!" Samaranch's connections were infallible. Sitting with him in Lausanne, he would know from his grapevine everything that was happening with Keller. Kim was the ideal alternative.' The extent of intimacy in Kim's strategic relationship with Samaranch was related by Manolo Romero, foremost specialist in IOC's television administration. 'I would be cautious in calculating Kim's role,' he said. '(The late) He Zhenliang from China, for instance, was much more outspoken. I sat through Executive Board meetings for fifteen years and seldom heard Kim speak strategically.'

Kim's own reflection on his role – in his post-Games publication *The Greatest Olympics* – was succinct. 'Our Organising Committee helped stage IOC Executive Board meetings, IOC Sessions, coordination meetings with the EB and other IOC commissions,' he wrote. 'It also helped with the General Assembly of the Olympic Council of Asia, the same with European NOC meetings and the Council of ANOC (Association of National Olympic Committees). Fourteen IFs had congresses during the Games. Samaranch said many times the key to the success of the Games is international cooperation. It's true. Without that, TV schedules, marketing, competition, referees, press security, all are impossible. I picked up the title of "Bridge", since I understood the positions of IOC, the IFs and NOCs more than anybody else. I went beyond the rules sometimes to make arrangements comfortable. We believed Seoul had to do a little more than other Olympic host cities. IFs are more technical, more concerned with their own sports and officials, yet as a body they would pledge full support to the Games of Seoul and those of the future, though at times it was difficult to do so. Most of the presidents and secretary-generals of the IFs had been my colleagues for many years.'

Seoul's bid for the Games had nearly defaulted, in fact, over the failure to reply to the mandatory IOC questionnaire and make a recommendation by the required date. The bid was only saved when Samaranch, by now acting as IOC President, insisted that the IOC Evaluation Commission visit Korea. For the Korean government, the Games were a political exercise from the start, as Christopher Hill relates in *Olympic Politics*: 'In pursuit of the Games, Korea enjoyed the advantage of a ruthlessly authoritarian government, which was, however, hampered in its dealings with dissenters by the need not to be too obviously indifferent to human rights. In 1972 Major-General Park Chung-hee, president since 1963, introduced the Yushin (Revitalising) Constitution, effectively making him president for life, but he was assassinated in October 1979. A period of chaos ensued from which Major-General Chun Doo-hwan emerged as president, confirmed in office under a new constitution in February 1981. He governed with a mixture of firmness and reluctant conciliation: after its first direct presidential elections in 1987, the country experienced its first peaceful transfer of power in February 1988. But although it was peaceful it was traumatic, and the run-up to the Olympics was conducted against the background of a continuing political battle.'

Hence the imperative coordination strategy by Kim, which sustained three objectives: a maximum number of attendant nations, irrespective of political alignment; the security of their athletes; and steps to lay the groundwork for Korea's diplomatic expansion across the world. These efforts, as Kim relates in his book *The Greatest Olympics: From Baden-Baden to Seoul*, became especially important following the Soviet-led boycott of Los Angeles in 1984. There soon came renewed calls from North Korea for a change of venue in 1988; subsequently, the DPRK moved to demand a co-hosting arrangement. Kim's liabilities in integrating sport with politics were mounting by the day.

Roh Tae-woo, a chair of the Seoul Games Organising Committee who would become president of Korea by the time of the actual Games, led a delegation to Lausanne in 1984 to challenge the DPRK's manoeuvres. It presented its first official report to the IOC at the Session preceding the LA Games, with a further consultant delegation to the assembly of ANOC in November; the latter adopted the 'Mexico Declaration' in total support of the Seoul Games, thereby raising moral pressure on the DPRK. The Asian Games of 1986 were an invaluable preliminary stage rehearsal for Seoul's administration, simultaneously providing an opportunity for Socialist bloc nations to view the Olympic preparations first-hand and to meet Korean sports leaders. Visiting the famed Lotte

Department Store – massive in its array of modern technological merchandise – some of them believed it was a propaganda display. While harbouring possible Soviet approval, Korea had to be cautious regarding South Africa, its NOC having been expelled in 1970. Kim's focus was essentially devoted to Moscow. 'When I was in the Soviet Union for a third time in June '88, their foreign ministry wished to open a temporary consular office in Seoul, which would be negotiated through the Soviet Embassy in Tokyo or Finland,' he recalled. 'I discussed this with our foreign minister, Choi Gwang-soo. It was, of course, for the Olympic period and through Olympic relations, yet I knew it would eventually grow into bilateral establishment.' One of the closest observers of Seoul's elaborate administration was Yugoslavian Artur Takac, the IOC's Sports Director. In his autobiography *Sixty Olympic Years*, Takac expressed his admiration: 'Two people stood out through their enormous determination and efficiency: Kim Un-yong, organising committee vice-president, and sports coordinator Moon Dong-ho. These were two remarkable officials, always at the ready with their dedication, their mastery of electronics and computer data processing. For a country which had little or no experience of hosting international sporting events, they were astonishing in the way they grasped the complexities of all the projects which, put together, make up the jigsaw of the Olympic picture. I never ceased to admire their abilities.'

The DPRK continued to be a scar on the face of preparations. Before the Korean War there had been a single Korean NOC, its seat located in Seoul, while the North had pressed, via Moscow, for joint allegiance or – with the South declining to contemplate either – a separate and independent NOC. With disagreement on both sides of the border, there was no North Korean team at Rome '60. Collaboration remained a distant prospect, and with the South continuing to reject the idea of a joint team – as had occurred with two Germanys – a solo North team had participated at Tokyo '64. The ramifications of a charade of IOC ne-

President Roh Tae-woo and First Lady Kim Ok-suk (centre right) visit IOC Lausanne headquarters, 1992, signifying Korea's expanding status.

gotiations to embrace demands from the North for involvement at Seoul '88 are detailed in Chapter 2 ('Seoul Spectacular').

An equal ongoing source of tension for Kim's organising committee concerned the government's response to public dissent, which emerged powerfully among the Korean middle class from the spring of 1987. President Chun reduced his unpopularity by dismissing ministers who might rival his expected successor Roh Tae-woo. Chun's ruling Democratic Justice Party staged a national convention to choose its preferred successor candidate against a mounting backdrop of public demonstrations provoked by Chun's decision to postpone the election until after the Games. However, he duly nominated Roh as his candidate; although Roh committed himself to more democratic governance, protest rallies mushroomed and thousands were detained. Pressed by US President Ronald Reagan to desist from using troops against protesters, Roh, and ultimately Chun, recognised the need for democratic change. Harassed by rival political parties, Roh resolved the crisis with a tactical speech. Now he became tolerated, promising to accept opposition parties' demands for wider democratisation, elimination of corruption, and the release of political prisoners. When the election came, Roh won with thirty per cent of the vote against twenty-eight per cent, twenty-seven per cent and eight per cent for the three opposition parties. Under the Seoul slogan for the Games ('Harmony and Progress'), Kim would retrospectively be able to celebrate an unparalleled achievement for his Games: 160 nations with 9,417 athletes and 3,887 officials gathered for an exemplary festival – nineteen more nations than at LA in 1984, and 3,538 more athletes and officials than at Munich '72, the last previous Games unaffected by any boycott. Press and broadcasters amounted to 15,740, the festival being celebrated with the aid of 74,000 volunteers. Though personally unobtrusive, Kim's landmark for his country's history was indelible.

If Kim Un-yong was riding high in the mid-Nineties – taekwondo having reached the summit of Olympic Programme acceptance at the Paris Centenary Congress of 1994, and Kim himself no doubt conscious that Samaranch quietly viewed him as a potential successor as ninth IOC President – life was suddenly to strike him from behind. The abrupt revelation, in December 1998, of widespread subterfuge in conduct of the 1995 election of Salt Lake City as host for the Winter Games of 2002 (see Chapter 4, 'Salt Lake Subterfuge'), and the appointment of Richard Pound to chair the investigation, dealt a blow to his reputation. Among the allegations of improper vote-inducement offered to IOC Members was the issue of a US green card work-permit for Kim's son John (Junghoon). On the one hand, the elder Kim denied involvement in the bureaucratic procedure; on the other, the application requires candidates to detail every element of their educational, professional and family background, and who would omit to include that his father was a member of the IOC? Every string is pulled to secure preferment, so why not by John Kim?

In response to a thunderstorm of revelations by Utah television naming a dozen or more gift-recipient IOC Members, Samaranch appointed Richard Pound, the legal sharp-shooter, as chair of the Ad Hoc Enquiry Commission. Although a US federal judge would ultimately

Richard W Pound, Montreal lawyer and IOC Member, leading candidate for the IOC presidency. Pound chaired the IOC's Enquiry Commission over the Salt Lake bid scandal, 1999, which imposed 'serious warning' on Kim Un-yong, his rival for the leadership.

dismiss all charges concerning the inducement conduct of Salt Lake bid campaigners Tom Welch and Dave Johnson – who had allegedly traded the incentives – expulsions and severe warnings had already been imposed by Pound's Commission in 1999, including a 'serious warning' on Kim. Yet Pound was simultaneously known to be the leading rival to Kim as potential successor to Samaranch in 2001.

Here was a prominent instance of potential legal conflict of interest. As a lawyer himself, should not Pound have been alert to conflict, and therefore withdrawn from his adjudication over the fellow IOC Member? Yet he seemingly felt no compunction about formal condemnation of his rival. When the US Justice Department dismissed the case against Welch and Johnson, should not the IOC's own internal conviction of Kim – based as it was on unconfirmed allegation – also have been deleted?

Issues surrounding Pound's authoritative position were further raised when it was disclosed that while he was supposedly giving voluntary service as IOC Vice-president, he was in fact receiving, on Samaranch's accord, substantial seven-figure 'legal fees' in secret. Pound stridently justified the fees as being separate and distinct, as his legal services, from his administrative services as 'honorary' IOC Member. Uncomfortably, the *New York Times* revealed in February 1999 – during Pound's Salt Lake adjudication – that Salt Lake organisers had arranged for Pound to be donated in 1997 a genealogical study by the Mormon Church tracing his Scottish-English ancestry. This study, based on extensive research and tracing of family history, was a gift from the Church's president Gordon Hinckley – although donated two years after Salt Lake had been elected – 'as a goodwill gesture,' reported Church spokesman Michael Otterson. A substantial family history could cost, according to the New York Genealogical and Biographical Society, as much as $50,000.

The global status of taekwondo in the 21st century would be nothing today without the vision and devoted application by Kim Un-yong five decades earlier. The founder of the modern sport could be said to have been General Choi Hong-hi, who in the 1950s left Korea for Canada, later moving to North Korea in 1979. President Park Chung-hee decreed that taekwondo, rather than football, should be the national sport, there being countless different factions of this leisure activity. Elected president of the Korea Taekwondo Association in 1971, Kim founded in quick order the Kukkiwon world taekwondo headquarters in 1972 and created the World Taekwondo Federation in 1973 (see Chapter 3, 'Asian Leadership'). He subsequently enlisted multi-experienced Dick Palmer of Britain as an advisor in its development expansion, which in 1980 led to taekwondo becoming a 'recognised' IOC sport. Michael Payne reflects: 'Kim's relationship with Samaranch was the key to taekwondo's arrival and expansion; this would never have happened years later. The sport was split, as judo had been. Taekwondo didn't have a clear profile, but the Olympic Games provided that. Its arrival was Samaranch's "thank

Prime Minister Kim Jong-pil (centre), Korean Sport and Olympic Committee president Kim Taek-su (right) and Korea Taekwondo Association president Kim Un-yong at the Kukkiwon opening ceremony, 1972

you" for Kim's mastery of the Seoul Games.' In 1984 a merger between WTF and the rival International Taekwondo Federation, predominantly based in the DPRK, failed to materialise, but Kim's creation of Kukkiwon, a Korean-based administrative headquarters, consolidated taekwondo's organisational self-confidence. The admission to the Olympic Programme of a fourth martial art – alongside boxing, judo and wrestling – at the Centenary Congress of 1994 was its apotheosis, a crowning moment for the man who masterminded its promotion. It is with no trite, gratuitous courtesy that Mike McKenzie, key promoter of the sport in Britain, should say of his early encounter with the influence of Kim, 'I sensed he had the aura of greatness.'

If Kim Un-yong's career trajectory suffered on account of the Salt Lake allegations, so too did his wife, emotionally, and his younger daughter Hae-jung, in a more practical sense. With both her mother and father being talented pianists, the musical gene flowed in Hae-jung, a child prodigy. Inevitably and justifiably, as with any parents, the Kims took every opportunity to help promote Hae-jung's development. Born

Hae-jung Kim performs Rachmaninoff Piano Concerto no. 2 in C minor with Moscow Philharmonic during the Olympic Culture Festival, 1988.

during Un-yong's embassy posting in New York, Hae-jung attended the exclusive Yewon Academy in Seoul before transferring to the acclaimed Juilliard School of Music in New York where, aged fourteen, she won first prize in 1980, her first year in the Pre-College Division, in the all-Juilliard Piano Competition, followed by a recital debut at the Lincoln Centre for Performing Arts. Further awards came her way in 1982–83, notably including first prize honours in the renowned Gina Bachauer International Piano Competition. Awards followed almost annually through 1992, when she won both the D'Angelo and Maria Callas international competitions as well as first prize in the Cologne (Tomassoni) International Pianoforte Competition. Her talent inexorably led to performing with major orchestras around the world.

Her acknowledgment of parental inheritance is explicit: 'The youngest among one son and two daughters, I received abundant love from my parents. Unlike my brother, in business, and my sister, a lawyer, I chose a career in music.... It was natural for me to become familiar with the piano as I grew up with both my parents playing at home all the time. For any of us, to rest in the shadow of one's father, one feels the warmth and magnanimity. As I walked down the aisle holding my father's hand at my wedding, I felt his hand tremble.... I felt sad as I noticed the tears in my mother's eyes – whereas my mother's love is obvious, my father's is more subdued and runs deep. Several times along the way I lost my self-confidence and fell into despair. Each time my father gave me strength and courage without fail – sometimes as a classical music-lover, at others as counsellor with candid advice and as my eternal supporter.'

What would be more natural, then, than for the father to open doors to Hae-jung's gifts through his professional contacts? Wherein, regrettably, lay dark repercussions: malicious criticism heaped upon the father regarding her career. With hindsight, it might have been advisable for Hae-jung not to have performed in Utah alongside Salt Lake's campaign as an Olympic host city, or to have declined her engagement, more audacious, to perform at the Session in her home city of Seoul at the height of the continuing Salt Lake controversy enveloping the IOC. The furore that surrounded the modern-day Leopold Mozart would ultimately serve to overwhelm the beauty of the daughter's art. Gratuitous critical reviews of Hae-jung's performances were penned by investigative journalists for no better purpose than to mount indignity upon her father.

Yet the father would not himself surrender to the media mob's insults during parallel campaigns bent on exposing, and destroying, the leadership both of FIFA – with some justifiable intent amid three decades of known collective and individual administrative corruption – and of the IOC, within which the extravagant lifestyle of some members, and blatant manipulation by bidding cities, had begun to threaten its very survival. I had written extensively for *The Times* of London about this cancer, which an otherwise astute Samaranch had misguidedly considered insufficiently significant for the brutal correction required. This

South and North Korean teams enter jointly behind the Korean Peninsula flag at the Sydney Olympics opening ceremony – a long-planned political triumph schemed by Kim Un-yong.

latter would be affected by Pound's stringent internal convictions, followed by Samaranch's root-and-branch Charter re-drafting, including appointment of an Ethics Commission and limitations on IOC conduct in pursuit of host-city elections, instituted under the direction of Samaranch, himself emphatically entrusted by members to steer them – and indeed potentially himself – clear of potential capitulation. An IOC with a cleaner face would emerge from its medical shower in 1999 in time respectably to stage Sydney's Games of 2000 (see Chapter 4, 'Salt Lake Subterfuge').

To outward appearances, Kim Un-yong retained his status, and the respect of a majority of fellow members, when receiving unanimous, gratifying approval for his accomplished negotiations, and the execution of a joint march at Sydney's Opening Ceremony by rival Korean states. A triumphant festival staged by gung-ho Australians – following an equivocal Winter Games at Nagano, which took place under a cloud

CHAPTER 1

IOC President Juan Antonio Samaranch with his initially intended successors, Kim Un-yong (right) and Dr Thomas Bach (left)

of questionable bidding tactics in the wake of their 1991 election at the expense of favourite Salt Lake – lifted IOC morale back to a platform of some dignity. Samaranch could retire in a year's time with his and the IOC's reputation at least partially repaired.

Yet the shadow of the Salt Lake 'serious warning' was going to continue to haunt Kim and, more to the point, his mentor and supporter Samaranch. Kim's remarkable achievements thus far entitled him to be ambitious – not merely personally but on behalf of his country and continent. Leadership of the IOC, in global perception, is one of the most prominent and intendedly non-political positions in world affairs. Prior to his election in 1980, Samaranch had confided to then Director-General Monique Berlioux of France, 'To be President is the most wonderful post one can ever hold. I would give up any assignment as a minister in my country to be IOC President. There is nothing like it.'

Kim was ready, emotionally and strategically, for the chance. Would Samaranch's loyalty hold fast? Would he at least stay neutral? The view

Chinese IOC Member He Zhenliang (left), source of influence in taekwondo's adoption as official event at the 1994 Hiroshima Asian Games – and constitutional adviser during Salt Lake scandal resolution

of Patrick Nally, sponsorship guru, an IOC aide to crucial economic security during Samaranch's reign, remains relevant to this day. 'Had it not been for Salt Lake, Kim would have been President,' Nally pronounced. 'Samaranch's intent was that he be followed by Kim, and subsequently by Thomas Bach. After the essential clean-up post-Salt Lake it became difficult to continue to support Kim, in terms of public relations. Pound, a dazzling lawyer, had been a possible early candidate, but in the event proved too emotionally irascible. Privately, Samaranch had to re-brief his influential place-men close to the election – it had to be an uncontaminated Rogge' (see Chapter 5, 'Presidential Turmoil').

Ser Miang Ng from Singapore, elected to the IOC at the Session prior to Nagano, was at the fringes of events during the pre-election phase at Moscow in 2001. 'It was difficult to measure the voting drift away from Kim, but Salt Lake did not help him,' Ng said. 'Yet I fully agree on the conflict of interest inherent in the conviction by Dick Pound's disciplinary commission. He should have recused himself, with Samaranch's backing. Kim had been a serious contender. You could have had a right or wrong conclusion about the Salt Lake decision, yet Pound was later revealed to having been substantially financially maintained by the IOC for his legal wisdom.' Dick Palmer (British Olympic Association) reflected, 'What Kim achieved, becoming eligible to make a presidential bid, was remarkable. On the face of it, he did not outwardly have a forceful personality; he was very self-contained, yet made sure he had widespread friends and only few enemies. As it was to be proved later, Korean politics and politicians are made of stern stuff!'

Kim's misfortune was that inadvertently he suffered a self-inflicted blow involving the new IOC Ethics Commission's hostility immediately prior to the Presidential vote. In an off-the-cuff conversation – I recollect with journalists – he proffered the opinion that IOC Members should receive a stipend for the expenditure of administering their domestic office, the responsibility of members officially being that they represent the IOC in their country and not their country within the IOC. They are there to promote the IOC and its ethics. Apparently, a journalist floated a sum of '$50,000'; the comment was leaked and subsequently 'went viral' as being part of his alleged manifesto for the job. The Crown Prince of Netherlands, an IOC Member, lodged a protest to the Ethics Commission; Kim received a public reprimand from chairman Keba M'Baye of Senegal (the same M'Baye who had sought a Seoul sponsor's fund for his son's proposed bank). Such was the hypersensitivity of the IOC post-Salt Lake that members had even been forbidden publicly to express in conversation their preferred candidate; Kevan Gosper of Australia was admonished for announcing his personal backing for Pound (see Chapter 5, 'Presidential Turmoil'). Tantalisingly for Kim, his unofficial proposal would be approved in principle by the Executive Board three years later . . . by which time he would be in prison. Paul Henderson suggested to the newly elected Rogge that the IOC President should receive such a stipend. On learning this, the retired Samaranch self-mockingly asked

Henderson, 'Can we make that stipend retroactive?'

Disappointed though he might have been with the election's outcome (finishing behind Rogge, but gratifyingly a vote ahead of an enraged Pound), Kim was not in the mood to take a back seat. The following year he earned widespread international acclamation for calming incendiary Korean emotions which erupted over a disputed speed skating medal decision during 2002 Salt Lake Winter Games. Yet he faced widespread media and governmental condemnation back home. Kim quelled a threatened walk-out by the Koreans, easing the anxiety of Rogge – a President still nervously finding his feet. Another year down the road, however, the IOC Session in Prague would pitch Kim into the furnace. Fate doubly twisted events in his disfavour: ironically, an unpredictably strong but narrowly-failing vote for Pyeongchang, alongside Kim's own second-option campaign for election as Vice-president – as well as his recalled and provocative failed presidential election two years earlier.

Kim might have debated forever whether he was right or wrong to seek the IOC vice-presidency in parallel with Pyeongchang's host-city bid. Yet a mathematical voting success for him against Norwegian candidate Gerhard Heiberg – a rival enjoying the backing of an IOC President known to be hostile to Kim – proved, alongside Pyeongchang's narrow defeat, to be Kim's cataclysmic nemesis.

There were historic comparisons to be made of this circumstance. The challenge by Kim himself in the presidential election two years earlier would have been marginally diminished by the host-city election of Beijing, at the same Session, for the Games of 2008 – an unwritten, subliminal disinclination of the IOC to vote twice within one Session for the same continent. It was similar to the case of Gunnar Ericsson of Sweden, who simultaneously ran for Vice-president at the 1988 Session in Seoul alongside the nation's Winter Games bid by favourites Ostersund (victory astonishingly being claimed by little Norwegian outsiders Lillehammer). When Samaranch had announced the decision on television, drawing the name from an envelope, he had glanced, uncomprehendingly, at an expectant King of Sweden in the front row of the audience: both had been optimistic for Sweden's first-ever Winter Games. In a correspondence from 11 July 2003, Thomas Bach of Germany had the following to say on the Korean-Pyeongchang debate: 'The results of the two IOC elections in Prague were a great success for Korea. The number of votes for Pyeongchang was unexpectedly high and is a great encouragement for future candidatures.... The two elections are not related to each other. I am convinced that IOC Members are looking at the election of an Olympic Host City and a Vice-president separately. This you can also see from the fact that Richard Pound (Canada) was even running for IOC President in the same Session of 2001 when Toronto was a candidate for the 2008 Olympic Games.' In the event, Canada lost both votes in the 2001 session in Moscow.

One of Kim's closest allies, the late Nat Indrapana of Thailand, remained visibly distraught about the disintegration which now descended upon Kim's career: the Pyeongchang bid organising committee returning home to vent their wrath on Kim, claiming his parallel Vice-presidency campaign had undermined Pyeongchang. This led to a media storm, with the public denouncing Kim as traitor and even calling upon him to take his own life. Indrapana reflected, 'Yes, we [IOC] say "country comes first", but I said to IOC colleagues that these were separate issues.' He insisted: 'The Pyeongchang vote came first. The way the government was to treat Un-yong was truly shocking. What did he do to deserve this? He had given his all to the country, but the public abuse nearly killed him.' The Korean parliament launched an investigation into the affair. Significantly, there was no IOC reaction to the controversy by Rogge in support of his new Vice-president, confining himself to stating merely that 'the election was a democratic process and Mr. Kim was an eligible IOC Member.' Rogge's partiality was later to be further exposed.

Ser Miang Ng, an increasingly important contributor to IOC affairs at that time, offered a special insight into the Prague events. 'Kim was unquestionably lobbying for Pyeongchang,' he recalled, 'because I remember him forecasting that the outcome against Vancouver would be "very close", so he knew from many contacts that Pyeongchang had strong support. Yet he was aware of [intercontinental] criticism that Asia was becoming a dominant event host – just as China would in the 21st century. It's difficult for me to comment whether he made an error in being a contender. Oddly, though, he had bad luck: a consequence of a decision in Beijing where China's minister of sport ruled against He Zhenliang – an increasingly articulate member of the Executive Board following Beijing's election for 2008 – running for the Vice-presidency. Chinese international policy veered against He becoming too powerful an international figure. But for He's withdrawal, Kim would have waited till the following year to run for a VP vacancy. The Korean press reaction against Kim in Prague was surprising. As a member of the Finance Commission, I was having a chat over a cup of coffee with Richard Carrion (Puerto Rican chair of the Commission) when a belligerent Korean journalist came up to our table shouting: "Why didn't you vote for Pyeongchang?" Carrion promptly tore the accreditation off the journalist's chest.' The mood in Prague was ugly. Paul Henderson adds that without Kim's extensive influence, Pyeongchang 'would never have come that close.' A matter of three votes.

As will be related in Chapter 6 ('Pyeongchang Reversal'), Kim Unyong's scandalous prison sentence prompted an outcry of moral protest across the world, with numerous IOC Members counted among those addressing the injustice of Korea's Supreme Court. Not least among them was Vitaly Smirnov, president of Russia's Olympic Committee and IOC Vice-president. His letter represented a global tide of dismay. He wrote:

I'm not in any way trying to interfere with the jurisdiction of your country but would like to express my opinion. I have known Dr. Kim for twenty years and I can say that during this period he did much to strengthen the authority of your country on an international level. The Olympic Games in Seoul which took place after two boycotts in 1980 and 1984 were brilliantly organised, and contributed to the authority of the IOC. It is difficult to over-estimate the great role that Dr. Kim played in this matter.

It was a very special case for my country: regardless of the fact that we didn't have diplomatic relations between our two countries. The team of the USSR received full support in all aspects – political and sporting – to a great extent thanks to Dr. Kim. May I remind you that in these Games the team of the USSR gained the greatest number of gold medals. Right after the Olympic Games, diplomatic relations between our two countries were established. I can celebrate almost the same about the activities of Dr. Kim as an IOC member, as a president of the World Taekwondo Federation, as president of GAISF. Can I kindly request Your Honour while making the ultimate decision to take into consideration everything mentioned above.

Smirnov's appeal to what would prove to be Korea's blinkered and repressive judicial attitude was echoed everywhere. William Schechter, a prominent and experienced public relations director in the US and known collaborator in Kim's international contacts, similarly addressed Chief Justice Choi: 'As an American citizen who frequently visited Seoul over the past twelve years for my business relationship with Dr. Kim and the World Taekwondo Federation, I offer the following insights from a global perspective, which I hope will be beneficial to you and your colleagues in evaluating the circumstances surrounding Dr. Kim.... I write as a professional public relations consultant who deals extensively with international media. Reporters and editors worldwide with whom I have been in close contact for a decade know Dr. Kim as a highly respected diplomat and sports executive, a symbol of Korean excellence and sophistication. Their impression of Dr. Kim is in stark contrast to the latest developments they have witnessed from Korea regarding allegations against Dr. Kim – a man with whom I worked closely over the years who never flaunted his wealth nor behaved in anything but a rightful and respectful manner in the many business encounters in which I was privileged to be involved.'

One figure intimately familiar with all of Kim's activities had been Morley Myers, for forty years an international correspondent for *UPI*. In a lengthy and articulate appeal to Chief Justice Choi Jong-young, Myers expressed his dismay, not to say outrage:

> This is an appeal for the release of Dr. Kim, who deserves complete exoneration from the politically motivated charges.... I have been fortunate to witness at first hand the matchless contribution that Dr. Kim has made to Korea in particular and world sport in general. Outside of Korea, Dr. Kim's imprisonment is viewed as an injustice, symptomatic of the political culling which has seen the incarceration of ten of the government's National Assembly.... I did not understand the ruthless political ambition of certain Koreans until the disgraceful events following Pyeongchang's narrow defeat by Vancouver.... Deceitful accusations that Dr. Kim verbally sabotaged Pyeonchang's bid were totally without substance.... When one IOC Member was interviewed by Korean television, he described how Dr. Kim had spoken to members routinely at breakfast, asking them to vote for Pyeongchang. The TV station said they would not use the interview because Korean people only wanted bad news about Dr. Kim.... The fact that Dr. Kim gained fifty-five votes (in the Vice-president's election) is indicative of the high regard and influence he wields in the Olympic family, an attribute which Korea cannot afford to cast aside. It is impossible to overstate what Dr. Kim has done for taekwondo and the wider Olympic Movement.... History will record Dr. Kim as a national hero for his extraor-

dinary deeds to foster the development of Korea from a third-world dictatorship to an emerging democracy and economic power.... The most influential figure in Asia, his power extends beyond continental boundaries as an IOC Vice-president and the president of GAISF.

Every allegation against Kim was unfounded. 1) Bribery in the selection for competition of taekwondo athletes: no connection with the WTF president. 2) Financial assistance to North Korea: none provided, any such funds having been forwarded following established cooperation for the 2000 Sydney Games and the Busan Asian Games of 2002. 3) Bribes in Korean Olympic Committee elections: all elections through normal transparent procedure, none with financial favours. 4) Embezzlement for opening WTF's IOC allocations account in Monte Carlo: common low-taxation practice for many IFs, taekwondo being a global rather than a Korean entity. 5) Misappropriation of funds from Samsung: the contributions by Samsung were for a broad range of sports promotion on public record.

As desperation mounted in vain attempts at his release, Kim's formal appeal for justice was unequivocal: 'In the hours before the decision by the Supreme Court regarding my appeal, I reached the following conclusions regardless of the outcome: I affirm my innocence of all charges. While I mean no disrespect to the Justices who had no role in bringing these allegations, the charges were baseless and politically motivated: they directly related to the Pyeongchang controversy.'

In a 2012 doctoral thesis, University of Kent Ph.D. candidate Choe Dae-hyun pronounced, 'The South Korean criminal justice system is often described as "prosecutorial justice". Most investigative and prosecutorial powers are exercised only by prosecutors. It is decisions made by prosecutors that usually decide the outcome of trials. On the basis of its extensive powers, the prosecution service has achieved a conviction rate exceeding ninety-nine per cent, which is one of the highest in the world.... The findings of this study are that a ninety-nine per cent of conviction rate does not demonstrate any great capability of the prosecution service. Rather, it leads to restricted constitutional rights of the defendants and meaningless trials which serve only to confirm the prosecutorial decisions.'

An indication of Korea's unabated distorted judicial practice are apparent in the broadcast by *KBS News* in May 2018: 'June 13 Nationwide Local Elections - 43% of National Assembly by-election candidates from Gwangju, Jeollanam-do, are convicts. In connection with the upcoming local elections, it has been revealed that four of the ten National Assembly candidates from Gwangju are convicts. Among the 970 candidates registered with the Gwangju and Jeollanam-do electoral commission for election to metropolitan councils, law-makers, superintendents of education, and National Assembly by-elections, 421 candidates have convictions.' In an 'Elections 2018 Situation Report' dated 31 May 2018, *MBC News* revealed, '49% of candidates for Gyeongsangbuk-do parliamentary seats are convicts, 143 convictions in total.' Likewise, *Yonhap News* reported, 'Of the 34 registered candidates for the National Assembly by-election, 14 have criminal records. For drunken driving and other crimes, one candidate has eight convictions.'

Years earlier, Anna Fifield of the *Financial Times* had reported in August 2005, 'On Monday, the day Koreans celebrate the 60th anniversary of liberation from Japan, President Roh Moo-hyun will pardon 4.2 million criminals. Reprieves will be granted for everything from traffic violations and breaching the national security law to business and political crimes.... This is the fourth largest amnesty in the fifty-seven year history of the constitution. The staggering scale of the amnesties reflects the criminalisation of South Korean society. The judicial system is at the heart of the problem – there is no civil code to speak of in South Korea, so every transgression becomes a crime, and lawyers complain about the politicisation of the judiciary and almost universal powers of prosecutors. Courts always approve public prosecutors' application for search and seizure warrants.' Kim Un-yong's name was conspicuous in its absence from President Roh's list of pardonees.

Circumstances were stacked against an innocent Kim, as reported by various newspapers in 2004. The Constitution of the Republic of Korea provides that citizens accused of crimes are presumed innocent until proved guilty. Despite this provision, Kim Un-yong was arrested on 27 January 2004 at Seoul's Severance Hospital without the issuance of a formal charge or an indictment. There is no right to bail in the Republic of Korea, and bail would not be granted him, though sick and aged 73. In the meantime, he was limited to one five-minute visit per day involving no more than three visitors, all conversations being recorded. Dr. Kim Sung-soon and staff members at Severance Hospital who were treating Dr. Kim for ailments including severely high blood pressure were threatened and intimidated by state prosecutors into altering their medical reports – suppressing evidence of a tumour requiring surgery, and thereby denying the 73-year-old diplomat and internationally renowned sports leader adequate medical treatment during his ordeal. Public prosecutors in the Republic of Korea operate next door to the courthouse, and routinely and quite openly lobby judges and threaten witnesses to do their bidding. These outrages followed a series of related injustices and slanders against the most conspicuous Korean and IOC official who, among other major achievements, was largely responsible for bringing the 1988 Olympics to Seoul and elevating the national sport of taekwondo to Olympic status.

Simultaneously, the *Wall Street Journal* Asia edition was reporting: 'News from the war in Iraq has overshadowed the unprecedented impeachment of South Korea's President Roh Moo-hyun. The few Western pundits writing on events in Korea fundamentally misinterpreted what transpired in that political theatre of the absurd.... To most Western observers, Roh's impeachment confirmed Korea's status as a robust, liberal democracy . . . but this facile interpretation ignores the impeachment drama's historical and cultural context: an illiberal, Confucian political culture that elevates naked power above the rule of law.... Roh's impeachment illustrates the propensity of East Asian political elite to disregard the law.... Kim [Dae-jung], a virtuoso flatterer of Clintonesque gifts, endeared himself to the West as a liberal crusader through the constant use of democratic rhetoric that seduced the Western press. The real Kim, however, evokes not Mandela or Gandhi, but Rhee Syngman, South Korea's charismatic president and a dictator known for democratic rhetoric coupled with undemocratic practice.... As once observed, Rhee ran "an imperial Presidency" – while he fought for democracy, he never fully understood that its rule applied to him as well.'

The 'rules' were eminently one-sided. When the Supreme Court rejected Kim Un-yong's appeal in 2005 it stated: 'Since Dr. Kim was unable to give convincing and rational explanation as to why he drew money and how he spent it, it can be *inferred* that he used public money for personal purposes.' Mere inference, therefore, amounted to guilt (see Chapters 7, 'Symbiotic Convergence' and 8, 'Squandered Icon').

Speculation surrounded Kim's imprisonment, as related by publication in *Segye Ilbo* of a June 2005 piece under the headline 'What is the truth regarding "deletion of article due to external pressure"?' The commentary reported that *Monthly JoongAng* had been due to publish an article detailing how Roh Moo-hyun had invited IOC President Jacques Rogge to the presidential Blue House for a meeting including the Busan politician Kim Jung-kil and allegedly received a guarantee on the maintenance of taekwondo on the Olympic Programme after Beijing 2008 and the election of Pyeongchang for the Winter Games of 2014 and his crony Kim Jung-kil as IOC Member. These were in return for securing a 'voluntary' resignation by Kim Un-yong from the IOC. It had become apparent that journalists were blocked in their attempt to report details of an alleged triangular agreement between Rogge, the Blue House and

IOC President Jacques Rogge visiting Korean President Roh Moo-hyun at the Blue House, June 2005, a controversial meeting preceding Kim Un-yong's forced resignation while in hospital.

Kim Jung-kil. Such a deal was vigorously denied by the IOC's media director Giselle Davies. At an initial meeting by a Blue House representative with journalists, Roh's request for censorship was rejected. The following day an executive of Samsung Group, of which the magazine is an affiliate, demanded that the article be blocked, resulting in the resignation of the journalists. The circumstance would never be clarified. Nevertheless, Kim's resignation was enforced by the Blue House.

Comments on Korean suppression of human rights were rife; *Newsis* in Seoul wrote, 'In South Korea, public prosecution has complete monopoly over all powers of investigations, conduct of investigations, and indictments, unprecedented anywhere else in the world.' *The Korea Times* noted, 'The National Human Rights Commission of Korea has played a limited role due to a lack of independence and transparency.... The NHRC has suffered statutory limitations since its inception.' *Yonhap News* wrote, 'Public prosecutors are not only conducting surveillance activities outside the boundaries of collection of criminal data information, but are also preoccupied with obtaining information with such deceptive means as falsification of identity or by impersonation.' The Asia-Pacific Human Rights Network observed, 'South Korea, although a relatively developed jurisdiction in comparison to other Asian countries, has not yet eradicated custodial abuse. When the NHRC was established, it received about 10,000 complaints of alleged abuse. Police brutality against demonstrators, sometimes resulting in death, has also been common. Rather than addressing the problem, the government has sought to restrict the right to assembly.'

Resigned to his fate, Kim Un-yong issued the following statement in June 2005:

> While I look forward to re-joining my family and ending this long ordeal, I would like to take the opportunity to maintain my innocence of all allegations against me. This has been confirmed by the most recent report by the United Nations Human Rights Commission, which described me as a 'political prisoner' and a 'prisoner of conscience' who was victimised by false allegations relating to the initial bid by Pyeongchang to host a Winter Olympics.
>
> I realise that controversies have been raised in the press relating to other issues. I cannot address any of them to comply with conditions and limitations to maintain my status as a parolee. I also note that I must immediately undergo surgery for a prostate condition which will require convalescence for an extended period.
>
> I have dedicated my life to serving the interests of the Republic of Korea and its people and I plan carefully to examine my options towards a continuation of such activities. I would also like to express my gratitude to friends and supporters across the globe who were unswerving in their support of and belief in me during my imprisonment. They should know how important they were in helping me to perse-

Nellie Vladimirovna Kim, legendary Soviet gymnast with a Sakhalin Korean father, three gold and silver medal-winner, Montreal 1976, personifies those with imperishable memories of a Korean icon.

vere.

Among many to protest to senior judges among Korea's judiciary was the renowned Nellie Kim, a multiple gymnastics champion from Russia and currently first vice-president of the International Gymnastics Federation (FIG) as well as vice-president of World Taekwondo. Her emotions were representative of an international community dismayed by Kim Un-yong's humiliation:

> I respectfully submit this petition to gain the immediate freedom from detention of Dr. Kim Un-yong, who by any standard has been recognised as a true national hero of Korea. It is impossible to overstate what Dr. Kim has done for the Olympic Movement. World leaders in

business, government, sports and public affairs have come to understand the greatness and potential of the Republic of Korea through Dr. Kim's personal intervention. The people of Korea have been the beneficiary.

As an influential principal in the IOC, Dr. Kim brought the 1988 Games to Seoul, and with it a surge in the development of modern infrastructure that transformed Seoul into the modern centre it is today. Dr. Kim's leadership of your Olympic teams has brought great honour to Korea, winning multiple medals at Summer and Winter Games, phenomenal results rivalling those of the world's greatest powers, awakening not only pride among Korean citizenry, but recognition that Korea is a nation of achievers who can produce excellent products and services for global export as well as young men and women who excel in athletic competition.

Dr. Kim led the joint delegation from South and North Korea at the emotional Opening Ceremony of the 2000 Sydney Olympics. This was a culmination of his personal peace diplomacy through sport. It paved the way for a national reconciliation which has been delayed for more than half a century. He also paved the way for taekwondo, the Korean national sport, to join the ranks of official Olympic competition. This not only brings an opportunity for further distinction worldwide via athletic achievement, but also provides needed resources for the continuing development of taekwondo.

It is absurd to suggest that Dr. Kim embezzled or misappropriated any funds from the WTF in light of the huge sums of private fortune which he has generously provided for over thirty years in founding and building up the organisation. I believe he committed no crime. Defamations against him are either politically motivated or the product of the misinformed or the misguided. History will record Dr. Kim as a national hero for his extraordinary deeds together with the development of Korea from a Third World dictatorship to an emerging democracy and economic power. Those annals will also reward those who answer their consciences to speak out against the injustices which Dr. Kim suffers today. The time has come for the authorities to acknowledge this great error and dismiss all charges against Dr. Kim, thereby restoring him to his rightful place of leadership and service to Korea

Nellie Kim

Dr. Kim Un-yong, ultimately pardoned of all charges in 2008, would proudly retain the title of 'IOC Vice-president (Retired)' – this having been forced upon him, as related in Chapter 7 ('Symbiotic Convergence').

It would be appropriate for the IOC posthumously to reinstate Dr. Kim's Honorary Membership, restoring his family's dignity. There is a comparable precedent for such reinstatement: the return of Jim Thorpe's gold medals from the Stockholm Games of 1912 by President Samaranch to Thorpe's daughter almost seventy years later, his medals having been crudely confiscated for the trivial offence of receiving a few dollars for playing, of all things, baseball. Moreover, as Nellie Kim relates, it is probable that Dr. Kim – contrary to (subsequently withdrawn) allegations of embezzlement – invested a substantial sum from private funds: some $200,000 per annum in the early years of taekwondo's promotion with Kukkiwon and the World Taekwondo Federation, totalling in excess of $1 million, even by the most conservative estimates. In promotion of the Olympic Movement over three decades, he privately donated more than all but three others over the previous century: founder Baron De Coubertin, Chicago property millionaire Avery Brundage and Mexican media mogul Mario Vazquez Rana.

CHAPTER 2

—

SEOUL SPECTACULAR

Alex Gilady, former European head of the NBC television network, believes that in the Olympic Movement, 'you have to make your own luck.' Seldom if ever has this more fittingly applied than to Dr. Kim Un-yong, who was self-determining to the ultimate degree. He was, by any measure, a remarkable individual of multiple talents – a unique figurehead in Korea and in Asia, most broadly in the regime of Olympic sport, his expertise at its zenith within the field of human relationships. In my six decades of international personal associations across life and across the sporting field, there was no one I more respected and admired for his or her genial breadth of perspective. Much more than a friend, he could be infinitely discreet. As Walter Troeger, his German counterpart, observed, Kim did not deal in casual public comment; you might not notice him in a crowded room, but his actions were to turn the pages of history. Uniquely in the exercise of international sporting influence, Kim Un-yong did not demonstrably exude power but quietly rode close to the shoulder of power.

His family was prosperous, educated, upper middle-class landed gentry, sensitively aware of the need, in under-developed early 19th-century Korea under Japanese colonial occupation, for international cultural attitudes. His parents exposed him as a child to foreign influence, notwithstanding his father's death from pneumonia, pre-penicillin, when Un-yong was five. Intellectually precocious, the six-year-old Kim was 'vice-president' of his class at Deoksan Primary School in Daegu, South Korea; from there, his mother moved to Seoul and he to Sakurai Primary

School, where only a tiny minority of the 1,800 students were Korean. One of few women at the time with advanced education, his mother quit Daegu to be free of impecunious relatives seeking financial assistance from prosperous family members. Both Un-yong's parents were accomplished musicians; his father in particular played the violin and organ. The musical gene so blossomed in Un-yong's younger daughter Hae-jung that she would enjoy an acclaimed early concert pianist career.

Un-yong was motivated at Kyungdong Middle School to keep abreast of his majority Japanese contemporaries in colonial Korea, both academically and at sport, and he became distinguished in athletics and sumo. Because of sport, and his experience of having been bullied, he was the best at fighting, the fastest runner, the strongest at sumo, boxing, karate and skating, as is recounted in the biography *A Big Man Who Embraced the World*, published by the Korean Sport & Olympic Committee (KSOC). Outside school he was extending his keyboard mastery of Chopin and Weber. By his third year at Kyungdong at the age of thirteen, Korea had been liberated at conclusion of the war in the Pacific, while Kim had been enlisted under a 'student mobilisation order', though too young himself to be a soldier. Following liberation, the school became all-Korean. Kim Un-yong accelerated his command in English by conversing with resident US troops. Inspired by an exceptional English teacher named Hong Jae-ik, Kim directed his studies toward a diplomatic career, enrolling in 1949 at Yonsei University's Political Science and Diplomacy faculty – a year before the start of the Korean War, during which he would fight to defend his homeland and experience military training in the United States. It would be eleven years before he graduated, yet the conviction had taken root. He would later recall one of Yonsei professor Baek Nak-joon's lectures: 'If you're capable of harbouring great ambition and making your time at university worthwhile, the country and the world will someday be led by you.'

Only days before scheduled diplomatic service exams, North Korea's invasion was launched on 25 June 1950. Twice escaping near death during the ensuing war, at times fleeing the occupying invaders as they advanced over the retreating South's forces, Kim faced a threat to his very survival. Sometimes living on forest acorns, he became involved in the Battle of Jincheon as a nineteen-year-old liaison officer for the combined UN forces, having deliberately inflated his true age to twenty-one. By 1953, he had transferred to military training at the US Army Infantry School in Fort Benning, Georgia, returning home as an intelligence officer for Korea's 27th Infantry Division. From there, he was further transferred to a US division, where the opportunity arose in 1955 for him to study Spanish at Texas Western College on the Mexican border while graduating from the US Army's Anti-Aircraft and Guided Missile School. In an extraordinary contrast of social skills, the ubiquitous Kim would entertain friends not only at the classical keyboard but with impromptu taekwondo demonstrations, splitting wooden boards with a lightning smash of the same hands.

By the age of 29, he was a lieutenant-colonel with top-flight experience in military intelligence as aide-de-camp to Korea's Army chief of staff, General Song Yo-chan. Kim Un-yong returned to Yonsei's College of Political Science and Diplomacy, graduating in 1960; within a year he was promoted to aide to the US Military Advisory Group. In May 1961 General Park Chung-hee would assume the presidency by a coup d'état.

Kim Un-yong's career as international diplomat now advanced with his roles as counsellor to the United States and to Great Britain in the 1960s and then as Korean representative at the United Nations General Assembly in 1965. Kim's grasp of international relations exceeded that of anyone else, in a nation tentatively emerging from almost total destruction – a metaphorical pile of ash. A crossroads for Kim Un-yong arose with a double national crisis in January 1968: a failed North Korean terrorist attack on the Blue House and the North's capture of the USS *Pueblo*, a US spy ship, in international waters. Kim's credentials, including his

At the International Shooting Federation meeting at Bern, 1974, Kim Un-yong (second right) successfully bids for Seoul hosting the World Championships 1978 – the launch of Korea's sporting emergence.

first-hand contacts with New York and Washington, DC, made him ideal for an appointment as counsellor to Korean embassies for US relations. Amid his multiplicity of responsibilities, Kim Un-yong's emotional attachment to sport remained vibrant. In 1971–72 he became president of the Korean Taekwondo Association and founder-president of Kukkiwon, the sport's headquarters in Seoul; the following year he became founder-president of World Taekwondo (formerly the World Taekwondo Federation, until it was re-named in 2017) and launched its inaugural world championships (see Chapter 3, 'Asian Leadership'). His sports administrative portfolio continued to grow at a gallop: in 1974, he became president and honorary general-secretary of the Korean Olympic Committee and vice-president of Korean Sports Association. In a nation with zero experience hosting international sports events, Kim Un-yong was impatient for advance and adventure. Perhaps the Olympic Games?

Sport's global dramas were a waiting invitation for Kim Un-yong's instinct to promote national expansion and the National Olympic Committee. An opening salvo was speculative: a bid in 1974 to host the world shooting championships of 1978. Korea's national shooting federation was led by Park Jong-gyu, the presidential security service chief in the Blue House. Following the assassination of First Lady Yuk Young-soo, Park was prevented from attending a conference of the International Shooting Federation. Being familiar with Kim Un-yong's capability from mutual army duties, Park sent him as deputy. The sole rival bidder at the conference in Bern, Switzerland, was Mexico, the transparent favourite led by media millionaire Mario Vazquez Rana, who was busy inviting voters to fancy restaurants. Who were South Korea, anyone might ask – economically uncertain and facing student demonstrations, with North Korea actively campaigning against their neighbours south of the DMZ? However, two advantages lay with the Korean outsiders: shooting's global sporting expansion needed an Asian breakthrough and, crucially, Kim's linguistic versatility with his fluent English was granted wider impact, with an international audience, than Vazquez Rana's Spanish. The key element of Kim's formal presentation was a bold gamble. Mexico having offered a competitive ten-dollar per competitor accommodation rate, Kim audaciously undercut it with a five-dollar proposal. Deal done: 62 votes to 40. South Korea had taken its first ambitious step onto the international sports stage. From this moment, Kim Un-yong began shrewdly broadening his and thereby Korea's administrative credentials, establishing valuable friendships for instance when attending the Olympic Winter Games at Innsbruck, Austria, in 1976, which marked the beginning of geo-political change in Asia.

'I never calculated in terms of immediate costs at Bern,' Kim recalled, 'but in the long term. At that moment Seoul had yet to be the stage for any major international championship, though we were already due to host the second Asian Athletics Championships the following year. Then came the shooting championships in 1978, followed by the first air rifle championships in '79 and the eighth women's world basketball championship the same year, and the twelfth Asian weightlifting championship in 1980. That was the sum total of our achievements at the time we went to Baden-Baden in 1981 to bid for the Olympic Games! President Park certainly went overboard with his belief in the need to eliminate anything that might be an obstacle to his homeland's modernisation. But then I think about how he committed himself wholeheartedly to food self-sufficiency, development into an export power, heavy industry development, and autonomous defence, only to lose first his wife and then his own life to assassins' bullets. President Park was an upright man, but also a humane one. The objective facts are a matter for history to determine. During the Games in Moscow in 1980, there had been a mood that everyone was the friend of Nagoya in Japan, who were intending to bid for '88, but I knew that this was not really so. *And* I knew we were capable of staging the Games. Our only handicap was not being known. We weren't that worried about the cost of staging the Games, but in April '81, immediately prior to Baden-Baden, I was the *only* Korean representative at a meeting in Lausanne between the IOC Executive Board and the International Federations, taekwondo having become a "recognised" sport only the previous year. We had not even the credibility, during voting in Baden-Baden, of being hosts of the Asian Games of 1986 because that was to be decided in the spring of the following year.'

A successfully staged world shooting event had sustained Kim Unyong's conviction that an Olympic bid was feasible in spite of the earlier failed attempt for the Asian Games of 1966. At the Blue House, Park Jong-gyu was also supportive, and in mid-1979 President Park Chunghee gave his conditional approval to bid. Temporary abrupt chaos descended with Park's assassination on 26 October 1979, sanity only being restored when successor General Chun Doo-hwan revived the project in September 1980 with the encouragement of subordinate Roh Tae-woo, then the minister of political affairs (and later chairman of the organising committee). Chun signed financial guarantees in February 1981, a task force having been formed and the International Olympic Committee having announced Seoul as candidate and invited them to make a presentation at Lausanne.

Christopher Hill relates in *Olympic Politics* that Seoul failed to respond, the bid only rescued when IOC President Samaranch sent the Evaluation Commission to inspect Korea's potential, aware that IOC respectability required a second bid besides Japan's after Melbourne and Athens had withdrawn. Hill further relates that Korean credibility was established when Kim Un-yong, by now promoted to head of international taekwondo, attended a conference of the Pan-American Sports Organisation (PASO) where a quid-pro-quo arrangement developed: Vazquez Rana would support Seoul in return for Korea's backing him for the presidency of ANOC which would grant him widespread continental power. Kim Un-yong consolidated his influential platform – on the foundation of his World Taekwondo (Federation) presidency and election as Executive Board member of GAISF – with a continuing tour of Central and North American nations, including the inaugural World Games in Santa Clara, California, in 1981. GAISF president Tommy Keller vainly attempted to stall Seoul's bid, suggesting it should be revoked; Samaranch countermanded, 'Wait and see.'

Korea's international grapevine now embraced authoritative support from a British-led International Table Tennis Federation and from British Olympic Association secretary-general Richard Palmer. By August 1981, sixty IOC Members had been canvassed. Hill calculated that prior to the IOC's vote, Kim Un-yong was optimistic of the backing of thirty members. Kim was to pull a strategic ploy at the Session, getting himself accredited not as a member of Seoul's bidding committee (despite being general-secretary of the NOC) but under his World Taekwondo hat, thereby gaining access to wider IOC meetings and extended lobbying potential. Nagoya, over-confident as the outright favourite, had their momentum compromised by Japanese environmental activists plastering Baden-Baden lampposts with protest posters. Seoul gained one-upmanship with elegantly attired hostesses at their hospitality salon, together with the presence of the renowned Olympic marathon champion from Berlin '36, Sohn Kee-chung, who had been obliged during the occupation to compete as a faux-Japanese. On the eve of the vote, international news agencies uniformly predicted a Nagoya victory. Seoul's publicity campaign had been bolstered by a substantial loan from Hyundai chairman Chung Ju-yung, who never requested a repayment.

Alex Gilady, an Israeli IOC Member, had a vivid recollection of Seoul's voting procedure. 'A clear advantage for Seoul was that most of their facilities were already built, besides which they were more socially collaborative than the Japanese,' he noted. 'My New Zealand colleague Lance Cross commented beforehand that he was in no doubt about what should be the outcome. I was aware that Samaranch felt Korea would be a better ally, that they would deliver, whereas at that stage Nagoya had almost nothing yet available. There was also the positive opinion behind Seoul of Horst Dassler, recognising the opportunity of expanding Adidas equipment deals in Korea. On the morning of the vote Yuri Titov, Russia's president of international gymnastics, having studied a financial article in the *International Herald Tribune*, pointedly asked how Seoul could afford the Games when the city had a six billion-dollar loan from Japan. Korea's treasurer promptly responded that Seoul's capability from its current GDP would make the loan seem like peanuts – that this was not a poor country needing patronage from Japan. Kim Un-yong's impact publicly was not conspicuous; it had been in his campaigning, and his shining light would become more apparent afterwards. When it was almost impossible for Lausanne to communicate with Seoul – everybody back home wanting to take the helm – it was Kim who oiled the wheels. In Baden-Baden it was evident that South Korea wanted to engage the world. Adverse comments by Japanese member Masaji Kiyokawa drew an adverse reaction among members. Samaranch recognised privately

Prince Alexandre de Merode, Belgian Member, IOC Medical Commission chair, 1967–2002, a central figure in Kim Un-yong's global liaison

that 'Korea could expand the Olympic Movement in Asia.' Behind the scenes, Kim Un-yong had adroitly sought the backing of IOC Members Kees Kerdel (Netherlands), Prince Alexandre de Merode (Belgium) and the Grand Duke of Luxembourg. Chung donated a further $100,000 for entertainment. Nonetheless, the *LA Times* predicted 'Nagoya by 20 votes'.

Following presentations by Nagoya and Seoul, a technical meeting was held between the IOC and the International Federations, with Kim Un-yong present as president of World Taekwondo. Without him, South Korea would not have had representation to discuss the items that emerged. Confronted with doubts about infrastructure and lack of hosting experience, Kim was able to respond emphatically that Seoul could cope. 'In simple terms, it was a fight between the nation of Korea on the one hand and the city of Nagoya on the other,' Kim recalled. 'We took government officials, diplomats, athletes, business tycoons – the heads of Hyundai, of Korean airlines, of Daewoo. Nagoya was represented by the Prefecture Council and Chamber of Commerce – they did not seem to speak English well and did not seem international. And yet the name Nagoya was big compared to Seoul at that time. We had to overcome the fear factor of the North Korean military threat. Indeed, in Baden-Baden information on terrorist attacks or demonstrations was received from

Eastern European countries that were pro-North Korea. We prepared an exhibition room where KAL stewardesses and former Miss Koreas entertained visitors with ginseng tea. Nagoya also had an exhibition but seemed less prepared.' IOC Members and IFs received a better impression from Seoul.

In peripheral attendance was Patrick Nally, soon to become a close associate of Dassler in the marketing field. He introduced Kim Un-yong to Dassler, who sensed that Kim was another door to Asia for Adidas, that Kim was ambitious – and not just on behalf of taekwondo. 'Dassler sensed that Seoul was commercially ahead of China,' Nally reflected. John Boulter, an Olympian middle distance runner and central figure in the Adidas machine, acknowledged how Kim Un-yong was to become an immense figure in the Olympic Movement. 'There were more significant players from Korea moving in and out of the Dassler suite in Baden-Baden than Kim, who was essentially a mover and shaker behind the scenes – not in power but manipulating power, talking to everybody.'

Richard Palmer, general-secretary of the British Olympic Association, was not unfamiliar with circumstances in Seoul. He recalled, 'South Korea had little experience of international affairs, but Kim Un-yong had a broad church of international friends and gave Seoul, and its bid, an international perspective. I was on the ANOC supervisory committee for the '88 Games, along with Jacques Rogge and others. What we knew was that the Olympic Village would be excellent and many facilities were ready, but the age-orientated administration, operating from the top down, was cumbersome and confusing, though we sensed their goodwill. Certainly, Korean sport was well-drilled, especially martial arts which epitomise the ethics of hard work.' Kevan Gosper, a long-time Australian IOC Member, had thought that Nagoya would be the winner, but reflected, 'The first time the Games were to be held on the mainland of Asia was appealing to many IOC Members, never mind the strained relations between North and South.' A sour note on the outcome would be lobbed into the debate when the decision became known by Peter Ueberroth, organiser of LA's Games. 'Seoul gave away two first-class round-trip tickets to each IOC Member,' he said. 'The tickets were easily redeemed for cash – many were.' In this context, who were guilty if indeed the tickets were traded for cash: the donors or the recipients? This element of financial exploitation would come to haunt the IOC.

Elected to host the Olympic Games by an overwhelming margin of 52 votes to 27, Seoul faced the gargantuan task of preparation, which not least involved financial equilibrium for the project. If the IOC had grasped a political nettle (thanks in part to the peripheral influence of Dassler), it was now to benefit immeasurably from a Dassler-oriented financial masterpiece. Michael Payne, then an executive with the advertising agency managed jointly by BBC commentator Peter West and Patrick Nally, was close to its heart as a prospective deal-maker. 'We were astonished at the IOC's decision. How could they do this?' Payne had wondered. 'The IOC was struggling, politically and financially, in the aftermath of the Moscow boycott. In 1982 I was head-hunted by ISL [International Sport and Leisure], a marketing subsidiary of Dassler's Adidas and Japanese advertising agency Dentsu. Under the leadership of its new president, Juan Antonio Samaranch, the IOC was concerned about its dependence on television income. In 1985, in collaboration with the Seoul Olympic organising committee and US Olympic Committee, IOC handed marketing to ISL. I was summoned to go to Korea to launch a revolutionary advertising scheme labelled "TOP" (The Olympic Partners) – an ambitious project designed to harness, exclusively, global industries. In Seoul, I witnessed first-hand the incredible transformation of a nation ravaged by war. In establishing such an innovative programme, Kim Un-yong was the diplomatic back-channel coordination between Samaranch, the IOC and Korea's political leaders, such as Games organising chairman Roh Tae-woo. Kim was the bridge, additionally embracing relations with the Kremlin. Korea had no diplomatic path within sport.'

In his seminal financial treatise *Olympic Turnaround*, Payne wrote, 'The concept generated by Dassler, Jürgen Lenz and me was to harmonise global rights – for the IOC, Seoul Olympic organisers and all NOCs – with a single exclusive marketing package, offering companies one-stop shopping for Olympic involvement. The biggest battle [was] with the US Olympic Committee, jealously guarding their control over domestic Olympic trademarks. USOC participation was critical, many prosperous sponsors being US-based.... By late 1985 we were desperate, with only three companies on board (Coca-Cola and Kodak were the first two) . . . and having already guaranteed millions of dollars to NOCs.'

In the event, 153 of the then 156 NOCs came on board in time for 1988, with sponsors including Philips, Time-Sport, Panasonic and Brother, on a modest $10,000 spread over three to four years plus $300 for every athlete attending Seoul. In the lead-up to Korea's Games, the power of the Olympic Movement, seen and unseen, rested primarily in the hands of three men: Samaranch, Dassler and Kim Un-yong.

If the IOC, and thereby Seoul, struck lucky with the crystallisation of TOP, progress through the seven years of fraught negotiations was threatened by the political nightmare of terrorism, cancellation or boycott by Communist-allied nations led by the Soviet Union, and not least by South Korea's northern neighbour, with whom they remained technically at war. Potential terrorism haunted Samaranch until the evening the participant athletes returned home.

Almost every bureaucratic move made by Seoul's Olympic organising committee was dependent on Kim Un-yong's ever-expanding sports diplomacy and on his network of contacts. Because of Korea's lack of formal diplomatic channels, Kim's personal sports connections were paramount for persuasive efforts with the Eastern Bloc. To lobby, say, Poland, he would attend a junior world fencing championship in Poznan, though well aware that Eastern Bloc policy on participation would essentially be determined by the Kremlin. At every turn, North Korean representatives within any allied Soviet colony would attempt to sabotage South Korean access. With few supportive Korean embassies, Kim's passport had to be for 'Olympic relations'. Tensions all but fatally mounted when in 1983 a Soviet fighter jet shot down KAL Flight 007 (New York to Seoul) off the coast of Russia's Sakhalin Island, killing all 269 on board. The Cold War temporarily boiled over: members of European NOCs, led by Franco Carraro of Italy, called for a change of venue, which was echoed in the US and West Germany. Many in the South Korean rank and file doubted whether their country wanted, or needed, the Games.

The following year, Kim Un-yong and organising committee chairman Roh Tae-woo were obliged to attend the Games in Los Angeles: to observe protocol, assure Samaranch of their loyalty, engage NOC contacts and win friends – notwithstanding that the Soviet Union figured a third successive boycott. Roh was targeted by relentless media interrogators: how could the Seoul project survive? Roh deflected doubts with calm conviction: 'Korea and the Olympic family have the responsibility, having been elected to organise the Games.' The strategically alert Samaranch – who had regularly attended the yearly conference of Soviet-aligned sports ministers – scheduled a change in the Olympic Charter: formal invitations to the Games would now be issued not by the host NOC but by the IOC, thereby bypassing Korea's political diplomatic famine.

Meanwhile Kim Un-yong was covering more ground than a marathon contender in training, using his multi-linguistic charm to establish liaisons that would keep Seoul buoyant. His tireless campaign would continue in 1985 alongside the IOC Session in East Berlin, the pulse-beat of the GDR. Kim's role as president of World Taekwondo Federation and Korean NOC vice-president gave him automatic access at the Session. Rumour suggested that GDR's gradual loosening from the Kremlin's strait-jacket policy had eased consideration by sports minister Manfred Ewald for its competing at Seoul. At a lavish reception, Ewald pointedly

Manfred Ewald, East German NOC president, prominent in persuading Soviet Bloc's participation at Seoul '88, visits Kukkiwon.

stressed that sports and politics 'should not entwine'.

Directly getting to grips with the Soviet Union's NOC was a protracted yet vital effort. Kremlin authority would determine the participation of most if not all allies. Bizarrely, East-West Olympic relations would precede political relations improvement. Kim Un-yong first visited Moscow in June 1987, attending a television commission meeting of the IAAF; it was an opportunity to negotiate 1988 television rights with the European Broadcasting Union. Kim was able to establish more intimate exchanges with IOC Member Vitaly Smirnov, a key administrative figure from Moscow '80, and sports vice-ministers Henrika Yushkevitch and Vyacheslav Gavrilin. They subjected Kim to examination by late-night vodka, his endurance proving equal to theirs. Kim and Gavrilin were to meet again in Tokyo in July, Kim having been authorized by the Blue House to give guarantees on athlete security, accommodation, transport and press accreditation. Trickier to handle was the Soviet demand for permission to dock a ship at Incheon Harbour, a similar move to previous operations at the Games in Melbourne, Tokyo and Montreal. It was not a spy-ship but a residence for non-accredited officials and cultural groups and a setting for supplies for athletes in the Games Village. Less provocative, Kim knew, would be the landing rights for Aeroflot; they had already been permitted for China during the Asian Games scheduled for 1986. Accompanying Kim Un-yong at these meetings was Kim Sam-hoon, international director for Korea's foreign ministry and the figure responsible for bilateral contact with Soviet bureaucracy – all foreign contact being conducted through the office of GAISF in Monte Carlo. The first official delegation of the Soviet NOC and sports ministry to Seoul came in August 1987, led by deputy minister Anatoly Kolesov and Yuri Titov, head of international gymnastics. Kim relates in *The Greatest Olympics*, 'I took them to Kukkiwon for a taekwondo demonstration. By the time the Games were finished, we had become real friends.'

Kim continued ceaselessly circling like a collie at sheepdog trials; in addition to the Soviets, he was maintaining contact with the entire Eastern Bloc brigade: Ivan Slavkov (Bulgaria), Alexandru Sipercu (Romania), and Tamas Ajan (Hungary). In September 1987, the IOC staged a reception to herald the issuance of Games invitations, having rejected North Korea's request to delay this formality. This function included a concert, and on Samaranch's request, Kim's younger daughter Hae-jung performed Beethoven's Piano Concerto No. 3 (a cultural invitation that would subsequently be manipulated to chastise Kim).

By now, the issue regarding a Soviet sealiner's docking at Incheon needed resolving. Kim Un-yong met Gavrilin in Tokyo in early December and consulted President Chun on precedents; Chun consented, and Kim was able to give Gavrilin unofficial approval on condition that the Soviets respected port authority, customs and security. The chemistry was evolving. On 21 December, the GDR became the first Eastern Bloc nation to announce its participation; it was soon followed by Hungary.

World Taekwondo Federation founding president Kim Un-yong at the 21st GAISF general assembly, 1987. International Weightlifting Federation president Tamas Ajan and International Swimming Federation president Robert Helmick provide authoritative support.

On 27–30 December the Soviets made their second official visit to Seoul and confirmed acceptance of formal communications, now to open through GAISF telex in Kim Un-yong's office at Kukkiwon. Acceptances quickly multiplied: in the first two weeks of January, Bulgaria, Poland, Yugoslavia, Romania and Mongolia came onside. USSR's formal acceptance, disclosed on television by sports ministers Marat Gramov and Gavrilin, was simultaneously matched by China. Samaranch and Kim Un-yong could privately celebrate – more so with Soviet cultural ministry approval of involvement in the Games' Olympic Art festival, alongside establishment of a 'temporary consular office'. Kim would recall, 'Socialist nations' first concern was participation, but this is now expanding to economic and cultural fields for after the Games.' Soviet consultation visits became monthly, as with their political allies. Kim Un-yong's one-time shooting gamble was paying dividends. Finally, on 1 September, he visited Beijing, collaborating with China's NOC on background management for the subsequent 1990 Asian Games in China.

The seven-year workload on Kim Un-yong was astonishing. He was wearing seven hats: in functional routine, he was the representative of the Korean Taekwondo Association, Kukkiwon, World Taekwondo, the Korean Olympic Committee, the IOC, the GAISF Executive Board (from 1986), and the Seoul Games organising committee. Most relevant of all, he was a discreet personal counsellor between Samaranch and the Blue House. No wonder contemporary administrators were in awe of him. Manolo Romero, technological master of television broadcasting, switched in 1985 from America's ABC network to EBU; the following year he was invited to join the IOC's Radio and TV Commission as consultant. He regarded Kim Un-yong's multi-faceted competence as profound. 'Dr. Kim was involved in every little piece,' he recalled. 'If a problem in Seoul's organising committee seemed insurmountable, he would intervene with an answer; his advice was paramount for efficiency, whatever the minute detail. From the start, I was so impressed by his grasp, even when an issue was not his responsibility.'

As Europe Director of America's NBC network, Alex Gilady spent countless days seated in Lausanne's Palace Hotel lounge – headquarters for visiting Olympic personnel – to monitor the interminable negotiations of the host city broadcast contract. He was similarly impressed: 'It was almost impossible for the IOC to communicate intimately with Seoul, with many in Seoul wanting to "take charge". Kim was well versed in the Blue House, understood Samaranch, spoke fluent English. Samaranch exploited Kim's shrewd communication skills from the start, and adroitly made him IOC Member following the Asian Games of 1986, steering his election to the IOC Executive Board in the year of Seoul's Games.'

Dick Palmer, no mean administrator for the British Olympic Association, knew as adviser to GAISF how complex the Korean political hierarchy was. 'The convention of bureaucratic direction coming only from the top led to a confused, cumbersome system of management,' he said. 'Within that system, Kim was the essential link, establishing cohesion with the IOC. In his coordination, there was always an element of wanting to please.' Nat Indrapana, an IOC Member from Thailand who was sensitive to the demands on Korea, admired Kim's breadth of allegiance. 'Un-yong was concerned not only for Korea but for Asia,' Indrapana reflects. 'At Seoul's Asian Games, a trial run for Seoul two years before the Olympics and dominated by China, Un-yong would say, "Let's work together." He was always looking for close friends, for collaboration. He embraced Samaranch on almost everything; they spoke twice a day.'

Kim Un-yong was the only organising committee member operating throughout the seven-year haul, which saw three different organising presidents serve: Kim Yong-sik (former foreign minister), Roh Tae-woo and Park Seh-jik (former chief of the Agency for National Security Planning). All three implicitly trusted Kim. Of 16 organising committee delegations attending IOC Executive Board meetings, five were led by Roh, three by Park and eight by Kim Un-yong. As he himself related in *The Greatest Olympics*, 'There were so many issues: early demands for change of venue, boycott and terrorist threats, participation doubts, television rights, protocol, accommodation, security, media venues, NOC cooperation, media facilities, doping administration, athlete eligibility, finance, each sport's venue, accreditation, translators, the IOC Session prior to the Games, and the Opening and Closing Ceremonies. An important example of NOC cooperation was support of African athletes, with a KAL charter at our expense, costing $1.5 million. I called KAL president Cho Choong-kun, and he agreed to fly the Africans both ways – 365 athletes and officials at three stops: Algiers, Abidjan and Nairobi. The deal was done with Lamine Ba, general-secretary of SCSA (Supreme Council of Sport in Africa), which agreed to contribute $500 a head.'

The Olympic Movement consists of three arms (exclusive of ancillary sponsors and media): the IOC, constitutional owners; the International Federations; and the National Olympic Committees. Over many years and many arguments during the IOC presidencies of Avery Brundage (1952–72) and Michael Killanin (1972–80), the IFs and NOCs had established their separate representative bodies: the day an Olympic Games begins, the IOC is effectively a bystander/supreme adjudicator, and it is the IFs (administering some 30 concurrent world championships) and the NOCs (supplying the ammunition) who create the live production – the action. Kim Un-yong was thus at the summit of a day-to-day festival embracing some 200 sports organisations, each with a vibrant vested interest. Central to Kim's liabilities would be negotiation of scheduled start times in association with (in particular US) television rights fees.

Foremost in self-importance among IFs are track and field (IAAF) and football (FIFA). In the autumn of 1984, Seoul staged a celebration event to mark the opening of the main stadium, the stage for Opening and Closing Ceremonies, the International Association of Athletics Federations (IAAF) programme and the football final. Ceremony ticket applications by officials and athletes, not to mention the public, are always a headache; so too is dovetailing the schedule of athletics and football. The demands of Primo Nebiolo, president of IAAF, were predictably a burden for Kim, alongside Nebiolo's negotiated financial compensation for start-time adjustment to US television peak-time viewing. A fourth function for the main stadium is equestrian show jumping, traditionally held on the final day prior to the Closing Ceremony. Equestrian events were a particular headache, administratively; as Kim lamented, 'six years ago we had nothing more than a few donkeys.' Extensive collaboration between Kim Un-yong and the president of equestrian sports (IFES), the Duke of Edinburgh – who was shortly succeeded by his daughter the Princess Royal, herself a contender at Montreal '76 – resolved the many issues. Show jumping, for instance, was to start at 8 a.m. to accommodate later IAAF events; horse and groom were not to be separated on arrival at immigration control. The equestrian schedule alone required 1,500 organising committee personnel.

A newly elected and proprietorial president of volleyball, Ruben Acosta of Mexico, sought to use the main stadium but was rebuffed: his alternative demand for a 20,000-capacity stadium was a major technical imposition, and Kim Un-yong was called upon to intervene in friction between Acosta and Seoul's protocol supervisor. Not least among the IOC policy leaders for his peremptoriness was Thomas Keller of rowing, who wrangled over the designated course and the massive operation of boat transportation – one of the few sports, Kim observed, 'where the president acted as frontline operator!' To boost audience figures (for television credibility) 10,000 free tickets were distributed at the rowing lake. Kim Un-yong was to succeed Keller as president of GAISF in 1986 – engineered by Samaranch specifically to stall Keller's blatant challenge to IOC authority on Olympic Games governance. Kim had expected possible difficulties with gymnastics bureaucracy, the IF president being Yuri Titov from Moscow, but Kim reported, 'He was reasonable and really a sportsman, impressed with the efforts we were making.'

Soviet antagonism towards the US-reliant South Korea regime might be dissolving, but the threat from the DPRK remained ever-present and was starkly apparent to those attending Seoul's hosting of the Asian Games of 1986, which served as a test bed for two years hence. A few days beforehand, a terrorist bomb killed five South Koreans at Gimpo International Airport, with security forces advising Samaranch that North Korea's infiltration of personnel into the South was increasing. Seoul's development of contemporary sporting technology in preparation for 1988 was not bulletproof.

Every IOC Member attending the Asian Games event, every floor of the official hotel, had 24-hour armed bodyguards. An additional ongoing political hazard came in the form of mounting student protests backing government opposition (New Korea Democratic Party), with ruling President Chun Doo-hwan due to retire three months before the Olympics. Here was an echo of the student riots prior to Mexico '68, which then resulted in multiple police killings. Could Korea move in time to meet a growing public demand for further democratisation? On the sporting front, yes. Into the Asian Opening Ceremony marched Iran and Iraq, separated alphabetically as a diplomatic gesture only by Jordan, Iran having been absent from Los Angeles '84. More to the point in terms of 'normalisation', 391 competitors now marched from ideologically opposed China. Park Seh-jik, now the Games' organising committee president, proclaimed, 'A new era in Asia is dawning.'

A month after Seoul's Asian Games ended, Kim Un-yong was elected a member of the IOC. He was the sixth in line from Korea, following inaugural member Lee Ki-bung (1955–1960). As already mentioned, Samaranch contrived for Kim's immediate swearing-in on account of the immediacy of his responsibilities. While Kim was unquestionably the appropriate candidate (as vice-president of the organising committee) to succeed Park Jong-gyu, who had died of cancer in 1985 just a year after succeeding Kim Taek-su, there had been subterranean counter-measures against this prestigious election within Korean sport – never mind the conventional practice by which the nomination for IOC Membership comes from the IOC, not the NOC. President Chun had dismissed the Kim 'nomination', speaking with Samaranch prior to the Asian Games as though it was his decision. Chun had previously forced Kim Un-yong's resignation as president of the Korean Taekwondo Association in 1983 to impose his own younger brother Chun Kyung-hwan in the post. Chun was known now to prefer Roh Tae-woo, currently still organising committee leader for 1988, or indeed sports minister Park Seh-jik for the Lausanne appointment. Samaranch resolutely backed Kim Un-yong: 'Korea can have Kim as IOC Member or hold the Olympics without any IOC Member.' Chun backed off and Kim was elected – a no-brainer.

The multiplicity of Kim Un-yong's management strategy included negotiation of television rights sales, a rewarding yet challenging arena. The task involving the prime objective of rights in the USA was magnified by Korea having hired Barry Frank from Mark McCormack's IMG; as an advisor, Frank proved to be out of touch with a huge but evolving market. As Payne relates, Frank's calculations 'in a scorpion war' were distorted by the extraordinary fee of $309 million paid by ABC network for Calgary's Winter Games (seven months previous), and he 'somehow convinced Seoul that their US broadcast rights could be worth up to $1 billion. This was totally unrealistic.' Frank also skewed negotiations with his attempts to intervene in event start times coincidental to television demands. Payne quoted ABC's chief negotiator for ten previous US contracts from Innsbruck '64 to Calgary as saying, 'We not only captured the market, we'd sucked it dry.' While the Calgary contract had taken less than six weeks to conclude, the one for Seoul was to require over six months, starting in September 1985.

In his Games anthology *The Greatest Olympics*, Kim Un-yong admits, 'I had to tell the Korean public many times that television rights involved more than just the fee. The side effects were beyond estimate. If Korea had paid for the television time to publicise its culture and images for 180 hours of live programming, it would have cost hundreds of millions of dollars – and that pounding the table does not necessarily result in higher rights.... I was caught between Korea's national pride and the cold reality of a maximum market price.' ABC's declining audience figures had resulted in ten per cent staff redundancies. Samaranch, aware of the 'sting' of the Calgary figure, sensed that the Summer Games US rights-holder must be allowed a profit; not to kill the goose, the fee allocated amounted to 20 per cent for the host's technical installation, with the remaining 80 per cent being split – two-thirds to the host nation and the remaining one-third divided equally between the IFs, NOCs and IOC (i.e., 9 per cent each).

Accomplished musician Kim Un-yong performs Chopin's *Fantasie-Impromptu* during a Korean visit by IOC President Juan Antonio Samaranch (third left).

Seoul's negotiations were jointly led by Canadian Richard Pound and Kim Un-yong, the former being Samaranch's legal hit-man. Pound recollects in his *Inside the Olympics*, 'It took much longer for everybody to be ready to negotiate US rights for Seoul.... The networks rebelled against a process that reduced the decision to one of money; they wanting to show what their plans would be for the broadcast of the Games.... The certainty of the Games actually taking place created some uncertainty.... The bids were much lower than imagined ... with Korea negotiating in Lausanne and their decisions being taken back in Seoul. Some of them slept in their chairs.... With the time difference between Seoul and Lausanne, they couldn't wake President Chun in the middle of the night.... When they saw the level of offers (from ABC, CBS and NBC), Olympic organising chairman Roh Tae-woo said they would accept the highest "with the greatest reluctance".' ABC and CBS were themselves in the midst of takeover bids by other companies.

Excelling at the keyboard with Chopin is a far cry from haggling with mega-buck TV executives, yet the remarkable Kim Un-yong was evidently in his element at both, unemotional as an accountant on behalf of an ambitious new Asian economic powerhouse. Outlining his strategy at the first rights meeting in Lausanne, Kim explained in *The Greatest Olympics*, 'I knew there was no market to warrant Frank's suggested $500 million.... CBS offered $300m, ABC $225m plus an additional guarantee from ESPN of a maximum $135m. NBC had two proposals: $325m, or $300m plus a maximum $150m additionally if advertising sales exceeded $635m – a risk-sharing system. These low offers surprised us, considering ABC paid the same for LA in their own time zone.... CBS and ABC were quite weak, awaiting takeovers, but NBC was strong, enthusiastic but very careful, not wanting to lose money.... A re-scheduled meeting was agreed for New York. We had to consider public opinion and face-saving, NBC to calculate production costs, insurance, etc. In New York, NBC discovered it was now the only serious bidder. Back home, there was pressure to reject this offer, preserving national pride.... I proposed a $300m guarantee plus a $200m risk-sharing bonus.... Not compromising with NBC could have accelerated calls for a change of venue.... NBC accepted my proposal at a TV press conference.... Most of the media reported only the $300m, not the bonus.'

The bargaining was not yet over: exhausting contractual details remained regarding Games cancellation insurance, with a 'letter of credit' from the Korean Exchange Bank for $330m and a reduction of fees in the event of Soviet withdrawal. The letter of credit was regarded as an insult to Koreans, necessitating lengthy debate among Kim Un-yong, Park Seh-jik and President Chun until approval was reached – under pressure from the IOC. Argument over a composite NBC logo for the Games further extended into 1986, before the signing of a contract in March at Lausanne: Samaranch and Finance Commission chairman Count Jean de Beaumont from France for the IOC, NBC president Arthur Watson and Kim Un-yong for the Seoul Games organising committee. An added $2m interest was received in respect of the six-month delay – which, a relieved President Chun told Kim in jest, 'you can keep.'

In a letter expressing mutual collaboration on the Games, Watson stated, 'It will not only be focused on sport, we will be putting South Korea, and its people, culture, history and development front and central.... My colleagues and I would like to discuss with you how to accurately represent the very special country that is South Korea.' IOC appreciation, in a note to Kim from Samaranch and Pound, was fulsome: 'We congratulate you on your outstanding accomplishment. This is an extremely difficult and important negotiation.... Your participation proved very effective.'

Rights for Japanese television were the next hurdle. Having paid $18m for Los Angeles with its wide time difference, a synchronised time schedule with a rich neighbour would raise the stakes, with a six-network consortium led by NHK – notwithstanding earlier colonial occupation. The project was complicated by previous behind-the-scenes negotiations for coverage of Seoul's Asian Games, so Kim Un-yong had to tread cautiously.

Public expectation, dissatisfied with the 'disappointing' but realistic US contract, was again over-optimistic. Kim Un-yong's opinion was that a projected figure of $80m was speculatively high and that $50m was negotiable, given Japan's GDP was only a third of America's. Japan's negotiators argued that event start times were already pre-arranged at inconvenient hours in favour of US consumption, and offered $40m. Through continued bargaining, Kim kept bidding high, up to $78m; his strategy was rewarded when Japan finally settled, in February 1987, at $50m – plus a $2m courtesy bonus. With pre-Games instalment payments, interest would raise the total to $60m. It was another value add by Kim Un-yong, which together with fees from South America (OTI) for $2.92m, Eastern Europe (OIRT) for $3m, Asia (ABU) for $1.5m, Canada for $4.9m and Africa for $170,000, brought the total of broadcast fees to $480m.

An impressed Samaranch, having expected no better than £35m from Japan, recognised Kim Un-yong's skill by appointing him chairman of the IOC's Television and Radio Commission. Over two decades, Kim would help IOC accumulate £3.3 billion in broadcast rights.

It was one thing to obtain financial equilibrium for the Seoul Games and another to defuse sustained attempts by DPRK, either to sabotage the event or, improbably, force the elected host city to accept 'co-hosting' with Pyongyang, which would run totally contrary to Olympic Charter decree (by which a city rather than a country is nominated). In my official biography of Samaranch, *Olympic Revolution* (1992), Kim Un-yong was explicit: 'During the IOC Session in Berlin in 1985, Roh Tae-woo and I met many socialist delegates. Manfred Ewald, the GDR sports minister, was optimistic. He had already had discussion with Samaranch, and really pushed the North-South talks. "That's your problem," he would say to me. "We will only work within the Olympic Charter." East Germany was much more of a leader towards participation in Seoul than the Soviet Union. Hungary and the others were just waiting to be given a guide. Four factors were of influence: the new détente between America and Russia, the damage of boycotts to sport, the unifying efforts of Samaranch, and our own efforts to be hospitable, whatever the cost, to show that our country was different to what people had heard. South Korea was still partially in darkness.'

The Session in Berlin was notable for many developments other than the dismissal of long-time Director-General Monique Berlioux, the demonstrative French former Olympian swimmer, who had resented Samaranch's authority from the start. It was now, for instance, that details began to emerge of timing adjustments in event schedules for Seoul that would accommodate the interests of NBC. Also emerging was news of the first series of meetings between the two Koreas that would eventually extend over two years, having initially been sounded out by Ashwini Kumar, an Indian IOC Member and Vice-president. 'The question of North Korea was really a side issue,' said Alain Coupat, aide-de-camp to Samaranch. 'But it was handy for Samaranch to have it as a second front on which to focus. The excesses of North Korea made it easier for other communist nations. I don't think that some ever understood, but Samaranch did not want to solve the Korean situation. The security would have been impossible. So the worse the controversy, in one sense, the better the situation. Persuading other people to enter into the debate, nation-to-nation, was one of the best things he ever did.'

Reflecting on Seoul's appointment, Samaranch recalled, 'In '81, I was contented enough about Calgary (being elected), but very worried about South Korea. It was hard to understand the Members' decision, but the hundreds of protesters were probably decisive against Nagoya. That is why, immediately after the Games in LA, I went with Vazquez Rana to Moscow to see Gramov, the minister of sport. What I achieved was not to talk of the past but consider the future. At that stage their position was still not clear – I think they were hedging at the time.... I could sense their uncertainty about the opinion of the IOC.'

Kim, in constant touch with the IOC leader, reflected, 'North Korea had been negotiating behind the scenes before the election and immediately demanded a change of site. Samaranch had made it clear there would be no such thing. For seven years we worked, through him, to make sure everyone knew they would be welcome in Seoul. The absence of diplomatic relations was going to be an obstacle, yet the Games served as a link to those countries with which we had no diplomatic connection. And the socialists realised that their athletes had been put at a serious disadvantage by boycotts, and that nothing had been gained politically. Once they realised we guaranteed security, they began to warm. It was Samaranch who persuaded our political leaders to open the continual discussions with the North. We knew we had to accept IOC advice, so our politicians were always prepared to talk. *We*, in Seoul, knew that co-hosting could not work, but if the IOC wanted to offer North Korea a share of sports, then we were happy to give it a try.'

Samaranch himself was frank: 'I told Kim to trust me. I was quite sure in my own mind that North Korea would never organise one single sport, even though they had a brand new stadium that they wished to use. I told Roh that he could offer the North whatever he liked, and of course, once we had entered this area of debate, everyone else entered the ring, Fidel Castro saying we had to give something more. I kept on saying publicly that we would never close negotiations with the North right up to the last minute. It was important for us that the meetings were always on our ground, not at Panmunjom. At *every* meeting there were secret service men in the delegation of both countries. The North's delegations were unable to change one comma of their instructions from Pyongyang. I was always saying to Roh these were not the South Koreans' Games, but the IOC's Games. I repeatedly assured Roh the proposals would never work because the North would never agree to accept free movement of media between North and South, which would have to be a part of any such agreement. I was aware that the Soviet Union wanted us to show we were "doing our best" for North Korea, although they still intended to take part. When I sent a delegation to Pyongyang, asking them to request permission to return to Seoul through the Panmunjom checkpoint, and this was refused, it was confirmation that the North would never agree to anything. They could not consistently open the border to television, sponsors and the rest of the Olympic family. Kim Un-yong was *officially* not in an important position, yet he was the perfect channel to the senior South leaders. I used him to judge how far I could go with offers to the North, and I spoke with him almost every day.... I tried to get to know Kim Yu-sun, the president of the North's NOC, but at private meetings translation tended to be a mess: Korean into Russian into English, neither of us really understanding the other. I went with Kim Yu-sun to the airport in Berlin together with Gramov, the Soviet minister, who confirmed Russia's intention was to participate, but [said] that the IOC must resolve the North Korean problem.'

There were multiple strands to political manoeuvres in the DPRK controversy. In his *Olympic Politics*, Christopher Hill reflected that in crisis, the IOC would have been able to find an experienced city that had already staged a Games to take over; that Korea's leaders believed this could happen if they allowed political demonstrations by students to become so violent that these had to be quelled by 'unacceptably harsh measures'. However, Hill further related the behind-the-scenes move by Horst Dassler at the Los Angeles Games, with an East-West meeting of ideological rivals attended by Valery Syssoev, the Soviet vice-minister of sport, and Manfred Ewald. One contentious issue was whether Korea would offer political asylum to would-be defectors. Kim Un-yong was in a cleft stick: Korea's accepted policy was refusal, but this risked contravention of international law. Commenting on the four joint negotiating meetings between DPRK and South Korea, from Lausanne in October 1985 to July 1987, and the North's ultimate rejection of the offered Games integration, Hill concluded, 'It is clear that Samaranch phrased the negotiations with extreme skill.... They were conducted as a search for conditions in which the North would feel able to send a team to the Games, but the IOC's broader purpose was to save the Games, not so much for the sake of Seoul, as for the whole of the Olympic Movement.' Kevan Gosper, a prominent Australian IOC Member and sometime Vice-president, remembers in his *An Olympic Life*, 'Continuing to negotiate with North Korea provided an outlet for frustrations on both sides of the border – kept the North inside the proverbial tent, rather than outside, attempting to destabilise the Games, while the upside for the South was the recognition it would gain from a successful Games to the North's discomfort. This overlooked, of course, widespread longing among the South's rank and file for re-unification.'

To any foreign observer, the tensions in the Korean Peninsula were – and are – frighteningly ever-present. One need only go to the Demilitarised Zone (DMZ) at Panmunjom, which stretches a hundred miles along the UN-designated 38th parallel. I was there prior to the launch of the Asian Games. A zephyr ruffles the muddy waters of the Imjingang River, catching the sunlight; ducks and pheasants cry overhead. A gentle peace, an autumnal tranquillity, lies on the rice fields and the rolling hills. It is a peace as fragile as a pheasant's egg. Assembled along the Northern side is the largest permanent peace-time armoured force in history. Here at a little farming village – which was obliterated seventy years ago and is still a joint security area, the volatile symbol of armistice – it was then, and is still, difficult if not impossible to believe in any kind of Olympic fraternisation across the border. In 1986, Samaranch was to have been a visitor to the scene of the little Bridge of No Return, the one forlorn remaining road link on Highway 1, where prisoners of war were exchanged in 1953 and across which, it was supposed, the Olympic family would pass if the North were to accept the offers from the South in a gesture of sporting unity. Wisely, Samaranch decided against such an appointment. Had he visited the invasion tunnel – driven through granite 70 metres under the demilitarised zone and discovered by the South in 1978 – and a third such secret tunnel to make mockery of the armistice, carrying 30,000 armed troops an hour and emerging 44 kilometres from Seoul, Samaranch might well have blanched. The larks sing in Panmunjom in the heart of the Demilitarised Zone, which has ironically become a wildlife sanctuary, saviour of the threatened Manchurian snow crane. But human hearts flutter. 'When the sun goes down,' a United States corporal said to me, gazing out at dusk at the invisible armaments around Jinbongsan Mountain to the north, 'this is the eeriest place on earth.'

Eerie it remained in 2019, whatever the latest speculative Tweet from vacillating US President Donald Trump regarding the Korean Peninsula. For Kim Un-yong, three decades ago, unification nonetheless was a constant emotional objective; in his growing partnership with Sama-ranch he was aware that the only route to a possible joint team for Seoul '88 must be directed via South Korea rather than by the IOC. The perceptive Alex Gilady, an Israeli Member from 1994 and peripheral analyst since the early 1980s, defined Kim Un-yong's status during the Samaranch regime: 'In Seoul, he *was* Samaranch, the conduit to the North.'

In *The Greatest Olympics*, Kim devotes 12 pages to the protracted and vain saga of theatrical political wrangling. It began with the North's recognition that Eastern Bloc allies were no longer in the mood for a boycott, whereupon they emerged with the unprecedented proposal for joint hosting. A progressive climate of détente between USA and USSR was diminishing DPRK's red rag posture. In February 1985 Samaranch had notified North and South that he was willing to chair a joint meeting to invoke the Olympic spirit, never mind the request by the North's dictator Kim Il-sung to the Kremlin and to Havana's Fidel Castro to undertake auxiliary provocation. As Kim Un-yong relates, that thorough exploratory discussion initially took place: Samaranch with both the Soviets and the GDR; Alexandru Sipercu, the Romanian IOC Member, with his Eastern Bloc colleagues; and Kim Un-yong himself with both the Eastern Bloc and the Seoul organising committee. Tensions had escalated with the Soviet sabotage of KAL 007 in 1983. In July 1985, deputy premier Chong Chun-ki submitted DPRK's demand for co-hosting and a unified team, under the banner 'Pyongyang/Seoul Olympics'. Samaranch responded that the Charter prohibited co-hosting and proposed the first joint meeting in October 1985 in Lausanne. This resulted in a stalemate, the DPRK going overboard by demanding the hosting of 11 sports, plus Opening and Closing Ceremonies in both Pyongyang and Seoul. Meanwhile, Ewald tangentially proposed sharing six sports. IOC Members Smirnov (USSR) and Slavkov (Bulgaria) each calculated the project had little chance.

In the second joint meeting in January 1986, DPRK continued

provocatively to pursue joint hosting. By the third, immediately prior to Seoul's Asian Games in June, they had shown no change: maintaining their presumption of co-hosting, and thereby presuming automatic host qualification for the football tournament, DPRK withdrew from a qualifying tie in Malaysia – and were promptly disqualified by FIFA. Many IFs (apart from conciliatory table tennis) were already reluctant to consider participation in the North. At the 1987 annual IOC Session in Istanbul shortly before the fourth joint meeting, North Korean IOC Member Kim Yu-sun peremptorily declared (in Russian) that their demand was now to host eight sports. Kim Un-yong, urgently briefed by Samaranch via aide-de-camp Coupat, responded in reply that this was nothing but a wish list from Pyongyang; none of it had been agreed upon, nor even mentioned. He was clear about the positions of the IOC and South Korea, stating, 'According to the Olympic Charter, the right to host the Olympics was granted to Seoul, but Seoul received a request from the IOC to allow for some of the events to be organised in North Korea, in the spirit of the Olympic Movement and world peace. Before discussing any important matters such as free transit between South and North, or the Opening and Closing Ceremonies, Seoul is waiting for North Korea to accept the IOC's offer. The door is still open.'

In consequence, the IOC sent a delegation to Pyongyang and to Seoul for further debate, led by Sipercu. On arrival in Seoul, Sipercu expressed exaggerated optimism for 'the greatest of festivals, including North Korea'. He was seemingly buoyed by the DPRK's construction of a new venue for gymnastics as well as its investment in a 150,000-seat main stadium and a guarantee of free access between South and North for all accredited personnel – a starkly empty promise, as his own delegation had been refused just such direct border crossing. Any lingering reciprocal optimism evaporated. 'I knew President Samaranch was testing to see how Pyongyang would handle this vital border crossing, and learned he was very discouraged,' Kim Un-yong reported.

Meanwhile, political demonstrations against President Chun were escalating in response to his 'Constitutional Protection' measures in April 1987 – an emotional tide that threatened Seoul's own equilibrium. This disturbing news spread globally, straining Kim Un-yong's credibility even among staunch supporters. An alarmed Kim went to discuss tactics with President-elect Roh Tae-woo, together with Games director Park Seh-jik. Roh appeared unduly relaxed, instructing his colleagues to stay calm and to advise an anxious Samaranch that all was well. The following morning came Roh's renowned 'June 29 Declaration' for extended electoral and democratic freedoms. The public furore abated. For the fourth joint North-South meeting, Kim Un-yong was ready to offer the North six sports; Samaranch instructed the offer to be five – both men's and women's competitions in table tennis and archery; women's volleyball qualifying; preliminary football; and the men's cycling road race. Both NOCs were asked to respond. Seoul did so immediately, while the DPRK requested further 'postponement'.

For the IOC, it was the end of the line in terms of tolerant generosity, though Samaranch would continue to leave the door open for the DPRK's unilateral rational adjustment. Neither party re-opened negotiations, the DPRK's fellow travellers recognising that its opportunity had been squandered. Kim Un-yong voiced his dismay: 'The South-North talks had a great impact on the thinking of some Koreans who strive for eventual unification. Those who did not understand the Olympic Charter, or did not care, thought that co-hosting was needed for joint participation of teams. They thought this could solve national sentiments. The outcome of the inter-Korean idea was a great disappointment.... Many social leaders and intellectuals believed in joint participation. However, you first need to think about why it is that the Olympic host city is selected seven years in advance. It means that seven years are needed to host the Games – if they could be held anywhere, there wouldn't be need for seven years of preparation. The same applies not just for the whole Games, but for competitions in a single sport in which you have to do all manner of work.... North Korea had neither the intention nor the capabilities to co-host the Olympics. It certainly was not prepared to accept all of the television and newspaper reporters, most of them from Western countries. They just wanted to prevent us from holding the Olympics. I cannot put enough emphasis on the significance of the IOC and Samaranch going beyond the Olympic Charter with such an historic proposal.'

In April, Samaranch made a final inspection trip before the opening of the Games. With the Korean election over and a new government headed by President Roh Tae-woo, he decided to visit the three leaders of the three opposition political parties. There was much debate on how this might be arranged. Kim Un-yong suggested that Samaranch invite them to breakfast, but it was alternately suggested that they meet at a reception celebrating the opening of the new swimming venue. This, however, was considered too public, and breakfast it was, the organisation being entrusted to Kim. The three leaders – Kim Dae-jung, Kim Young-sam and Kim Jong-pil, plus a representative of the Democratic Justice Party – engaged in a resume regarding the political balance in South Korea's volatile constitution. It was further proposed that Samaranch and Kim Un-yong, as the IOC Member for Korea, should meet with civilian groups to explain the IOC position. After meeting the three Kims, Samaranch issued a press release stating that he would leave the door open until the day of opening of the Games, and that he was ready to visit Pyongyang if invited. Inevitably, there was no reply from Pyongyang. North Korea stayed away, as did Cuba and six other nations. In the event, following the Games Kim Young-sam would open diplomatic relations with the Soviet Union through his northern diplomacy policy upon taking office as president in 1993.

Opening Ceremonies come and go; they have little to do in the main with the festival that follows, yet are a moment of national celebration and an opportunity for the host country to express itself to a global audience. Never was this truer than for Seoul. They opened their arms to 159 other nationalities and 5 billion television viewers, and we saw them for what they are: tranquil yet with inner strength, graceful yet energetic, moulded by ancient dynasties yet ambitiously modern. Seoul gave us not assertiveness or aggression, but gentleness and humility. The people were determined yet poetic: their pageant was a picture of history, colour and elegance. On a morning when the gods graced Seoul with sun and an autumn blue sky, the emphasis was not on achievement, which was as much a part of the South Korean story as it is of the Olympic Games, but on harmony and friendship, simultaneously capturing that mystic, indefinable quality that is the essence of the Olympics. There was about their presentation a sweetness, at times a naïveté, that was enchantingly oriental, embracing thousands of children that epitomised a basic premise of the Games: that our future lies with youth. Into the stadium came the flame, and the climax of a journey through South Korea that had brought emotional involvement for hundreds of thousands in countless villages, the torch now carried by a national hero – Sohn Kee-chung, aged 76, winner of the marathon at the Berlin Olympics as a forced and reluctant Japanese in 1936. Later that evening, a small Korean woman, Choo Nan-yool, sat on a stool with an expression of intent concentration, gazing privately ahead. At that moment she represented not merely herself but her country. At stake was the first gold medal of the Games – never mind that it was in the demonstration sport of taekwondo, and therefore unofficial. Facing her on the other side of the competition mat was Maria Angela Naranjo of Spain; seated in the gallery was Juan Antonio Samaranch, who would be presenting the medals. For Choo it was the sporting moment of her lifetime; many of her compatriots felt the same. At the end of three rounds, there was no doubt about the winner, for she had attacked throughout this national sport that was to become global. The medal which Samaranch hung around her neck had no price.

As Kevan Gosper recorded in *An Olympic Life*, 'The Games allowed the South Koreans to put their stamp on the world. More than 13,000 athletes and officials from 160 countries participated, as well as almost 16,000 media and 23,000 volunteers. Not known as a sporting country, Korea surpassed its own expectations by finishing fourth in the medal rankings. The Koreans took seriously the slogan they used for the Games: "Seoul to the World and the World to Seoul". Later Samaranch would say of the Games: "Never before has a city, a people, a country devoted so much enthusiasm, goodwill, inventiveness and sacrifice in carrying out with zest, intelligence and organisational talent, the mission entrusted to them in 1981. It was phenomenal and universal. Friendship and goodwill were everywhere." The Games were a huge coup for the Koreans, a mirror image of how important the 1964 Games had been to Japan in the aftermath of World War II in bringing the country back into international respectability.... The Games gave Korea a new international standing.'

Eminent American historian Professor John Lucas reflected on the element of professionalism making its substantial impact on the Games in the wake of the IOC's acceptance at the previous year's Session at Istanbul. Lucas wrote in his *The Future of the Olympic Games*: 'Scores of nations promised big money to any of their athletes who returned with a medal – any medal. Philippine President Corazon Aquino showed her nation's gratitude for a light flyweight bronze medal with an $18,000 gift. Korean pride was Everest-high, all of its gold medallists awarded pensions of $16,600 a year for life. No nation has greater pride than the French, and they awarded 200,000 francs for gold, 100,000 francs for silver, 75,000 francs for bronze.' Yet Lucas went on to quote a disenchanted Derek Johnson, a British 800 metres silver medallist from 1956, who had stated, 'It does not matter what happens to the Olympic Games. They have become such a political thing that it is actually desirable that they should be cut down to size. The Olympics are of emotional value without intrinsic value. Their disappearance would be of no great loss to society.'

Of the official film of the Games, British commentator Simon Barnes observed, 'The film was one great saccharin-sweet, ultra-nationalistic Korean love feast, filled with half-baked clichés, soft soap, flannel, and lies produced for the gratification of the Seoul City Fathers.' Interestingly, Barnes simultaneously had much praise for many things that took place in the Seoul festival, while as an aside Lucas recalls the massiveness of the security operation 'needed not only on the ground but also in the water, in the air and under the sea, while the USA, apart from its 40,000 troops along the border manning the Panmunjom checkpoint, stationed two aircraft carriers off Seoul as a warning to the North.' According to Games chief Park Seh-jik, all shopkeepers at the airports were recruited as surveillance agents.

Few Olympic Games are without a hitch, but one in particular arose on 22 September in the boxing ring. Byun Jung-il, a likely medal-winner, was ruled to have lost his bantamweight bout to Bulgarian Aleksandar Khristov. On the referee's verdict, Byun's trainer, Lee Hong-su charged into the ring along with other coaching staff and proceeded to rough up New Zealand referee Keith Walker. The furore became physical; security staff attempted to intervene, while NBC enjoyed the drama, covering the story globally for the best part of an hour, thereby rousing antipathy towards both Americans and its own operation. An appeal was held by the International Boxing Council, and Walker was suspended, making a hasty and discreet return to his homeland. An upshot of this was the resignation of Kim Jong-ha, president of Korea's Boxing Association – but following a meeting with Samaranch and Kim Un-yong, he was persuaded to withdraw from his well-intentioned gesture. Disruption in the ring did not end there, with further controversy in a light middleweight bout in which American Roy Jones was deprived of victory, having visibly outclassed Korean Park Si-hun. Dick Pound subsequently revealed in *Inside the Olympics* that following the fall of the Berlin Wall, evidence emerged from the records of the Stasi secret police to show that bribes had been paid to boxing judges. 'They certainly had not been paid to ensure that the American would win,' he wrote. 'The jury of appeal established by the IF for each major competition routinely upheld the judges officiating at the bout, so the injustice became a matter of Olympic history. The outrage was so thoroughly felt that even the IF responded with a gesture that it thought would calm the waters, but that in fact simply demonstrated how corrupt the judging had been and how impotent the leadership of the sport was in dealing with corruption.'

If boxing was an embarrassment in presentation of the friendly Games, far worse – through no fault of the Koreans – was to be the doping revelation surrounding Ben Johnson of Canada, who won the 100 metres against arch-rival Carl Lewis with a new world record of 9.79 seconds. Samaranch, for the first time in the Games, awarded the gold medal to Johnson; the sporting world paused in admiration, but one of the greatest scandals in Olympic history was about to explode. As Lucas related: 'Absolutely nothing has accentuated the public's confusion about the Olympic Charter's fundamental principle, talking about moral qualities, peace, international understanding and goodwill, more than the case of Ben Johnson in 1988. There may have been hundreds of athletes taking steroids at those Games, but "poor Ben" made headlines on every continent.' Some said that he and his entourage were no more than an aberrant band of greedy specialists. Others saw a direct line of fuzzy, ever-changing and impossible-to-follow Olympic rules, with profit rather than principle their main thesis, which had in turn carried Johnson and many others into the swirl of chemical manipulation. 'Big Ben has led us to the bottom of the pit,' wrote Pierre Hurel in *Paris Match*. Geoff Dyer in *New Statesman and Society* found in monomaniac Johnson 'a kind of life in the Faust lane'. Worst of all was Johnson's worldwide publicity in the wake of his shame, which earned him several hundred thousand dollars in Japanese appearance fees and $25,000 from French television for advice on anabolic steroids. Johnson was tarnished, but so was the whole

Olympic Movement.

Kim Un-yong became first aware of the crisis two evenings after the race when told by Samaranch, 'We are in trouble.' Kim then heard that Richard Pound, the Canadian IOC Member, was suggesting that somebody could have spiked Johnson's urine. The calmest expert on the scene was Arne Ljungqvist, the Swedish head of the IOC Medical Commission, who relates the profundity of the moment in his *Doping Nemesis*: 'Johnson's abbreviated career caught people's attention long before the Olympics. Rumours that he was doping abounded.... Ahead of the competitions I met him at a reception, and when I saw his eyes I was a bit uneasy. The whites of his eyes were very yellow, a sign that the rumours were true. Steroids taken orally affect the liver when used over a long period of time.... I hurried down after the final to the doping control station to ensure everything followed protocol.... I've never seen such a circus of screeching hangers-on. We sat there staring at each other until Johnson was ready to give his sample. . . When I returned to the hotel the next evening, there was an envelope under the door: Johnson's A test was positive with the steroid Stanozolol.... The following day Johnson's B sample confirmed the positive test. One of those who hurried to Johnson's defence was Pound, member of the IOC's Executive Board but representing the Canadian Olympic Committee and leading their delegation. He argued that the test had been interfered with and that this could have happened because security at the doping station had fallen apart.... I replied that at no point do IOC rules stipulate who should be allowed in the doping control station, only who may be in the room where the sample is taken. Pound's attempt to discredit us lacked weight and when Manfred Donike (West German Doping Authority) said that Johnson's sample revealed long-term use of Stanozolol, the defence did not have a leg to stand on.'

Ljungqvist's account of the process, and the reluctance of Primo Nebiolo to head the inevitable subsequent press conference, was indicative of some prominent Olympic leaders' failure to get to grips with a trend that could destroy the Olympics. Kevan Gosper recalled Samaranch having announced that 'doping is death' at the IOC Session in Seoul preceding the Games; here now was evidence, with Johnson's shameful revelation that the IOC was doing its job of surveillance. Gosper added: 'Samaranch proclaimed "the gap between our aims and those who are cheating is narrowing" – nevertheless the IOC should have been more vigilant after the Johnson case.... People were starting to question how some athletes managed to have such a big jump in performances. Comments were made about the female star of the Seoul Olympics, American Florence Griffith Joyner, who won gold in the 100, 200 and 4×100 metres relay – she was always found to be clean but rumour swirled on how much better she had done in Seoul than at previous major meetings including the LA Games. Suddenly the drug debate was out in the open, and out-of-competition testing was established in the early 1990s.'

Irrespective of the Johnson shame, Seoul's Games remain to this day an event to be remembered, not least for the Pierre de Coubertin Award to Lawrence Lemieux, a Canadian sailor in the Finn class. While lying second and likely to win silver, he abandoned the race to save an injured competitor, relegating himself to 21st place. Such is Olympic honour. Christa Luding-Rothenburger of the GDR became the first and only athlete to win Olympic medals in both the Winter and Summer Games in the same year, adding a cycling silver to a speed skating gold at Calgary. Anthony Nesty of Suriname won his country's first Olympic medal in the 100-metre butterfly with a defeat of acclaimed American Matt Biondi by 0.01 seconds, thereby blocking Biondi's attempt to break the seven-gold record of Mark Spitz in one Games and making Nesty the first black swimmer to win an individual gold. Six golds went to the GDR's remarkable Kristin Otto. US diver Greg Louganis won back-to-back titles in both diving events after hitting the springboard with his head in the three-metre event final – encountering subsequent contro-

Kim Un-yong brings taekwondo to the world's attention with this demonstration by the Korea Army Airborne team: at the Seoul Opening Ceremony, September 1988.

versy when he declared he had been HIV-positive, though the condition is not contagious in water. The Games were innovative for the introduction of women's judo, the return of tennis after a 64-year absence, and the introduction of baseball and taekwondo as demonstration sports.

As I walked away from the Closing Ceremony of the Seoul Games, a haunting oriental chorale still drifting upwards into the night sky, I was more than ever in love with Korea. Confronted with the largest Games ever, they had been the perfect hosts. The debt which the Olympic Movement owed them was immense. The Koreans had the organisation of the Germans, the courtesy and culture of the orient, and the sense of money of the Americans. They could hardly fail. It is true that the Games always tend to bring out the best in a host nation, but few if any had given so much, and on such a scale, as had the South Koreans. The worst had been expected. The IOC had been condemned for allowing the Games to go ahead there. Yet what had been achieved by a nation that thirty years earlier had been a bomb site – and, when it was awarded the Games in 1981, was a pariah to most socialist countries – was phenomenal. Considering some of the logistical problems (accentuated for the most party by the lack of linguistic communication), the Koreans had been more helpful, more accommodating than the hosts of any other Games I had attended, in spite of the intensity of security. The competition facilities were without parallel, advancing public perception of what a Games can provide more than anybody since the West Germans in 1972. The friendship had overflowed. At the Closing Ceremony, Arabs and Israelis walked around the track with total informality, side by side. And behind it all lay the tireless imagination and coordination, the foresight, of one Korean with a gamble on a shooting contest 14 years earlier: Dr. Kim Un-yong.

ASIAN LEADERSHIP

The extent of the influence of Kim Un-yong in the Olympic Movement exceeded that of many administrators throughout its illustrious history, beyond the original initiative of founder Baron Pierre de Coubertin. Perhaps his most remarkable contribution lies in the establishment of taekwondo as a major global sport, achieving its inclusion in the Olympic programme within two decades of becoming president of Korea's national association – a status that had eluded, say, table tennis for the better part of a century. Testimony of this feat flows from many. Jean-Claude Schupp, forthright administrator of GAISF, worked in league with Kim during the Korean's most instructive years. He reflected, 'What [Kim] achieved, I would say, is the promotion and advance of taekwondo, so to speak his own sport. At that time in the 1970s, there was rivalry between karate and taekwondo. From the moment he arrived on the scene, Kim was significant – lobbying day and night. What he did inside the sport was transformative – not an easy task to make it competitive, which previously it was not; it had been about ideology, a lifestyle. To convert it to competitive tournaments, with rules and referees that everyone understood – that was a huge accomplishment.'

Ser Miang Ng, a fellow IOC Member from Singapore whose prime place in history was masterminding the inaugural Youth Olympic Games of 2010, is equally fulsome. 'Kim Un-yong modified a leisure activity, gave it an exciting competitive structure with objective judging and presentation for an audience, judging that could be understood – a sport that is dynamic, powerful yet safe,' he said. 'He simultaneously founded Kukkiwon, the world headquarters, and almost immediately also the World Taekwondo Federation (WTF, renamed WT in 2017), which blended within conventional IOC administration. Among other martial arts, judo, boxing and wrestling, the global appeal of taekwondo is its strong moral code and strict hierarchy, making it easy to create local competition. Kukkiwon represented the spirit of the sport – a clever move.' Taekwondowon, the national training, development and educational complex subsequently established in Muju by the government in 2008, is the ideal 'university' of the sport, representing Korea's emotional philosophy: international sport + traditional art + amateurism + honourable spirit = modern taekwondo.

Richard Palmer, for many years general-secretary of the British Olympic Association and member of the IOC Evaluation Commission for cities bidding for the 1988 Olympic Games, recalls the rivalry between WTF and the International Taekwondo Federation (ITF), which emigrated, temporarily via Canada, to North Korea. 'The two were at loggerheads,' he said. Palmer had witnessed the early years of Kim's energy when living at Harrow in North London while serving at Korea's embassy: 'By the time of the Seoul Games, he was already a star!'

So what are the origins of taekwondo, that amalgam of physical force and mental discipline embracing internal peace and serenity, which was claimed as the 'national sport of Korea' by President Park Chung-hee in 1971? The first recorded history of Korean culture is over four thousand years old. Martial arts initially exploited many weapons in defence against wild animals and robbers, yet fundamentally coordinated all four limbs and leveraging powers. Legend holds that techniques were refined by an Indian Buddhist monk, Bodhidharma, who allegedly transported his skills to China; Buddhism then transferred the art to Korea, though evidence suggests these techniques may have pre-existed in Korea. A mural in North Korea from the Goguryeo Kingdom (37 BC–AD 668) depicts contestants in taekwondo-style combat. Taekwondo sculptures survive from the Silla Kingdom (57 BC–AD 935). When Confucianism succeeded Buddhism, martial arts seemingly fell into disrepute in Korea, no longer serving as a discipline within a military career. Occupation by Japan in the 20th century further limited the art; many immigrant Koreans discovered varied martial arts in China and Japan. All this changed with the liberation and the creation of the Republic of Korea in 1948, and the development of multi-disciplines in schools, consolidation only arriving in 1965 with formation of the Korean Taekwondo Association, and with it acceptance of coordinated moral discipline.

Kim Un-yong's introduction to taekwondo in high school was educational. It was subsequently refined under private guidance of 'great-grandmaster' Yoon Byung-hee, with the realisation of the art's true complexity. Aged thirty, Kim was professionally employed at the Blue House government headquarters as Assistant to the Ministry of National Defence – in consequence of his extended military education in America – yet without the prospect of advanced diplomatic involvement, his career seemed stalled. At forty, his life took a profound turn when he was offered the post of deputy director-general of the presidential security service, with responsibility for US relations. Unexpectedly, he was presented with the task, in 1971, of becoming president of KTA, a position which had just experienced five incumbents in nine years. In his *Challenge to the World*, he wrote, 'I experienced a tremendous amount of conflict when I quit my career as a diplomat and became an aide at the Blue House – that dream (of a diplomatic career) was something I still kept when I became a scholastic director. Yet taking on the presidency of a sport association, usually something for retired officials, meant my hope would be extinguished completely. . . The more I thought about it, the bleaker my future seemed. . . before I finally accepted the KTA post.... [It was] an unpaid, part-time position but [one] demanding a sense of responsibility and mission, so you were under tremendous pressure. I set out with four visions for taekwondo: full adoption as a national sport, globalisation, promotion of national prestige, defence of the country.'

Marketing strategy formed part of the background to the adoption of taekwondo as Korea's national sport, as Kim Un-yong explains: 'In March 1971, the then-president Park Chung-hee granted to me a plaque stating "National Sport Taekwondo" in his own calligraphy. When I first became president of WTF, taekwondo was not the national sport which both wrestling and football claimed to be. We made many copies of the plaque and asked all taekwondo schools to display it and thus it became the national sport, seen in taekwondo schools all over the country; furthermore the title becoming etched in the media.'

Alongside these visions Kim Un-yong had immediately proclaimed seven objectives as KTA president: publication of a taekwondo magazine, confirmation as national sport, institution of a school development programme, construction of a taekwondo training centre, delineation of taekwondo ethics, standardisation of official management rankings, and publication of a taekwondo regulation textbook.

For construction of the ambitious training centre initially titled Central Hall of Taekwondo (and later renamed Kukkiwon), formidable hurdles were confronted in locating an available site and in funding a three-story, 7,600-square-metre building of architectural elegance, capable of seating two thousand, all amid the global petrol crisis precipitated by the Arab-Israeli War. Funding was amassed from 31 independent donors, Kim Un-yong himself contributing some £13,000 from his private family wealth (the equivalent of approximately £182,500 in 2019). An opening ceremony arrived in 1972, with Kim declaring, 'To show the world the true face of taekwondo as Korea's national sport, I intend to stage a world championship next year, inviting teams from forty countries worldwide, where Korean instructors have been sent from Seoul.'

Kim further relates, 'In November 1972, the Kukkiwon opened as a central hall of the Korean Association. Far from being a splendid ceremony, it was a rather shabby affair. The roads were all unpaved, there was no telephone service, electricity or running water.... Despite the cold winter, heating was out of the question. But once the hall had been built, the next objective was to host a world championship – the first step towards global status. A world federation was essential for the globalisation of the sport. An international federation would have to have all the national federations as members. The existing International Taekwondo Federation (ITF, as opposed to WTF) was not an international organization along those lines though there had been discussion on integrating the Korean Association with ITF, which was not accepted. The first WTF championship was held at Kukkiwon in May 1973, an historic event.'

Come that day, 161 athletes comprising twenty teams from 17 countries contested the first World Championships at Kukkiwon, which was conducted in three 3-minute rounds without head gear. The day following its completion, 35 representatives from 17 nations gathered for the foundation of the World Taekwondo Federation; Kim Un-yong was elected as inaugural president, Roland Demarco (US) and Leo Wagner (West Germany) as vice-presidents, and Lee Jong-woo as secretary general. In his opening address, Kim Un-yong stated: 'I am sure an international organisation with traditional taekwondo spirit will play a vital role in providing the basic foundation of the opening of a new era of taekwondo on a worldwide scale.' Meanwhile, Korea's Culture and Education Ministry had moved a month earlier to dissolve the International Taekwondo Federation (headed by Choi Hong-hi) for irregular conduct, leaving WTF as the sole legitimate body, based at Kukkiwon.

The following year, Kim Un-yong received the President's 'Outstanding Service Award' for 'dedication to social welfare and physical fitness of the community, and promotion of taekwondo as a world sport'. Kim said he was ashamed to be thus rewarded 'for the little bit of work I did for the development of the national sport.' He also reflected on the duality of the sport: 'Taekwondo is definitely a sport since it is recognised by the IOC as such. Yet its traditional aspects as an art cannot be disre-

At the IOC Session at Baden-Baden, 1981, meeting with West German general secretary, Walter Tröger (right), admirer of Kim's international expansion

garded; whether it is more sport or more *art* is a matter entirely for the individual practitioner. It is flexible enough to be both at the same time.'

Within less than five years, Kim Un-yong had already become a figure of note on the world's sporting stage. Walter Troeger, a central figure in the planning and administration of Munich's Olympic Games in 1972, had a worm's eye view of sport and quickly detected Kim's emergence. 'He broadened the flavour of Asian sport,' Troeger recalled. "Being multi-lingual was invaluable in gaining approval. He was a smooth diplomat, most essentially in negotiating the promotion of taekwondo, persuading IOC Members that this was important. He quickly enjoyed the backing of John Coates of Australia, and members from all five continents.' All this while Kim harboured doubts about attempting to project little-known taekwondo in the face of seemingly dominant interest in football across all continents.

It was one thing to stage the first World Championships and create an international federation, and another to gather strategic momentum towards gaining a coveted place on the Olympic Games schedule. This difficulty was magnified by taekwondo being largely viewed, across the Olympic Movement, as a 'new' sport inferior to the better-known karate. The door towards this goal would come by gaining hands with the influential NGO known as GAISF. In 1974, the President of IOC was newly elected Michael Killanin from Dublin, an amiable Irishman who already had enough difficulties stabilising an evolving membership without needing to bond with an as yet unfamiliar Asian motivator who was starting to make waves. For now, Kim Un-yong would have to continue to cut his own steps up the mountain face. As he would recall in an article published in 2011 titled 'How Far Had Taekwondo Come?':

The greatest goals of the KTA were to achieve results internationally and make use of an international umbrella (GAISF). Karate was too powerful and we could have ended up as just an ad hoc group. In October 1974, the first Asian Taekwondo Championships were held at Kukkiwon and an Asian federation was established. In 1975, the second World Taekwondo Championship was staged with 30 countries participating. The event was attended by GAISF secretary general Oscar State, who urged us to pursue GAISF membership. At the GAISF general assembly in Montreal that year, the WTF was unanimously approved for membership, over objections from judo, karate, ITF and swimming representatives. The prevailing belief at the time was that Taekwondo was just one school of karate, representing the same martial art – some overseas instructors even advertised it as 'Korean Karate'. It was a pivotal event for us. Thanks to its GAISF membership, the WTF became an official international federation, competing and co-existing with other Olympic and non-Olympic sports federations. We had taken our first formal step on the international stage. After this, the WTF went to work taking advantage of the GAISF umbrella from above, while obtaining certification and budgetary support from the scattered national associations under the auspices of individual NOCs. Rather than developing from the bottom up, it was a matter of using diplomacy, taking advantage of the GAISF umbrella to expand quickly from the top down.

The conference of GAISF at Montreal in 1975 had proved initially tortuous and discouraging, under the gaze and demonstrative opinions of such prominent Olympic figureheads as FIFA's supremo João Havelange of Brazil, American Harold Henning of FINA (swimming) and boisterous Charles Palmer, Britain's executive member of World Judo and known opponent of taekwondo's ambitions. Kim Un-yong's already established friendship with Oscar State seemed a hollow trump card, with WTF needing unanimous acceptance. Palmer posed an armoury of objections, the worst being WTF's perceived 'split' from ITF, his obstruction strengthened by his having now succeeded State as secretary general. In the event, the debate on WTF acceptance lasted two hours, with international judo president Antonio Garcia de la Fuente countermanding Palmer when declaring taekwondo and judo to be 'distinct individual sports'. The vote was, astonishingly, unanimous in WTF's approval. To have out-manoeuvred karate and China's rival wushu, to be the only Asian international federation among sixty others with a home base, and to become eligible as Olympic contenders was truly a majestic feather in Kim Un-yong's cap. Six months later followed inclusion in the Council of International Military Sport (CISM). Taekwondo aficionado Dr. Allan Bäck would pronounce:

Taekwondo has emerged as a world sport largely due to its strong central leadership, spear-headed by Dr. Kim Un-yong. The WTF, more than any other martial art organisation, has regulated the activities and behaviour of its members. It is this self-policing that is primarily re-

Kim Un-yong awards an honorary taekwondo *dan* certificate to Muhammad Ali during Kukkiwon visit in 1976 – a promotion coup.

sponsible for the recognition of Taekwondo by the larger sports community and for its dominance among the martial arts. Dr. Kim's leadership has led to the establishment of Kukkiwon and its standardisation of the techniques that are taught. At the same time, Kukkiwon has been progressive. Instead of conservatively stifling new developments, Dr. Kim has instituted many changes in what is studied, not for the sake of novelty but of improvement. He has organised conferences where techniques are carefully scrutinised and compared with other martial arts by many grandmasters. Such perseverance has given Taekwondo international stature. We owe Dr. Kim gratitude for his unyielding pursuit of the ideal martial art.

Momentum began to gather internationally, having started with America's Amateur Athletic Union adopting Taekwondo as a competitive sport in late 1974. The European Taekwondo championships took root in Barcelona in 1976, twelve nations having formed the European Taekwondo Union, a *volte-face* from some European opposition to WTF within GAISF. The Pan Am Taekwondo Union followed suit in 1977 during the third World Championships in Chicago, and the Asian Union during the third Asian Championships in Hong Kong in 1978. Africa's amalgamation was tabled during the first African Championships in Ivory Coast in 1979, and Oceania's amid the first Oceania Championship in 2005.

Kim Un-yong's nest egg had developed into a global farm, ceremoniously acknowledged in June 1976 when legendary three-time world heavyweight boxing champion Muhammad Ali graced Kukkiwon with his presence. With Taekwondo's comprehensive training, Ali suggested, no other martial art was comparable. The visit of Ali would be surpassed, bureaucratically, by that of newly elected IOC President Juan Antonio Samaranch in 1982, following his own election at Moscow's Olympic Games – and thereby the launch of a behind-the-scenes strategic partnership with Kim Un-yong that was to determine part of a revolutionary Olympic road map. In the presence of international NOC members from around the world, Samaranch solemnly announced, 'The time has come for taekwondo to be adopted as an official Olympic sport.' Kim Un-yong thus had one foot in the door – yet domestic crises in his own back garden had begun to threaten Samaranch's and Kim's own future.

The assassination of Korean President Park Chung-hee in October 1979 had provoked political upheaval, with a military junta led by Chun Doo-hwan and Roh Tae-woo seizing power and exploiting armed forces to quell violent demonstrations demanding democracy following closure of the National Assembly and formation of a Special Committee for National Security Measures. The social abrasion of military dictatorship rocked the foundations of more than just Taekwondo's equilibrium. In his book *Challenge to the World*, Kim Un-yong, for a time under effective house arrest and his future as KTA president in danger, observed:

I don't know who was responsible, but the military administration began seizing taekwondo figures right and left, carrying out arrests in an effort to suppress them. I think some of them had it in for me personally. It may be that after taekwondo's great strides as a national sport since I took over as KTA president, certain people felt insecure and jealous, or coveted the KTA presidency. There was one person, a relative of one of the key administration figures, who was very open and deliberate about wanting to take the KTA post away from me. He resorted to methods like requesting anonymous letters from five or six overseas instructors. The authorities put pressure on me and other taekwondo school heads to resign. We all had no choice but to give our notices. The military administration at that time wielded more powerful authority than ever before. These were frightening dictators, who had used tanks to quash the democracy movement; nobody at the time knew what to do. So we all resigned and were subjected to internal investigation. I was just lying low and waiting for an opportunity. For the previous ten years, KTA executives, taekwondo officials and I had worked purely for the advancement of the sport. We had not been seeking for any kind of personal gain. They could investigate all they wanted: they were not going to find any irregularities. Believing that the truth would come to light, I quietly tended to my own body and mind, working out intensely during that period – the equivalent of running a marathon from Seoul to Daejeon. It was enough to make people at the gym wonder if I were an ageing athlete or a coach.

Amid the domestic political turmoil, the safety valve for Kim Un-yong was, in the wake of Seoul's spectacular election in 1981 as host city for 1988, the blossoming allegiance with Samaranch. In the tense communication relationship between Lausanne and Seoul – heightened as it was by language incompatibility – stability and continuity were wholly dependent on a single conciliatory link: articulate, fluent Kim Un-yong. The testimony to his adroit negotiations between the Blue House and IOC President is widespread. Israeli IOC Member Alex Gilady, who was situated at the heart of NBC's protracted TV negotiations for coverage in Seoul, closely observed the Samaranch-Kim coordination. 'With Kim's mounting involvement with GAISF, and then the inaugural World Games, he was for Samaranch the heart of global sport strategy – not so much having influence in Asia, but directly to the top desk at the Blue House,' Gilady recalled. 'Out of the military came the president of the nation, and the president of the Seoul Olympic organising committee. It was almost automatic, following the "dress rehearsal" of Seoul's Asian Games in 1986, that Samaranch should make Kim an IOC Member, two years later promoting him to the IOC Executive Board. Another element was Samaranch manoeuvring Kim's elevation as GAISF vice-president in 1984, thrusting Kim into place in preference to Primo Nebiolo, premier of international athletics. Kim was the master communicator, an effective tool for Samaranch. Nebiolo as GAISF leader would have been too powerful (as had been predecessor Tommy Keller, Swiss head of international rowing and challenging IOC authority). Samaranch needed to close that door. Kim's value to him was not that Kim was making decisions in Seoul, but [that he was] relaying Lausanne's strategy to the real seat of government.' Historian Christopher Hill reflects in his *Olympic Politics* that Kim, conscious of IOC interests, was an obvious place-man for Samaranch with GAISF 'because IOC needed such collaboration'.

Jean-Claude Schupp of France, a member of Horst Dassler's Adidas team who would transfer to GAISF as secretary-general, fully recognised the harmony, the mutual collaboration between Samaranch and Kim. 'Samaranch was looking for someone who would provide GAISF's support for his objectives, his advice and philosophy,' he said. 'It was Samaranch who steered Kim's election as vice-president and then president. When I was appointed, my prompting from Samaranch was "don't change anything". In a couple of minutes, I knew exactly what I had to do: "Follow Kim!" Of all IF presidents, Kim was the closest to Samaranch. Politically, it was oil on the water – indeed, at that time, oil on the whole

Olympic Movement. Kim would not act without Samaranch's direction. They were hand-in-glove.' Following the successful Olympic bid in 1981, Kim had proposed to the new culture and education minister, Lee Kyu-ho, the reinstatement of all taekwondo officials who had resigned amid the military takeover.

Patrick Nally, a sponsorship guru who would have a major role in Samaranch's revolutionary TOP sponsorship innovation in the late 1980s, observed the Samaranch-Kim liaison. 'When Lance Cross of New Zealand, chairman of the IOC's Radio and Television Commission, died shortly after the Seoul Games, Kim was the straightforward replacement,' he remembered. 'He was a faultless diplomat, understanding Samaranch's wish to amalgamate WTF and ITF, ensuring North Korea were involved in the delicate debate, even though Kim himself was against the union.'

Kim Un-yong's ascent of the administrative ladder in pursuit of Korea's international status – triumphantly celebrated with Seoul's election for 1988 – had been preceded the year before in 1980 when the IOC's Programme Commission, chaired by Director of Sport Arpad Csanadi of Hungary, had recommended taekwondo to be accepted as a 'recognised sport' – on condition that other marital arts were not to be likewise promoted. The proposal was mandated at the IOC Session immediately prior to Moscow's Olympic Games, reflecting increasing trust in the reputation of Kim, and celebrated back home by a banquet for 800 guests at the Shilla Hotel attended by dignitaries including Korean Sport and Olympic Committee (KSOC) president Cho Sang-ho. Kim Un-yong's message from Moscow contained a pardonable sense of collective triumph: 'The approval of an Olympic event less than five years after taekwondo's admission to GAISF is the reward for efforts by all taekwondo practitioners for its globalisation and modernisation.' Attempts by the IOC to examine the co-existence and possible merger of WTF and ITF were terminated, thanks to Kim Un-yong's overriding character at the IOC Session prior to the Los Angeles Olympic Games of 1984.

In the interim, Kim had cemented his reputation when masterminding the GAISF-promoted World Games – embracing IOC's non-accredited but 'recognised sports' – at Santa Clara, California, in 1981. After a congratulation message from President Ronald Reagan, Kim Un-yong's opening address as World Games president welcomed the wider world of sport: 'This event is not intended to oppose the Olympics, rather to bring non-Olympic events together in one place and nurture a sports festival. I hope in future we will all come together under the GAISF banner, forsaking politics in favour of cooperation.'

Less than two months after Seoul's election for 1988, a meeting in New Delhi of the Asian Games Federation – later to become the Olympic Council of Asia – had voted for Seoul as host city for the Asian Games of 1986. Nothing could have better prepared Seoul for '88. In the space of eight weeks an East Asian city, raised from ashes and inspired by the vision and energy of one ex-diplomat, had become a doubly scheduled date on every global sports calendar. Kim Un-yong records that Seoul's success in staging the Summer Games was an inestimable boon to the globalisation of taekwondo. 'The best way of promoting the sport was to invite guests to the Kukkiwon whenever they came to see our preparations for the Games and we would stage demonstrations for them,' he explained. 'In April 1982, IOC President Samaranch arrived, simultaneously with a meeting of the WTF Executive Board. We were able to give him an exhibition, where he was presented with a bouquet by a student, Kim Hye-soo, who later would become a famous actress. Following Samaranch, other IOC and NOC members would visit, together with officials of IFs from different sports and cabinet ministers from different countries, so we gained confidence from gathering many allies from around the world. Now came the time to have taekwondo adopted as an official event at different international competitions. In 1982 it was adopted by the African Games, next by the Pan Am Games. The sport having established itself within the US and Central America, there was significant symbolism in its being adopted by the Pan Am Games, which at that time (1983) was staged in Caracas. Mario Vazquez Rana of Mexico recognized the growing importance of the sport. WTF standing in South and Central America duly rose, taking the lead in rivalry with karate and the ITF.'

It would be hardly surprising that at the IOC Session in East Berlin in 1985 it would be agreed taekwondo should be a demonstration sport at Seoul '88. It had been the IOC's intention for badminton and baseball to be demonstration events, but persuasion by Kim on Samaranch secured badminton's replacement by taekwondo. Kim Un-yong's own promotion continued when, in conjunction with hosting the Asian Games, he was elected as an IOC Member – making him the sixth Korean to earn that distinction – thanks to Samaranch's firm recommendation of him in the face of President Chun's reluctance. A week later, additionally through Samaranch's veiled influence, Kim succeeded Tommy Keller as president of GAISF. In recognition of such twofold prestige, Park Seh-jik – who had succeeded Roh Tae-woo as president of the Seoul Olympics organising committee – declared, 'Dr. Kim's selection as IOC Member and GAISF president is a result of outstanding skill and leadership, his great achievement over the years.'

Taekwondo had become a rolling snowball of ever greater dimension. In 1987, a select demonstration from Kukkiwon was invited to perform at an Olympic Week in Lausanne. The televised Opening Ceremony performance at Seoul '88 by a Special Airborne Force group drew a worldwide gasp of astonishment, while Hiroshima's Asian Games of 1994 was obliged – despite all Japan's historic denigration of Korea – to include taekwondo alongside karate and judo. Only by Kim's intervention with Samaranch was taekwondo embraced as an exhibition event at Barcelona's Games in 1992. Kim recalled in his *Challenge to the World* that while taekwondo was adopted as a demonstration event in '88, it was omitted from Barcelona. 'For the sake of the sport's promotion, I had to get it adopted and immediately discussed the issue with Samaranch,' he recalled. 'He reminded me that demonstration events had already been decided, that only two were allowed. So I thought up something: "We'll call it an exhibition game; there's nothing in the rules about that." If the Barcelona event becomes a historic setting for unveiling various new competitions, it will be that much more memorable around the world. It may not be in the rules, but from the spectators' standpoint, they are going to think the more the merrier.' By this roundabout route, Kim ultimately was able to establish taekwondo as a third demonstration sport, its programme extending over four days, and even attended by King Juan Carlos. Kim Un-yong's Korean-oriented march across the global stage was further crowned a year later with the 11th World Taekwondo Championship and fourth Women's Championship being staged at Madison Square Garden in New York City. Kim extended the promotion to an all-American audience with a $300,000 broadcast of the entire event by NBC – the ultimate in show-biz. It says much about the myopic self-interest of some insular Koreans that Kim was blamed for

Opening Ceremony for 11th World Taekwondo Championships at New York City's Madison Square Garden, 1993: massive TV promotion across USA

CHAPTER 3

taekwondo's absence from Atlanta's centenary Olympic Games of 1996 – from which demonstration events were excluded.

With the goal of having taekwondo officially adopted at the 1994 IOC Congress in Paris, Kim Un-yong solicited IOC Members he thought would be influential, including IOC Sports Director Gilbert Felli, American member Anita DeFrantz, Atlanta Games organizing committee chairman Bill Payne and many others. 'Having seen only the Olympic demonstrations in the past, they changed their minds about taekwondo's status after witnessing the championships at Madison Square Garden,' he said. 'To maximise the publicity, we needed television coverage and signed a contract with ABC for a broadcast for one hour. The Garden event had participants from around 90 countries.'

Kim Un-yong's ultimate objective was taekwondo's addition to the programme in Paris, via recommendation from the IOC Programme Commission and thence by the Executive Board. So there was dismay when this was rejected by the Programme Commission in 1993. Yet significantly – though at first glance it may seem irrelevant – it was this year that Sydney was chosen as host for the Millennium Olympic Games of 2000. The clandestine Samaranch-Kim conspiracy was about to move up a gear – never mind that the Programme Commission was adversely guided by a continuing WTF-ITF conflict and doubts about inclusion of multiple martial arts in an already alarmingly overcrowded Olympic schedule. However, subterranean uncertainty in 1993 was to prove misleading, as Phil Coles, then a prominent Australian IOC Member of elite canoeing heritage, relates:

Sydney having been elected, narrowly, at the IOC Session in Monte Carlo, Samaranch summoned me and my IOC colleague John Coates, to tell us, 'We need two new sports: triathlon and taekwondo – that's what I want. Tell everyone!' This opened my eyes. Taekwondo? Here were athletes not of the ordinary: schooled in courtesy, strict regard for rules, all thoroughly trained before entering competition. Nor would you find drugs in the sport. Having been so involved for Seoul's election for '88, Kim had advised our campaign on Sydney's strategy. Internationally, he was one of taekwondo's many forces, its father figure.

Fekrou Kidane, a refugee and campaigner for Ethiopian – and African – democracy, had become African adviser to Samaranch during South Africa's anti-apartheid convulsion and subsequently Samaranch's personal aide-de-camp; he knew the score. 'One of Samaranch's objectives had become taekwondo's inclusion. Aware of Japan's and judo's opposition to taekwondo, he knew that the project would need the majority support of IOC Members, yet required an informative, close collaboration with Kim. To underpin the project, Kim needed the allegiance of influential IOC Members. So he co-opted several, such as Coles and, I think, Gunilla Lindberg of Sweden, onto taekwondo's Executive Board.'

One of Kim Un-yong's most effective lobbyists would be Philippine IOC Member Francisco Elizalde, for many years trusted scrutineer of IOC elections. He has intimate memories of Kim's wizardry: 'I was not there at Baden-Baden in 1981 for Seoul's long-odds defeat of Nagano. I

Francisco Elizalde, Philippines IOC Member, long-standing supporter of Kim Un-yong, dismayed at his imprisonment

CHAPTER 3

remember dismayed Japanese journalists questioning the IOC, "What were you people thinking of?" At the Asian Games in 1986 in Seoul, everybody associated the success of the event with "Dr. Kim"; he was so friendly, bosom buddies with so many, always very accommodating, always so well-informed. I recall that Sheikh Ahmed of Kuwait coveted the presidency of the Olympic Council of Asia, with Bob Hasan of Indonesia being a rival candidate. Kim was overheard mentioning, "I have other ideas." Kim was so clearly on a mission, on larger goals, bent on achieving them.' Elizalde continued, 'Dr. Kim so avidly spread the taekwondo gospel, his national sport. At the Shilla Hotel, where the IOC stayed during the '88 Olympics, there was a taekwondo exhibition station at the end of the driveway, in walking distance. We passed it regularly, popped in for a chat. We practised taekwondo in the Philippines – not widespread but popular in schools and clubs. We'd had karate a long time, but not that much developed, no connection to Olympic ambition. It was Dr. Kim who established taekwondo's set of rules and regulations, the system of judging . . . and the rest is history. I remember at some international gathering, the North Korean predecessor of ITF leader Chang Ung, speaking in Russian, interminably pressing on about ITF's status, and Kim not responding. Why not, I asked him? "Because every year he has to justify his existence," Kim responded nonchalantly.'

With the Samaranch-Kim liaison in full swing, the fate of taekwondo's Olympic inclusion hung in the balance at IOC's centenary Session in Paris in 1994, in the wake of the first Congress since Baden-Baden and a preceding Executive Board meeting. (IOC Congresses are intermittent debating platforms, organised at the President's discretion and embracing all those involved in the Olympic Movement, IFs, NOCs and stakeholders including sponsors.) Such was the obfuscation surrounding the taekwondo factor that Samaranch did no more than hint at discussion of its inclusion a month beforehand. Kim Un-yong duly raised Korean media expectations prior to the EB meeting when he stated, 'Taekwondo's status is higher than ever since its adoption as a recognised event for competition around the world. At this Session, it has the opportunity for adoption as a full Olympic event.' Despite pessimism among the Korean media, a survey on eligible Olympic events (16 mandatory and 26 optional), by Karl-Heinz Huba's widely distributed and respected English-language German website *Sport Intern*, placed triathlon 24th and taekwondo 25th, ahead of archery, golf and baseball. Inevitably and expectedly there was hostile publicity from karate and the ITF, including sabotage letters to IOC Members from ITF President Choi.

Meanwhile, Samaranch and Kim had covertly agreed to avoid thrusting the issue before the EB, which would have raised public debate; Samaranch was merely asking the EB's opinion prior to the Session. There were no objections, and Samaranch felt able to announce, offhand, that a decision would therefore be made by the Session, 'limited to the two additional sports for Sydney'. His unspoken moral contract with Kim Un-yong was about to be sealed: Kim having persuaded Samaranch to adjust his initial proposal for a single weight-class each for men and women to two weight classes each. Kim, trusting in Samaranch's unfailing support, had proposed to the EB three classes each, men and women. Kim discussed presentation tactics for the Session with chief backer Jean-Claude Ganga of Congo and Libyan Bashir Mohamed Attarabulsi. The key moment arrived, with hundreds of expectant taekwondo supporters in attendance around the conference hall.

The Session's opposition began with Vladimir Cernusak of Slovakia demanding, 'Why does this sport have two different federations?' Kim Un-yong blandly responded, 'The reason taekwondo has been raised as an official Olympic event is because I am confident in its unlimited potential as a sport. I don't know anything about similar groups such as the ITF. But the WTF has been staging international competitions continuously since it was founded in 1973. It was admitted to GAISF in 1975 and received IOC approval in 1980, adopted as an official event in the 1983 Pan Am Games, the 1986 Asian Games and the 1990 African Games. It was a demonstration event at the Olympics of 1988 and 1992 and has 140 member countries around the world. Over the past twenty years, taekwondo has made rapid strides as a global sport. It possesses its own set of rules and equipment that differ from other martial arts. With its value having been improved this way, I don't see it unreasonable to be included in Olympic competition.'

There were no further questions, while several IOC Members made statements expressing support. Samaranch asked for objections, then enquired if any wished to abstain. Silence. When announced, the vote was unanimous: all 85 IOC Members present in approval. For triathlon's attendant vote, the results were 83 in favour and one against, with one abstention. Speaking to the Korean press afterwards, Kim stated, 'I was 99 per cent sure it would pass, but the other one per cent could have been an issue. I had to remain prudent until the outcome was in my pocket.' That evening, he received a call from South Korean President Kim Young-sam in congratulation. The two would meet for breakfast at the Blue House on Kim's return, and for a bevy of interviews. Previously the government had shown scant interest in the project; now it was offering funds for travel and expenses. Kim declined. 'The IOC Session is over, everything's done, and now you offer your support?' he responded. The offer was less than half what had actually been spent on a project that would give South Korea a unique place in sporting history.

The Session's decision dumbfounded IOC director-general Francois Carrard, an astute and renowned Swiss lawyer who was widely respected for his comprehensive and loyal grasp of IOC's complex affairs. Twenty-four years later, Carrard reflected, 'At the time of the Seoul Olympics, I'd not yet weighed the Samaranch-Kim relationship, but subsequently it became more and more obvious. When I became director-general in '90, Primo Nebiolo and Mario Vazquez Rana were the more prominent influence, but Kim and GAISF became something else. Samaranch knew that in Kim he had found someone to keep GAISF under control. I had discovered that taekwondo was an intricate world, but I was truly shocked to find it suddenly emerge as an Olympic sport, without apparent previous consultation! I would have expected some debate, yet suddenly Samaranch is announcing, "We consider taekwondo as an Olympic sport." I had many IOC Members say to me privately, 'We should never have introduced it. We already have enough problems!" Yet somehow the Session at Paris in '94 had been totally silenced, and taekwondo approved almost unannounced. Dr. Kim knew exactly what was going to happen. It was at this moment I realised the power of his influence on Samaranch. A big defender for taekwondo and triathlon had been Gunnar Ericsson of Sweden, chair of Barcelona's Olympic Coordination Commission. At every EB meeting, Ericsson at the close would prompt Samaranch: "Remember the issue of triathlon." I had commented to Samaranch that it might be best to consult the IFs of swimming, cycling and athletics, the individual federations of triathlon's three disciplines. Yet in comparison to Ericsson, Dr. Kim never openly mentioned a word about taekwondo.'

IOC Vice-president Kim Un-yong celebrates the IOC's certification of taekwondo as an official event at the 2000 Sydney Olympics, IOC Session, Paris, 1994.

British IOC Member Sir Craig Reedie, who had trailed Samaranch for several years in the 1980s in his travels around the globe in pursuit of badminton's programme inclusion – achieved for Barcelona in 1992 – observed that in the IF environment, taekwondo was viewed 'as Kim's reward for the Asian countries'. Jon Tibbs, a prominent sponsorships promoter and host bidding-city negotiator, reflected, 'I mainly followed Kim's expanding influence in the columns of *Sport Intern*, his astute sensitivity in promoting ideas. I recognised we were watching a smart man, he regularly being referred to in reverent tones. Yet I encountered the Olympic election of taekwondo almost with disbelief, hardly having experience of the sport. The achievement added to the aura surrounding this man.' Such personal fame, such acclaim as now enveloped Kim Un-yong and the esteem he had generated for Korea's national sport back home, had sown the seeds of what would, in due course, become motivation for brutal political revenge.

For the moment, reflected prestige upon Korea would lead to such international sporting expansion that this Asian peninsula's southern republic was to become – as an envied performance power-house and international event host in multiple sports – temperamentally damaged by its sense of self-importance. Simultaneously, Samaranch's revolutionary rehabilitation of IOC finances by sponsorship ingenuity, fanned by the gratuitous city publicity garnered through television coverage, would create a distorted optimism among expanding, ambitious bid cities that, within two decades, would generate the reverse phenomenon: a widespread reluctance and withdrawal from bidding campaigns on account of ever-increasing hosting expenditure. Samaranch's hesitant successor, the soft-spoken but dogmatic Belgian orthopaedic surgeon and former Olympic sailor Jacques Rogge, largely marked time, leaving the next incumbent, German lawyer and Olympic team fencing champion Thomas Bach, to confront turbulent waters with his imaginative and necessary Agenda 2020 revisionist adjustments.

Following Paris's grotesquely expensive (reportedly $15m) centenary Congress and Session and taekwondo's promotion, South Korea was to exploit its prestige with host appointments for a parade of major international events, the trend coinciding with Kim Un-yong being elected on consecutive days in February 1993 as president of both the Korean Sports Council (KSC) and Korean Olympic Committee (KOC), alongside the instalment of Kim Young-sam as Korea's first democratic non-military President. Kim Un-yong was thus quadruple sports administrator, embracing the IOC vice-presidency and leadership of GAISF – a platform of power second only to that of Samaranch.

However, Kim Young-sam's reign would see the termination of the Ministry of Sports and Youth; it was replaced by the Ministry of Sport and Culture, a body less disposed towards Kim Un-yong's domestic responsibilities. The result was a loss of harmony with Kim Un-yong's ambition to elevate the KOC's performance levels – fourth on the medal table in 1988, and seventh at Barcelona '92. Reduced government funding would impede further development, yet Kim Un-yong forged ahead with an upgraded Olympic House, accommodation raised from 200 to 600 with advanced training facilities – especially for Winter Games disciplines, such as a ski jump tower at Muju, joined in 1998 by a high-altitude training camp (1,300 metres) at Hambaeksan Mountain – together with raised Olympic medal pensions of ten, five and three thousand dollars respectively.

Expanding Korea's, and his own, international respect, Kim Un-yong negotiated hosting appointments for the first competition of the Association for International Sport-for-All (TAISFA) in 1996, embracing 500 IF representatives, the Winter Universiade at Muju/ Jeonju and the Busan East Asian Games in 1997, the IOC Session of 1999, the FIFA World Cup and Busan Asian Games of 2002, and the Summer Universiade at Daegu in 2003.

The most ambitious of these seven international events was FIFA's

World Cup, which had been secretly promised to Japan by authoritarian Brazilian president Joao Havelange, acting behind his own executive committee. Havelange's home city of Rio de Janeiro was simultaneously bidding both to host the IOC Session of 1999 and the Summer Games of 2004. As chief sports correspondent of *The Times* (London) at the time of the election campaigns during 1995–96, the author was closely in touch with Lennart Johansson of Sweden, chair of UEFA. I was thus aware of a strong tide of European support for Korea; that with the breakdown of the 25-strong FIFA Executive vote likely to split 13-12 either way, the opinion of Johansson and his European colleagues was that joint-hosting was the solution – specifically to avert antagonism between the Asian rivals in the defeat of one or the other.

The Korean bid committee – led by Korean Football Association president Chung Mong-joon of Hyundai Industry renown, who was conscious of my 40-year contact with FIFA and my being a member of FIFA's media commission – invited me to Seoul on a non-financial basis to give advice (a leather briefcase offered as a gesture is still in use). Korea was intent on an exclusive bid and reluctant to lose face by publicly agreeing to joint hosting. My opinion, given at a government reception, was to maintain Korea's solo bid, but to issue a formal statement accepting that 'if it was FIFA's wish', Korea would accept the principle of joint hosting. This they announced a week later.

While Havelange was, improperly, hand-in-glove with Japan, Kim Un-yong's trump card was his intimate contact with Samaranch, who as IOC President could lean on Havelange on both World Cup and Olympic Session issues. As journalist, I had the ear of all three men (all of whom have since passed away). Their private negotiations remain undisclosed, but what is known is that Samaranch contrived to persuade Havelange that to leave the outcome to a secret FIFA vote would embarrass Havelange should Korea win. On election day, Havelange arrived at the meeting to announce: 'Gentlemen, I have an excellent idea – that we should accept co-hosting!' It could never be proved, but there can be little doubt that Kim Un-yong's influence on both the 1999 IOC Session, which Seoul secured by 57 votes to 31 – in spite of a Latin bloc solidly behind Rio – and World Cup 2002 will have favourably swayed the decisions. If, as seemed increasingly probable, Kim Un-yong was to run for the supreme post in world sport when Samaranch eventually retired, what was now to stop him?

In the event, fate in the form of domestic political revenge and IOC antagonism towards a formidable Asian would confound Kim Un-yong's ultimate ambitions during the next few years. In the wake of his vindictive treatment during the years 2003–2006, and shortly prior to his sudden death in 2017 shortly before a taekwondo championship to be staged in his honour, Kim Un-yong gave a rare and extensive interview to a publication by the Italian Taekwondo Federation (*"Taekwondo and the Olympic Dream"*). Conducted by Angelo Cito, it was an interview of historic reflection on the remarkable evolution of Kim Un-yong's national sport. It is presented here in abridged form:

When I was elected president of KTA, this was one of our few well-organised national associations with an international perspective. Despite the poor reputation of taekwondo in Korea at the time – because of internal struggles – the KTA began spreading knowledge of our sport and sending some instructors to America and Europe. Outside Korea, taekwondo was then known as 'Korean karate'. Korean society itself looked down on us. Times weren't all that good, let's say. People expected a lot from me, because they knew how much I was devoted to my work, aware of what I could achieve. They had hopes of coming together in a single entity with common values, like other sports federations. The dream of taekwondo athletes was to have a central gymnasium that could represent a point of reference for everyone, an official HQ where we could welcome visiting foreign athletes. Back then, Korea's economy was unsteady. Today, people know about us, but back in 1971 no one could even say where Korea was geographically. I remember taking part at the first meeting of all NOCs, as president and general-secretary of KOC, organised in Rome by Giulio Onesti in 1975. (Onesti was the motivator of the organisation of collective NOCs within IOC.) I had to stay quiet in a corner together with Taipei and Vietnam, as Korea had no power. I didn't forget, however, the dream of having a central gym, and during the press conference declared I wanted to build such a centre for the KTA, which was to be the Kukkiwon that you all know today. Building the gym was not an easy project; we did not have an adequate location, let alone a budget. I managed to gather six hundred thousand dollars, which was incredible for those times, as Korea was not well developed as yet. I met many public figures from whom I received not only funds, but also cement, steel, glass and all we needed to complete the building within a year – and without government support.

Another dream was to organise a World Championship. To do so, I had to work for the unity of all different styles, convinced that if we wanted to integrate the world, we needed to be united, to standardise our evaluation of competitive criteria, as I thought the level of preparation of instructions was paramount.... Today, the level has much improved and many of our instructors are excellent, PhD holders at the head of university institutions, whereas in the past many had an elementary educational level.

To gain the inclusion of taekwondo on the Olympic Programme, it was important to register all our disciplines. Therefore taekwondo needed to be a member of GAISF, of FISU, of the international university federation and of the Military Sports Council and to take part in all major intercontinental events.

Becoming president of GAISF – a role I held for twenty years – and organising the World Games allowed me to embrace taekwondo in continental competition, which was a breakthrough towards the Olympics. Korea's domestic situation in those years was very unstable, yet becoming an IOC Member kept me working for the Olympic Games of 1988 in Seoul.

It became urgent to write adequate competition regulations that would be accepted worldwide. It was during the LA Games of 1984 that I had the idea, from boxing, of introducing a helmet to ensure safety. The Western world could never have accepted kicks in the face… [I]t wasn't easy to organise the first World Championships. We didn't have funds . . . so we decided to involve all our instructors who had been sent abroad, who held talks with respective local governments, and managed to gather 15 countries and 19 teams. A dream come true.

When I first tried to register taekwondo with GAISF, the president of the International Judo Federation claimed we were just a branch of karate. There was much opposition. My mission was complicated by instructors in America putting up signs on their gymnasia reading 'Korean karate' – which was hard to explain to the IOC. The World Taekwondo Federation began with our small World Championships, where the stadium was sold out. I had wanted to name the federation 'International Taekwondo', but General Choi, who had branched out in Canada, had already used the title, so I chose 'World Taekwondo Federation' – to become the first of all national sports that anyone of any age could practice and then to globalise it and show the world our Korean potential. Korea had nothing to show during previous Olympic Games. In 1960 in Rome, Korea did not win a single medal – it took 30 years to do that in Montreal in 1976.

At the Seoul Olympic Games, I was able to bid for taekwondo to be included as a demonstration, even if medals were not considered. To bring taekwondo to the Games as an official sport was not easy. We were lucky to have an IOC President such as Juan Antonio Samaranch, with whom we often worked during the organisation of the Games –

on television rights negotiations and helping the Soviet Union and East Europeans to take part, while avoiding boycotting actions from some nations. Taekwondo was part of the Opening Ceremony, thousands performing in unison, leaving the world in amazement and allowing us to show the martial art aspect alongside the sporting aspect.

During the Games of Barcelona, I suggested taekwondo again as a demonstration sport. Reaching this objective was not easy if you compare it with Seoul, both baseball and badminton being introduced in the Programme before taekwondo, with a real risk of exclusion for us. The President of IOC, who had visited Kukkiwon in 1992, saw with his own eyes what had been achieved, how I had managed to develop a new sport. All this had helped in Seoul. At the Barcelona Games, Basque pelota and roller hockey had already been introduced as demonstration sports. I argued with Samaranch that were taekwondo not demonstrated in Barcelona, all our instructors in Europe would lose face. Fortunately he agreed, and we managed to place taekwondo as a third demonstration sport, competing over four days. Taekwondo was now well positioned, present in all five continents. At the Paris Session in '94, however, during discussion on taekwondo's inclusion, Samaranch had suggested its introduction along with triathlon, with one medal each for men and women. I objected, now that I had necessary political power. I argued that taekwondo could not begin with only two medals – it was impossible to combine eight men's and eight women's categories in a single event per gender. Without this, it would have been better to cancel everything. Long negotiations did achieve eight categories: four each for men and women. During the Paris Session, I was asked to explain the behaviour of ITF, which had sent a documentary complaint against WTF, while karate threatened legal action against the IOC. My strategy was to say nothing – only that I knew WTF as a member of GAISF, of the Pan Am Games, of the All-Africa Games, FISU, CISM and World Games, etc., and specifying our number of national federations and the number of world championships we had organised. There was then the vote. I was the only one admitted in the conference hall; our supporters all had to wait outside – and we obtained a unanimous favourable vote, 85-0.

From then on, taekwondo has undergone many changes; more national federations soon managed to be acknowledged by respective NOCs, the Italian Federation among them. Maintaining our traditional values, it was essential to have a new vision.... [W]e had grown enormously in Asia and managed to achieve the necessary stability. Then and now, it is paramount that all the various institutions have a common vision in maintaining unity instead of fighting against each other, as has often happened in Korea. It took twenty years for us to achieve inclusion, where some other sports took a century; still others have had to merge different federations (like badminton and baseball). Thanks to my work with President Samaranch, we managed to achieve inclusion without having to unite WTF and ITF. There is still talk of this, but I doubt it will be possible – a great idea but not technically easy.... [T]he promotional work of our taekwondo instructors across the world was fundamental to WTF's success. The work I did in unifying the sport in Korea, all without help from the government, could not have been done without the work of our instructors overseas and the assistance of Samaranch.

Regrettably, Olympic sport has become too market-driven. Of course we need more money to fund development, but Olympic values are something different – the solidarity, friendship, peace. We often lose sight of these and become slaves to the market. There is too much professionalism, too much ego, all creating problems, as we witnessed at the last Olympic Games in Rio. This is why many cities now don't want to become hosts. In the 1990s, many thought that hosting brought increased income, yet expense is too high while revenue diminishes.... [T]he IOC should work to reduce costs and contribute more themselves. The same goes for taekwondo itself, in the building of a healthy society. I learned during my career what can be done in society – that you need to have a dream. Through these, young people can learn to share, to achieve; the Games are meant to teach the importance of this. Korean modern history saw two main events: the war on the Korean Peninsula, which was intended to protect the nation, and the Games in Seoul. People forget; they should remember that before the Games, South Korea was marginalised not only in sport, but also culturally and economically. In the end, the positive always comes through, and Korea saw great development in politics, diplomacy, society, economy, medicine and sport. A country that in thirty years had won only one gold medal at the Olympics won twelve during the Seoul Games – success which was then confirmed in Barcelona and maintained in later editions. I think the number of medals may decrease in the next Games at Tokyo, because we focused too much on the present, not investing in future athletes.... [I]n conclusion, the Olympic Games of Seoul brought the country to global development, from the individual all the way up to big corporations like Samsung, Hyundai, Korean Airlines and the rest. We now need to be careful not to be over-confident, or we'll be in trouble. There are changes in the Olympics, but the IOC is not a factory, like say Fiat, relying on marketing too much of its logo at the expense of its ideals. Due to the huge income, the IOC is easily exposed to criminal organisations, leading to scandals like doping, as with FIFA or IAAF and other federations. IOC leadership needs to focus on re-establishing focus and harmony in today's complicated context of international terrorism, refugee crises, financial tensions etc.

I visited Italy on many occasions, took part in my first IOC meeting in Rome in 1975. During the years of spreading the gospel of taekwondo, I often met with Italian officials and asked for help where necessary, gratifyingly being appointed Knight Commander ('*Commendatore*'). Young people need to stay united, give their best, contribute to the development of taekwondo. They need to have a big dream.

That dream can have many dimensions. Just listen to Mike McKenzie, the accomplished National Director of British Taekwondo and coach in Sheffield (GB), which was the stamping ground for a flourishing teenager named Sebastian Coe who would go on to become a legendary middle-distance Olympic champion. McKenzie represents the definitive educational element of taekwondo, which an inspired Kim Un-yong lifted from remote Asian obscurity into one of the most character-formative occupations available to mankind. McKenzie offers a textbook of taekwondo's virtues.

'The heart of taekwondo lies in its self-discipline. Emotionally, mentally, it makes you more balanced as an individual. It can help develop both parents and child, a family activity, beneficial to both in confidence and skills. You can have mixed classes; it's family friendly. For adults, it's a deviation from the stresses of every-day life; it improves fitness and health – more interestingly than regular gymnastics, more varied, needing no mechanical or equipment devices. Many participants were motivated in the 1970s and 1980s by the Chinese-American star Bruce Lee.

The standardisation of this competitive sport was probably Kim Un-yong's finest achievement, preventing its fragmentation. It could be said there's now criticism of World Taekwondo, the federation, for lack of sponsorship and media coverage, but that's the same for most low-profile sports. It needs to be more spectator-friendly, but that's not the fault of president Choue, who wanted to move the HQ to Lausanne, alongside many Olympic federations, although this was resisted. Yet a strength of taekwondo is that it is so cost-effective in simple stadium layout. For the 2012 facility in London, the hall was converted from fencing to taekwondo in 72 hours. Taekwondo is thus for anybody, for everybody, for any overweight child. Every child is eligible for this graceful martial art.'

The significance of taekwondo in the Olympic programme was further emphasised at a celebration of the 25th anniversary of the sport's inclusion at a gathering at Lausanne in April 2019. IOC President Thomas Bach joined the hosts (WT president Choue Chung-won and ITF president Ri Yong-son) and mutual promoters, together with former German Chancellor Gerhard Schroeder, Association of Summer Olympic International Federations (ASOIF) president Francesco Ricci Bitti, EB member and United World Wrestling (UWW) president Nenad Lalovic, International Hockey Federation (IHF) president Hassan Moustafa and Internatonal University Sports Federation (FISU) president Oleg Matytsin.

President Bach reflected, 'Ever since taekwondo became an Olympic sport, WT has transformed a Korean martial art into one of the popular sports in the world, and WT has developed the men's sport into one with gender equality. WT has opened a pathway to participation by refugees, helping motivate the creation of the Olympic refugee teams and establishment of the Olympic Refugee Foundation.'

Choue responded, 'It is an honour to have been included in the Olympic Games programme for the last 25 years, during which taekwondo has grown significantly thanks to the global exposure the Games has provided. We have innovated and made the sport more exciting, ensuring it can be practiced anywhere, anytime, by anyone regardless of age, gender or ability.' Ri added, 'To the sport's profound philosophy and characteristic spirit, ITF has devoted itself to building a civilised society and will continue this cause in conformity with Olympic ethics to encourage the creation of global peace.'

—

SALT LAKE SUBTERFUGE

In 1984, as a writer on Olympic affairs for almost three decades, I recognised at the Los Angeles Games that the IOC and host cities were running a tight ship. LA's chief, Peter Ueberroth, masterminded a privately funded Games in the wake of Montreal's cash-strapped budget in 1976 and Moscow's financially shrouded 1980 organisation; he provided the media with antiquated school buses without springs, ran a porta-cabin office – and made the definitive profit that paved the way for new IOC President Samaranch to revolutionise future finances. The tone had changed by the IOC's Session of 1986 in Lausanne: whereas LA had been the sole bid for 1984, now there were 13 launched simultaneously, six for the Summer Games and seven for the Winter Games of 1992. It was a frenzy of lobbying, inducements and veiled invitations. This embarrassing rash of expanding ambition, encouraged by Samaranch's decision to televise the award ceremony – free city advertising! – obliged his appointment of Marc Hodler, Swiss IOC Member and veteran head of international skiing (FIS), to establish restrictions on souvenirs, exhibition booths and luxury inspection visits. It was all in vain: the gravy train, the tide of which would serve to spawn blatant IOC and city misjudgements over the coming years – and, by uncorroborated inference, ensnare Kim Un-yong – was up and running.

Evidence of blatant malpractice was often visible, sometimes unidentifiably furtive in the pursuit of votes, and included transparent seduction of media, which I learned as a target. As correspondent of *The Times* (London), I was duly entertained modestly at the Racing Club de

Kim Un-yong with Marc Hodler (centre) and Kevan Gosper, respective IOC Members from Switzerland and Australia, during the Seoul Olympics. Hodler would notoriously elaborate on the Salt Lake scandal ten years later.

Paris by genteel veteran Alain Danet, who was promoting Paris, and likewise by Amsterdam. When I drove independently to Barcelona (my son then resident in Spain) to assess the city's bid, a smart new travel bag appeared unannounced in my hotel room – though at no time over the year did I receive one word of supplication from Samaranch for his home city. Professionally, I wrote in favour of Paris; Barcelona was elected. I favoured Sofia for the Winter Games; Albertville in the Savoie Alps was elected. It was the IOC's mute apology for preferring Barcelona to Paris.

The indulgence of bid cities towards IOC Members was ever escalating, the surveillance of the IOC minor and ineffective. Media condemnation of IOC excesses reached fever pitch in 1990 when Atlanta was preferred over inadequate Athens for the Centenary Games of 1996 – allegedly on the back of Coca-Cola funding. Privately, bid leaders for Toronto and Manchester respectively advised Samaranch of purported underhand demands from certain IOC Members; without documentary proof, no action could be taken. Samaranch, as President, was too busy consolidating IOC's new financial security – on the back of Kim Un-yong's spectacular Seoul Games and the mushrooming TOP sponsorship – to focus on a handful of bad apples and manipulative bidding cities in the IOC awards barrel.

Three years on from Kim Un-yong's Korean masterpiece, I had a close sense as journalist of the destructive cloud overhanging the IOC – and not just because Samaranch's observant wife Maria Teresa had privately said to me that 'something has to be done about the excesses.' In the campaign for the Winter vote in 1991 at Birmingham (UK) for the Games of 1998, I was transparently aware of Salt Lake's superiority over its two rivals. I had visited Nagano – competent, but markedly inferior to Utah's magnificent facilities. My *Times* preview forecast Salt Lake, though I agreed, on request, to assist in composing an acceptance speech for Nagano, in English, should they win the vote.

Following Nagano's shock victory, I was offering condolence at Salt Lake's hospitality boutique. Campaign director Tom Welch's wife Norma was in a mood of quiet fury, muttering, 'We ran out of money!' The clear inference was that Nagano had not – that incentives changed hands. Welch decided there and then that if this was the strategy, Salt Lake would emulate the practice. And they did. Ironically, they need not have bothered; four years later they won by a landslide in the first round in Budapest. But the hidden explosives had been planted . . . and Nagano's financial records seemingly became unavailable.

When Samaranch had succeeded Michael Killanin in 1980, IOC reserves had been a vulnerable $200,000. With the concerted wisdom of Peter Ueberroth and Horst Dassler, Samaranch had adroitly consolidated Olympic Movement finances – for the moment. Host elections in 1991 (Nagano '98), 1993 (Sydney '00), 1995 (Salt Lake '02) and 1997 (Athens '04) would continue with unabated media criticism of flaunted cities and IOC extravagances within an unrestrained bandwagon. The proverbial was about to hit the fan, just as Kim Un-yong had reached the apogee of his influence and power in harmony with Samaranch. Emerging He Zhenliang of China was also a rival to other change-makers, Canadian Richard Pound and Australian Kevan Gosper.

The equilibrium rupture sprang from a comparatively anonymous Salt Lake City television station, KTVX, to which had been leaked, in November 1998, a letter dated 1996 from David Johnson, senior vice-president of the Salt Lake Organising Committee for the Winter Games of 2002. It was addressed to Sonia Essomba, daughter of a Cameroon IOC Member; Johnson advised her of termination of 'our scholarship programme with you', enclosing a final instalment of just over $10,000. The leak, metaphorically equivalent to the Watergate break-in, reached the desk of December's IOC Executive Board meeting, Samaranch having already requested clarification from Salt Lake. Marc Hodler roused his colleagues, delivering an impromptu and incendiary lunchtime press briefing. Within hours the rest of the world gasped at the exposure.

The eminent 80-year-old Hodler had claimed that IOC votes 'were sold'; that Atlanta, Nagano and Sydney were implicated; and that 'eligible' lists of available corrupt IOC Members were circulating. At this point, Kim Un-yong was unblemished. Seoul's election campaign had arisen when the IOC was struggling to survive amidst a succession of three boycotts. Kim had studiously negotiated votes on a promise of security and inclusivity, not dollars. His ascent of the IOC ladder had been by cultural, diplomatic and linguistic collaborative charm and persistence. 'Yes', recalls Dassler cohort and sponsorship guru Patrick Nally, 'Kim had sought financial favours for his taekwondo development projects. He did expect to be funded for expansion, for the inaugural World Games – not a surprise for us over the years that he was receiving benefits, not shy of asking, sometimes borderline, but always for sport not for himself.' A man of principle, Kim was adamant that his elder daughter return her engagement ring when retreating from a proposed marriage.

In the shortest time of any IOC Member, Kim Un-yong had become an Executive Board Member in 1988 – doing so within two years of initial election. Four years on, he was elected Vice-president of IOC, prior to Barcelona '92, by a surprise but emphatic 54-29 margin over favoured Chiharu Igaya of Japan, who had been celebrated as Asia's first slalom silver medallist at Cortina '56.

In 1995, a year after the triumph of taekwondo's promotion to the Olympic Programme, the IOC instituted an Evaluation Commission to scrutinise accredited bidding cities prior to their presentation for election. Selected by Samaranch to chair the commission, Kim inspected the contest among Salt Lake, Jaca (in the Pyrenees), and Sion (in the Swiss Alps). In his *Challenge to the World* – written in the wake of his own achievements and Korea's performance rise to fourth and then seventh place in the medals table of the Seoul and Barcelona Olympics, respectively – Kim reflected, 'There is not some special secret of success that applies on the international stage. The most important thing is that IOC Members are fairly assessing your strengths. After that, it's important to value human relations, with respect and esteem for people's character – close human relationships where you treat everyone fairly without distance or taking sides. I always treated all IOC Members equally, whether they represented a small African country or a world-dominating power. I think that I was recognised for my achievement in raising taekwondo to the stature of a global sport, and for my ability in safely handling the television broadcasting rights issues and ensuring the Seoul Olympics' success.... For good results to come, you have to do your job diligently, reward your faith in yourself, and live up to your words throughout the process.'

By 1996, Kim Un-yong – now IOC senior Vice-president – had the sensitive task of steering Lee Kun-hee to becoming Korea's additional IOC Member. Back in 1993, two months after his election as president

Kim Un-yong with South Korea's Lee Kun-hee (centre) and North Korea's Chang Ung (right), after their election as IOC Members, IOC Session, Atlanta, 1996

of both KSC and KOC, Kim had been summoned to the Blue House by President Kim Young-sam, who was intent on the IOC promotion of Lee, at the time the president of Korean wrestling and KOC vice-president as well as chairman of the Samsung Group. The plan to have Lee installed at the Paris Session of 1994 was stalled by Lee's public clanger during a visit to China, but re-surfaced – with Samaranch meeting Kim Young-sam – in time for the Session prior to Atlanta '96, where Lee was elected alongside North Korea's Chang Ung. Kim Un-yong/Samaranch synergy? Kim had agreed to support Chang's nomination, thereby backing Samaranch's global expansion.

Supervising the evaluation of Winter Games cities intensified Kim Un-yong's ambition to complete the double: Korea's hosting of the winter event, and the value of such an achievement in further expanding

CHAPTER 4

Korea's international prestige. The staging in 1997 of the Muju/ Jeonju Winter Universiade (snow events in the former, ice in the latter) further fuelled Kim's intention. Financial setbacks at Muju subsequently opened the way to Pyeongchang, Gangwon-do province, hosting the 1999 Asian Winter Games – originally scheduled for 2000 but moved up at the demand of the Olympic Council of Asia. Backed by Prime Minister Kim Jong-pil, Gangwon-do's Asian Games were a low-key launch-pad for the major objective; fate, however, was ultimately to twist cruelly against Kim Un-yong.

Central to the turn of events, as Samaranch and his IOC colleagues attempted to smother and repair the volcanic damage of the erupting Salt Lake scandal, was He Zhenliang – sphinx-like in outward appearance but a man of outstanding intellect and unpretentious charm. Emerging from Beijing's contentious host city defeat by Sydney at Monte Carlo in 1993, he was one of a minority of those Chinese involved in the bid at the government level to retain his equilibrium in the narrow controversial defeat. He was a calming voice of rationality during a period of IOC chaos that veered at times dangerously close to panic. Conscious of He Zhenliang's infectious tranquillity, Samaranch had invited him to attend the EB meeting of December 1998 in a non-voting capacity, He having just ended a four-year term. Following Hodler's uncharacteristic outburst, the EB was in a quandary – all the more so when Frank Joklik, chair of the Salt Lake organising committee, was summoned to Lausanne and confirmed some of Hodler's worst allegations. Widely circulating among others was the story that Salt Lake had given Samaranch a valuable ceremonial sword – instantly presented, as with all other gifts, to the Olympic Museum. Samaranch reflected, 'I am worried these revelations are just the tip of an iceberg.' He had reason to be: Paul Henderson, as related, had given specific but undocumented and unattended warning. According to He Zhenliang's biography *China's Olympic Dream*, he had written in his diary, 'The festering corruption in the bid process has finally burst open. Traced backwards, it will probably not stop at Salt Lake. If it is handled well, it could solve the problem of vote-buying. If not, the IOC's reputation will be greatly damaged.'

Kim Un-yong could not have imagined, as Salt Lake's manipulation was forensically laid bare, that danger loomed for him personally. Some of those IOC Members named as offenders might be supportive colleagues of his, but he was, he could aver, uninvolved in having received any 'freebie' inducement – trips to Disneyland, Las Vegas and Niagara Falls; scholarships for relatives; funds for domestic political campaigns; or the quarter of a million dollars lavished on Jean-Claude Ganga, the Member for Republic of Congo, including cosmetic surgery for his wife and hip replacement for his mother-in-law! Kim Un-yong had sought assistance – for the advancement of taekwondo.

With every thread of IOC and Salt Lake activity under the media microscope of investigative journalists – a licence for many to print anything they could imagine – there was a false assumption that the supposedly ideological IOC had previously been perfect; in fact, it had only been as perfect as the better of its administrators. Benevolent, selfless yet obsessive founder Baron de Coubertin, for instance, gave Hitler the blessing for Berlin '36 – having been nominated by the Nazis for the Nobel Peace Prize, an honour perhaps more deserved by the organisation than the individual. De Coubertin's successor, Henri de Baillet-Latour, stood to profit from the merger of his family-founded bank with Deutsche Bank, while President Avery Brundage had a contract to build a new German Embassy in Washington. In vain might Robert Helmick, former IOC Member from the US, proclaim that Samaranch should immediately retire, Helmick himself having resigned in 1991 for conflict of interest-plagued business deals.

The stricken global festival which Kim Un-yong had ambitions to lead was being assaulted on every front. Wolf Lyberg, an eminent Swedish NOC official who had been involved in six unsuccessful Swedish bid campaigns and was an exhaustive Olympic historian, had protested about irregularities in 1986: now Christer Persson, who had led Ostersund of Sweden against Salt Lake, was demanding $14 million in compensation to the losers, including Quebec and Sion. Graham Stringer, a Labour Member of Parliament who coordinated bids by Manchester, admitted, 'Everyone knew there was a small number of IOC Members who were corrupt, and you just accepted that's the way it was.' Anita DeFrantz, an American bronze medal oarswoman in 1976 and one of four IOC Vice-presidents, lamented, 'I heard of people spending weeks at Le Clarion, the top hotel in Paris. It costs a hundred dollars just to breathe the air in the lobby.' DeFrantz had been one to complain that Kim Un-yong had offered first-class airfare for Members inspecting Seoul's facilities, which had allegedly been redeemed by some for cash. Who is to blame: recipient or donor? At what point does goodwill become bribery? British IOC Member Mary Glen-Haig, an Olympic fencer, welcomed first-class fares to anywhere, irrespective of her intent.

And scholarships? Kim Un-yong's campaign for taekwondo's expansion had privately funded coaches and students across the world. Kevan Gosper, an Australian track silver medallist and regular EB vice-president who was a potential successor to Samaranch until age precluded him, recalls in his autobiography *An Olympic Life*, 'I didn't automatically associate talk of scholarships with a problem in the bidding process. Scholarships, including for foreigners, are a way of life in the US.... I had been a beneficiary of one. (Records revealed $400,000 in scholarships or financial aid from Salt Lake) Sydney had an extensive programme for assistance for African athletes to come to Australia to train in lead-up to the Games.... yet over time I had become increasingly uncomfortable with our process for selecting cities – that it allowed every IOC Member and an accompanying guest to visit.... By 1995 and the decision for 2002, some one hundred and fifty people, including partners, could be continually visiting cities over two years.'

What did emerge in January 1999, as Samaranch and the EB contemplated steps to repair the ethical carnage, was admission by John Coates, president of Australia's NOC, that on the evening of voting in 1993 for the 2000 Games, he had offered $35,000 each 'for sports development' to Charles Mukora and Francis Nyangweso, respectively IOC Members from Kenya and Uganda, Then, and now amidst the storm, there was no reproof for an action possibly decisive in the two votes by which Sydney surpassed Beijing. He Zhenliang pronounced, 'This was absolutely improper.... The Olympic image has been tarnished. Personally, I would agree to cancel Sydney's qualification. Nevertheless, since the EB has decided not to change the venue, and in consideration of Australian people who are innocent, I can respect the EB's decision.'

In turmoil, Samaranch contemplated quitting. Following the Coates revelation, He Zhenliang sent Samaranch a fax stressing that the President alone was capable of rescuing the IOC – but if Samaranch resigned, worse confusion would follow with appointment of a successor. 'In the midst of the tempest, everyone realises the value of the helmsman,' He noted. 'We will steadfastly stand by you.' This was not remotely a scenario in which Kim Un-yong could have presented personal public guidance.

Samaranch's initial response to crisis had been to assign an Ad Hoc Enquiry Commission to be headed by Montreal lawyer Richard Pound, along with EB colleagues Keba M'Baye, Senegalese Judge at The Hague International Court of Justice; Jacques Rogge of Belgium, President of European Olympic Committee; Pal Schmitt of Hungary; and lawyers Thomas Bach (Samaranch's next-but-one intended successor) and director-general Francois Carrard. They were given to the end of January to formulate proposals. The instant recommendations from the EB had been a temporary suspension of six accused Members; further investigation of three others; creation of an Ethics Commission; extension of enquiries into bid cities without cancelling Sydney or Salt Lake; reforms to the bid process; and creation of a 15-strong 'selection college' to elect the Winter Games host for 2006, which would be composed of eight IOC Members, three athletes, one representative each from IFs and NOCs, plus the most senior IOC Member and chairman of the Evaluation Commission. No longer currently on the EB, He Zhenliang approved its determination to be swiftly decisive, yet considered it defective not to challenge bid city conduct. He also opposed the 'selection college' which violated the Charter and deprived innocent IOC Members of their voting rights.

He Zhenliang moved to make his opinions known; here was a parallel to the situation that would confront Thomas Bach as President, almost two decades later, when attempting to uphold natural justice in determining between guilty and innocent in the notorious Russian doping scandal of 2011–14.

Pound was clearcut from the outset in his direction of the Ad Hoc Enquiry Commission, stating he did not believe that inappropriate conduct from Salt Lake and some IOC Members had risen to a criminal level. 'We have found evidence very disappointing from a number of Members, their conduct completely contrary to everything the Olympic Movement has worked so hard to represent, in the process by which the Games are awarded,' he said. He proposed prohibiting Members from visiting bid cities, but added that they should continue to vote on the award. 'We will do whatever is necessary to ensure that IOC Members are held to the highest standards,' he stressed. Pound praised Samaranch's vision and leadership in making the Olympic Movement financially secure, saying that 'the stability achieved by Samaranch was needed now more than ever'.

Pound's was a potent moral code for upholding Baron de Coubertin's foundation, to which he had donated, as an Olympic swimmer, subsequent twenty years of strenuous IOC service. However, that service, which now involved stringently imposing penalties on errant colleagues via an internal emergency disciplinary committee, had a double context of serious ethical and moral issues: while he was on the one hand a supposedly 'honorary' Member, his law firm had received – with Samaranch's accord and hitherto undisclosed – in excess of $4 million over six years from 1985 for his legal service to the IOC on 'contractual issues'. Pound strongly asserted, on exposure of his secret deal, that there were clear demarcations between his lawyer's service and 'Olympic service'. 'There was no conflict of interest,' he insisted. 'When I acted as lawyer, my law firm billed the IOC. I specifically did not benefit. I tried to separate time as Olympic lawyer from IOC membership.' Yet culturally the actions were functioning in the same rowing boat – double sculls, one might say, raising 'very serious moral issues'. Many of his IOC colleagues, including Sergei Bubka, were less than happy to learn subsequently of Pound's personal commercial operation, when he was about to mete out punishments to colleagues for their (albeit sometimes improper) financial acquisition. And Kim Un-yong was about to feel the force of Pound's in-house 'jurisprudence'.

Foremost of the penalties was the expulsion of six Members: Agustin Arroyo (Ecuador), Sergio Santander (Chile), Abdel Gadir (Sudan), Jean-Claude Ganga (Congo), Lamine Keita (Mali), Paul Wallwork (Western Samoa) and the deceased Rene Essomba. Already resigned were Bashir Attarabulsi (Libya), Pirjo Haggman (Finland), Charles Mukora (Kenya) and David Sibandze (Swaziland). Pound and his emergency committee colleagues well knew that a worldwide self-appointed inquisition was waiting upon the imposition of the IOC's own calculation of the ultimate sentence, even if some offending individuals were comparatively minor offenders. For instance, Salt Lake had voluntarily and spontaneously given Sergio Santander a donation to a domestic political campaign. The Utah city had invited Attarabulsi's son to university; the moment the controversy was exposed, Attarabulsi attempted to repay the full amount – even selling family jewellery – moving Samaranch to say that 'cities should bear fifty per cent of responsibility'. Haggman had resigned out of embarrassment, having broken no Olympic oath; her husband had taken an advertised job in Ontario during Toronto's bid, whose leader Henderson had provided temporary accommodation.

The lesser judicial lash of a 'severe warning' befell Vitaly Smirnov, president of Moscow Olympic Committee in 1980, and, with greater long-term significance, Kim Un-yong. In this decision lay a prime legal conundrum. Samaranch's reign as IOC President, repetitively extended by changes to the IOC Charter, would run to 2001, but it was Pound's overt and much publicised ambition to be his successor. With Kim increasingly galloping forward as Pound's potential rival – and Kim avowed by some, prior to Salt Lake's scandal, to be Samaranch's choice – was it not a legal conflict of interest for Pound to be instrumental in imposing a conspicuously damaging decree upon his opponent? Whether the same legal inhibition might have embraced the Ad Hoc Enquiry Commission member Jacques Rogge is uncertain – unless he himself had already privately decided he would be contender, as Europe's most prominent figure, in the succession contest.

Pound's situation was unintentionally equivocal. He was appointed by Samaranch, resolute in his convictions to rescue the IOC's, and his own, reputation amid a stark moral crisis. The question, legally, would not only be whether there was a conflict of interest, but the potential for this to exist.

Either way, how had Kim erred, if indeed at all? Pound's Commission acknowledged that Kim was *not* privy to obtaining a US green card for his son Jung-hoon (John) with a bogus job; it lacked documentary proof, and Kim Senior denied the alleged collaboration. The Ad Hoc Enquiry Commission nonetheless imposed the warning on Kim Senior, on account of the irregularity of Kim Junior's actual employment – the sins of the son being vested upon the father. David Simmons, a Utah businessman/ CEO at Keystone Communications whom Kim Un-yong did not know nor had ever met, had pleaded guilty to a misdemeanor tax infringement (for submitting a 1992 tax return that falsely deducted the salary of "employee" John Kim); in his plea settlement, Simmons had stated he had created a fake job for John at Keystone's New York office, with Salt Lake indirectly paying the salary. Simultaneously, John was indicted for using the green card, granted in October 1992 on the basis of the job with Keystone, to enter the US repeatedly, and lying to federal investigators about Keystone. Family and close associates agree that father Kim was demonstrably disinclined, financially or otherwise, to aid the errant conduct of his son – irresponsibly selling family property. John has never called or visited his sick mother despite her stroke in November 2014 (notwithstanding her emotional defence of his waywardness), and was later absent from his father's funeral in October 2017. If indeed Kim Un-yong was uninvolved, then the long-term damage inflicted upon his ambition as IOC President was arguably invalid on two critical counts – possibly diverting the path of Olympic, and Korean, history.

Something of a legal parallel exists between the Kim Un-yong issue and that of a sports body's *internal* judgement by Professor Sir Harold Thompson, illustrious Oxford scientist and chairman of the Football Association of England, when imposing a ten-year ban on Don Revie, manager of the England team – though it is not comparable in terms of Revie's transparent guilt. This former successful manager of Leeds United, appointed by the FA in 1974 in the wake of dismissal of World Cup-winning Alf Ramsey, had abruptly and secretly abandoned his England post mid-season in 1977 to accept employment in the United Arab Emirates. It was a shocking betrayal in the middle of England's qualifying tournament for World Cup '78. However, at Revie's High Court appeal in 1979, Justice Cantley, while openly condemning Revie's conduct, ruled in his favour and dismissed the ban: Thompson and his FA disciplinary colleagues had exercised *prejudicial interest* (including some critical comment reported by the author in the *Daily Express* prior to their private verdict).

Responses by IOC colleagues to the Pound Commission's judgement on Kim Un-yong are uniformly supportive of the victim. Ching Kuo Wu from Taipei, the acclaimed architect of Milton Keynes New Town (a grand social development in Great Britain) and for many years president of International Boxing Federation, recalled a confused arena. 'You have to look at the background,' Wu said. 'There were no regulations. Anybody could do almost anything. What did IOC or cities officially restrict? That's how Salt Lake became a tragedy for the Olympic Movement's future.' The memory of Walter Troeger, motivator of Munich '72, is clear eyed: 'I saw nothing devious (in Kim Un-yong). All my contacts with him revealed his being direct and responsible. He was always identifying the game at hand.' Close ally Alex Gilady admitted, 'Pound's verdict was a slap in the face, a shock to Kim's credibility.'

Jon Tibbs, respected international agent for sponsorship and host city commercial negotiations, was hired by the IOC to engage public promotion experts Hill-Knowlton for the IOC's attempted rehabilitation. Tibbs observed, 'Kim had an aura of invincibility, of strategic cunning, and he emerged at the time seemingly unscathed – it was *only* a warning, while most of the other cases were so much worse.' The green card issue is itself nebulous. Paul Henderson, the authoritative Canadian businessman, Olympic yachtsman and some-time head of the International Yacht Racing Union and IOC Member, reflected, 'Canadians apply for green cards by the thousands. Applicants have to supply their life history, every justification. Of course John Kim would say, "Oh, by the way, my father's a member of the IOC." He wouldn't need to seek his father's intervention.'

Manolo Romero, IOC guru of television broadcasting, describes the ambience of relationships endemic across the Olympic Movement: 'Within the Olympic family there existed a network of doing favours for friends; it was viewed as normal. It can be difficult to differentiate between one culture and another. In the 1990s there was still an element of 'open university', who can you help – so much a matter of a moment in time. Many people sent their kids to the US; it didn't seem to be an offence. I had the impression that Kim would have approved of his son using him as a reference. So what? When I applied for a green card, I had to give the story of my father and grandfather. Yet the difference in cultural attitudes between continents is still the same today. As for financial donations, I think Salt Lake's were petty cash compared with some commercial deals done decades later.'

Kim Un-yong had acquired many friends in the Olympic Movement, as would be evident before and after injustices were meted to him. None was more supportive than Francisco Elizalde of the Philippines, who adroitly perceived the possible exploitation of a father. 'Kim's son, whom I met casually, was a complete zero; all he wanted to do was to take advantage of daddy's position to make a buck,' he remembered. 'I was sure he was that kind of person who would try to make use of his father's name – especially as Salt Lake were utilising people in a certain manner to gain votes. I don't think Dr. Kim would have had anything to do with this young guy's attempt to obtain a green card, but I do know John was always willing to take advantage. I totally agree that Dick Pound saw in Kim a principal rival, that Pound viewed himself as heir-apparent to Samaranch, so there was definitely a conflict of interest. We all knew that Dick always went out of his way to crucify Kim.'

There was widespread comment, some adverse, on the extent to which Kim Un-yong, through administrative influence, assisted in his younger daughter Hae-jung, a talented concert pianist, receiving engagements with international orchestras at Olympic-related functions. This would inevitably provoke envy and criticism within the intercontinental divide on ethical propriety, as opposed to legality. IOC opinion was equivocal. Hae-jung was a prodigious young musician from accomplished musical parents, someone who had won many international prizes after studying at the renowned Juilliard School of Music in New York.

She was entitled to her appointments. Was father's influence on behalf of the daughter, within the self-acclaimed elite Olympic environment, retrospectively wise for himself? Elizalde agreed that her appearances stoked comment, even though her performances were truly outstanding. Equally loyal friend Gilady recalled, 'Father pushed too hard!' Romero considers that what was possible in the 1980s and 1990s would have had no chance following introduction in 2000 of the IOC's stringent Ethics Commission. Many reflect – as does Craig Reedie, chair of the World Anti-Doping Authority (WADA), which was introduced almost unobserved in the spring of 1999 amidst the Salt Lake crisis – that 'any dutiful father would have done the same.' Intercontinental shades of cultural attitudes widely differ, as Romero suggests.

The old school-tie preferment in Anglo-Saxon appointments across the English-speaking world – including at times within the governing UK Cabinet – are no less offensive than Asian, African and Latin American financial sidekicks. What could be more objectionable than the former long-standing, separate entrances onto the field, at England's hallowed cricket ground Lord's, for 'gentlemen' and 'players'? Notoriously, inverse snobbery by the lower middle-class regime which guided British athletics in the 20th century excluded Sebastian Coe, double Olympic champion in 1980 and 1984 from Seoul '88 on account of financial envy for the boy from a working-class grandparent background who had made good: 'Have you seen the size of his house?'

Uncomfortably for Kim Un-yong, son John's irregularities would keep re-emerging, sustaining a shadow on the father that would inevitably cause Samaranch to re-estimate his alleged consideration of Kim as his potential successor. In August 1999, Simmons pleaded guilty to tax evasion in relation to John's employment, admitting that John's salary was being paid by Salt Lake's bid committee, citing that the purpose was 'influencing the father's vote in favour of Salt Lake'. This invited a contentious comment from US IOC Member James Easton, suggesting Kim 'could be stripped of his powers', as quoted in an interview by Associated Press correspondent Hannah Wolfson. Being simultaneously president of international archery and chairman/CEO of the leading archery equipment company Easton Technology, Easton himself was *knowingly* representing a potential conflict of interest through his parallel commercial activity.

If personal, social and administrative positions were at risk within the Olympic Movement's elite bubble, so more alarmingly were financial loyalties. Would the multi-national sponsors of TOP withdraw the support first enrolled at Kim Un-yong's Seoul Games, and by now quadruple in value? Public antagonism to IOC in America was partially driven by fear of collapse of what was widely regarded as America's controlling finance of common parlance 'Lympics' – the majority of TOP's 11 clients being from US and currently paying $55 million each for the two-festival package of Salt Lake '02 and Athens '04. Visa International, which had long before trumped American Express for TOP inclusion, proclaimed, 'We expect the IOC to continue to review the opportunity to rebuild public trust and support.' With no fewer than four separate enquiries being staged within the US, there was evidence of a potential takeover of the IOC by its prime funding backers.

Samaranch and Kim Un-yong were both damaged by the crisis, the former in the short term and the latter in the long term. Their survival hung in the balance; for Kim, the fact that the regular IOC Session in autumn 1999 – as opposed to the earlier Extraordinary Session that handled reconfirmation of the Pound Commission's verdicts – was scheduled for Seoul meant it would be an occasion for measuring his surviving prestige. The pressure in February '99 had been on Samaranch, with Senator George Mitchell, leader of the US Olympic Committee's Ethics Enquiry, calling for 'reform at every level'. Mitchell, prominent as international peacemaker for terrorist-torn Northern Ireland, declared, 'Ethical governance has not kept pace with the *paid* expansion of the

Olympic Movement.... We do not exclude or condone those from Salt Lake from the "giving", but they did not invent the culture; they joined one. This culture was made possible by the closed nature of the IOC. In each improper transaction there was giver and taker.... We believe it's a replacement of priorities to focus on any individual as opposed to systemic change.' Mitchell did not call for Samaranch's resignation – and changes were at hand.

Following He Zhenliang's private exhortation to Samaranch not to quit, there had been the inaugural meeting to establish WADA, with the US and European Union jointly countering that it should be led by the IOC. However, WADA's foundation, overshadowed as it was by the Salt Lake crisis, was approved under a so-called 'Lausanne Declaration'. It was during this conference that the attendant forty or so Members – guided by He and compatriot Lu Shengrong, president of international badminton – rejected the proposed Selection College for appointment of a host city for the Winter Games '06. He Zhenliang stressed that the IOC should trust its own Members, irrespective of a dozen renegades. He was congratulated by Italian Member Mario Pescante: 'This is a meeting of historic input – demonstrating we are people with brains.' Meeting in private days later, He finally convinced Samaranch that he must stay to lead the IOC's recovery, withdrawing from external enquiry debates to design the internal restructure. 'Without the skin, on what will the hair grow?' He asked.

Friends and colleagues of Kim Un-yong identify that his strategic ploy was always covert personal diplomacy rather than overt public utterance. In the career path of Asia's two most prominent individual IOC Members, Kim and He Zhenliang, the latter was often the more visible leader – notwithstanding the fact that dictatorial political control in Beijing archly limited his capacity for accumulating international celebrity. However, in IOC's escape from ignominy, He was the more instrumental in fashioning the collective path to safety while his Korean counterpart was stealthily regrouping in the bid to succeed Samaranch – though it could be that age (by 2001 he was 70 years old) might tell against him alongside Rogge, a 59-year-old Belgian who in 1999 was not yet perceived as a front-runner.

When the IOC had assembled for its Extraordinary Session to conclude the Pound Commission's penalty recommendations and implement reform proposals, He Zhenliang and his EB colleagues were anxious – lest convincing penalties on errant colleagues failed, to their embarrassment, to earn the necessary two-thirds majority, which would be an even worse potential situation for Samaranch. He Zhenliang arrived early in Lausanne to debate procedures. To consolidate a position of authority in the face of a doubting global audience, it was agreed to stage a vote of confidence in Samaranch. This was achieved by an 82-2 margin. It was further announced, after appeals were heard from the accused, that the EB would resign en masse if Pound's recommended verdicts were not accepted. The necessary majority was obtained on six expulsions, along with nine warnings and severe warnings; in addition to four resignations, 19 Members had been penalised for misconduct. Kim Un-yong may have winced, but he was still alive and scheming.

Next came reform on procedures for the 2006 Winter Games election. Taking the floor, He reasoned, 'There is shock treatment, and there is gradual reform. We should heed the Chinese proverb which recommends, "Feel for the stones to cross the creek."' The restoration of a membership vote was accepted. As for a Reform Commission, he proposed it should be jointly composed of IOC representatives and independent opinion from objective public figures under the idea that 'the monk from the outside recites the better scriptures'. From all sides, He's wisdom was accepted.

Awareness of IOC's ruptured morality was evident among many older Members. Veteran French mountaineer Maurice Herzog, who had retired in 1994 after 24 years' service, reflected, 'It's true the IOC has always seemed anachronistic. It lives among itself. The Members are like Cardinals at the Vatican. Governments come and go, but it doesn't matter to us. The mass of new Members (42 introduced by Samaranch) has changed the family feeling quite a bit. I think that's positive, because we have to be associated with international federations. But the discreet side, the Vatican element, has altered a lot. There are sports professionals arriving.' In such an innovative environment, the subtle negotiations of Kim Un-yong within GAISF had been vital to Samaranch's autocratic administration.

Prior to formation of a Reform Commission (tagged the '2000 Commission'), there had been the creation of the Ethics Commission, which included Howard Baker (the former White House chief of staff) and was chaired by Keba M'Baye (Senegal). The other members were Robert Badinter, former president of the French Constitutional Court; Kurt Fursler, former president of the Swiss Confederation; Kevan Gosper, IOC Vice-president; Javier Perez de Cuellar, former UN secretary-general; and Olympians Chiharu Igaya (Japan) and Charmaine Crooks (Canada).

The 2000 Commission would be composed of 82 members, 36 of them from outside the IOC, including former US secretary of state Henry Kissinger; Giovanni Agnelli (Fiat); Peter Ueberroth; Boutros Boutros-Ghali, UN secretary-general; and Olympic historian John MacAloon. Twenty-six were Olympic athletes, 44 IOC Members (twelve of them past or present IF presidents), 24 NOC presidents. The Commission was divided into three groups: in consideration of constitutional reorganisation, the IOC's future and host city selection. Central debate was led by He Zhenliang, who was particularly alert to US intervention promoted by US Senator John McCain, who had proposed the IOC 'should send the Senate a monthly work report'. He Zhenliang quoted esteemed American historian John Lucas as saying, 'McCain's knowledge of the Olympic Movement could be written on the back of a 33-cent stamp. If politicians have the slightest influence, the Games will meet their doom before the second decade of the 21st century.' He requested that Kissinger extend his message 'imploring the Commission to "maintain" 20th century independence, transparently adopting Members' respect of different continental cultures and geo-political considerations in host city election.' The Commission's resolution included a ban on Members' bid-city visiting, a practice begun in 1986; Members to undergo re-selection every eight years; and future Presidents being limited to twelve years. Samaranch's previous anxiety having been dispelled, he asserted, 'I hope representatives realise that for the future we have had to make drastic changes. We cannot miss this opportunity.'

For Kim Un-yong, the long-term opportunity remained. A benchmark for him within the IOC's constitutional upheaval of 1999 would be the regular Session of June, which was scheduled for Seoul. Tension remained. At the previous EB in Lausanne, there had been a confrontation, with Kim adopting a dramatic taekwondo pose of purported attack against Secretary-General Carrard; in fact it had been no more than a ceremonial militaristic gesture, comparable to a rifleman's parade-ground 'Present Arms!' Here was momentarily the theatre of the absurd, as Kim sent a written apology for his excess. The Pound imposition had left him emotionally treading on ice. Although scheduled many months beforehand, the appearance of Hae-jung to perform at the Session's opening ceremony was an open invitation to critics of an ambitious Asian sports fanatic who was also an indulgent father.

If the winds of Salt Lake might have largely blown through, occasional eddies remained in the wake of the 2000 Commission revision. There had been no fewer than four American enquiries: by the Salt Lake Ethics Panel, the US Olympic Committee, the US Federal Bureau of Investigation (FBI) and the US Department of Justice. In December 1999, Samaranch was scheduled to testify before the Congress in Washington, DC but was assured he would not be grilled by the FBI. 'If he is going to Washington, he's confident there is no problem,' Carrard announced.

Samaranch would appear before the House Subcommittee on Oversight and Investigation – but the tide of American self-importance was on the ebb.

However, back home for Kim Un-yong, tectonic political plates were shifting uncomfortably. In the relatively new democracy of South Korea, with its hierarchical Confucian-oriented structure, a major development necessitated his political allegiance. Kim Un-yong had been a master of the social art in the advancement of sport, associating seamlessly with the Blue House in his multiple sporting manoeuvres. He had nonetheless resolved never to be personally involved in the illusory, hypocritical chemistry of politics itself. Yet now President Kim Dae-jung demanded in 2000 that Kim join the Millennium Democratic Party in an advisory capacity. He had no option but to accept – a move he would come to describe as his worst ever.

There had been minor friction between Kim Un-yong and Kim Dae-jung in early 1997 when the latter was campaigning for presidency – a trivial perceived put-down in the second-row seating arrangements at Busan's East Asian Games, with Kim Dae-jung anxious for the local vote. The pair would meet again in October, close to the election, where Kim Dae-jung would ultimately succeed. Three years on, Kim Un-yong suddenly discovered – having reluctantly agreed to be an inaugural member of the new Millennium Democratic Party on the pretext that it could be beneficial for sport to have a government voice – that his inclusion in the National Assembly had been announced by the press. It was a further political appointment that he had earlier declined, but from which he could not now withdraw. What would now subliminally occur was that, in the public – indeed international – arena beyond the corridors of the Blue House, the Korean President could be upstaged by a figure more famous than he. The concept was fanned by sly comments from Kim Un-yong's subordinates. The seeds of political envy would take time to germinate. As he would recall:

Newspapers began publishing the list of the Millennium Democratic Party's proportional representation candidates. I discussed the situation with my wife, who was absolutely against – joining the National Assembly would be a burden for me, we concluded. I called the National Assembly's secretary-general Kim Ok-du. I said I would not be accepting a proportional representation seat, and he seemed quite taken aback. I called the Blue House but could not get through. The list containing my name had already been circulating in public. I still regret having been unable to stop this from happening. The general election took place in April 2000, the National Assembly convening in June. When law-makers were being assigned to standing committees, I was hoping to join the Culture and Tourism Committee, but because of my conflicting interests with KSC, I was assigned to the Unification, Foreign Affairs and Trade Committee.

Undeterred by the political discomfort, Kim Un-yong characteristically maintained his dedication to sporting objectives. Soon there arose discussion of South-North reunification and he was able to debate sports integration with DPRK's 'dear' leader, Kim Jong-il, during a visit to Pyongyang. An interventionally minded but discreet Kim Un-yong could sense – through his own multiple presidential duties with national and international bodies – the prestige potential for Kim Dae-jung, who would subsequently receive the Nobel Peace Prize. Kim Un-yong recalled, 'As Korean Sports Council chairman, I was considering ideas for inter-Korean athletic exchange. A joint march at the Olympics seemed an idea worth pursuing. There had already been the precedent of East and West Germany holding a joint entrance and then competing separately. I checked with German IOC Member Thomas Bach. A unified team posed many issues, but a joint march, in contrast, would be both feasible and very effective. At an EB meeting I met with Samaranch and mentioned the idea of a joint entrance at the Sydney Games. The IOC's ideals concern youth education and peace. The instant Samaranch heard my idea, his eyes widened in approval, and he expressed his enthusiasm to the EB, saying he would do whatever it took for the IOC to make it happen. He sent an official letter proposing the joint march to the two respective heads of state, and announced it to the media – so the joint entrance at Sydney was an idea of mine pursued by the IOC and agreed to by the South Korean government.' Consulting with the North's dictator, Kim Un-yong was able to emphasise Samaranch's suggestion for a joint march, recalling the joint table tennis team that had competed in Japan in 1991. Kim Jong-il seemed unexpectedly enthusiastic, as Kim Un-yong recalled in his *Challenge to the World*:

> I had been interacting with North Korean sports officials for decades on behalf of South Korean sports, so I expected at some point to have the opportunity to meet Kim Jong-il, but I never imagined I would meet him there at a historic inter-Korean summit accompanying President Kim Dae-jung. Chairman Kim Jong-il seemed to be an intelligent person with leadership ability and sensible judgement. He was dynamic and had an excellent sense of humour and an open way of thinking. He exuded confidence in everything, and he was the type that acts decisively according to what he thinks is right. There's a story about how Prime Minister Thatcher of the United Kingdom met with Gorbachev when the Cold War was coming to an end, and told him, 'I can talk to you.' The impression I got from Kim Jong-il was that you could talk to him. After the inter-Korean summit ended, I returned to Seoul, but there was no response from the North on the joint march issue. I proposed another idea to Samaranch – inviting the South and North state leaders to the Sydney Opening Ceremony. He thought it a good idea but expected no response from the North – as would be the case, Kim Jong-il claiming he would be too busy to attend.

Further dialogue between Kim Un-yong and Chang Ung – the North's force behind taekwondo rival ITF – recognised the catalyst of a joint march for peninsula peace, leading to the pronouncement in June of an Inter-Korean Joint Statement embracing sports collaboration. As negotiations continued, there were anxious moments not only from Korean Cold War activists but from the IOC and from Sydney's organising committee. Phil Coles was a long-serving IOC Member from Australia who had received a warning from Pound for over-extended visits to Salt Lake with his partner, and had been obliged to resign from Sydney's organisation. He remembers, 'Korea's joint march was just *one* event in an opening ceremony which for us in Australia was a momentous occasion. We didn't want Korea's reunification emotions to overshadow our own.' Simultaneously, Samaranch himself lived on a knife's edge, his anxiety an echo of 1988: in grave anxiety, according to Alex Gilady, that the spectacle of the joint march could crumble even at the moment of entering the stadium.

Symbolically, it took a month for Lausanne to receive a response from the North on the Kim Un-yong/Chang Ung collaborative proposals. The IOC's recommendation was that the amalgamated team should carry three flags: IOC, South and North. The teams would wear identical uniforms but compete separately. The North's protracted reply was instead to carry identical peninsula flags, as at the table tennis event in Japan. Stalemate. Kim Un-yong raised the proposition of inviting both heads of state to the opening ceremony. No go, responded Pyongyang, as opening day approached.

Chang's early arrival in Sydney revived optimism. At the airport, he told the press, 'If we respect the spirit of the Joint Statement, I don't think it's a strange idea to enter together and compete separately.' Chang, Kim Un-yong and Samaranch met urgently. Prolonged debate ensued. Kim Un-yong reconfirmed the identical uniform, with Samaranch proposing that the number of athletes should be a hundred from each nation;

Chang proposed that the unified team's name should be 'Korea' and that its members should carry the peninsula flag, which would be used for medal ceremonies. Chang's compromise was for North's officials from their NOC to augment their team in the march to maintain level numbers. A press conference was staged immediately prior to the opening ceremony of the IOC Session preceding the Games. Kim Un-yong had rejected Samaranch's suggestion that each team additionally carry the Olympic flag. 'We cannot carry anything but the peninsula flag symbolising unity,' he had insisted.

Prior to the acclaim for the televised joint march in the stadium, there was discord in the 14-year liaison between Samaranch and Kim Un-yong. Samaranch seemed to try to gain acclaim for the unified accord by suggesting a slogan flag reading 'Thank you IOC,' which was flatly dismissed by Kim's nationalistic response. 'South Korea is home to seventy million people, one of the world's top ten powers, and a sports power with a 400-member team participating in the Olympics,' he replied. 'It has the world's 11th highest economic trade volume. Don't treat us like we're East Timor or Herzegovina, or some other country with four athletes and a population under a million.'

A further rift arose on payment for the joint uniform. Samaranch had promised to meet the bill of $150,000; in the event, he offered first $30,000 and finally $40,000 – one-quarter. If the march was a public triumph for Kim Un-yong, it may have concealed a moment when he further lost the allegiance of his most valued Olympic partner. Following the Games, President Kim Dae-jung held a reception at the Blue House for the Korean squad, admitting to Kim Un-yong that without medals in archery and taekwondo 'we would have been in real trouble'. Kim Un-yong replied, 'We had the joint march this time, and the key aspect next time will be fielding a unified team. North Korea's competitive capabilities need to improve enough to match ours, and that will require a lot of support.' President Kim, enthusiastic, pleaded for Kim Un-yong's continuing innovations. Subsequent discussion with Chang Ung led to an unofficial agreement for such a unified team at Athens in 2004 – but before that initiative could gain a foothold, Kim Un-yong's career would be frozen by political revenge.

CHAPTER 5

—

PRESIDENTIAL TURMOIL

Of all elections for successive presidents of the IOC, none has witnessed the same complexity of emotions and rivalries as surrounded the personality battleground of 2001, when veteran Juan Antonio Samaranch finally departed. Here was the closure of a revolution that had transformed the Olympic Games: from traditional amateurism to professionalism; from fragile finances to seemingly billionaire wealth; from ancient honourable fair play to a playground where an immeasurable minority of cheats threatened the festival's historic nobility and where three contrasting characters from different continents – Asia, North America and Europe – vied for the throne. Never before had there been two outstanding characters with eminent credentials who were simultaneously opposed by the cultural mores of other continents. Olympic history had not previously experienced such morally perplexing alternatives as among Kim Un-yong, Asian 'outsider' from emerging democratic South Korea; Richard Pound, abrasive Canadian lawyer, personable to the restricted company he respected; and, quietly, Jacques Rogge, a courteous yachtsman/orthopaedic surgeon from politically undemonstrative Belgium who was also, crucially, a European.

Unknown to any IOC voter was a significant incident in 1997. It had confirmed the conviction of John Boulter and Jean-Claude Schupp (as related earlier) that it was the firm intention of Samaranch to manoeuvre Kim Un-yong into position as his successor, both to maintain Samaranch's administrative legacy and to broaden the IOC's intercontinental influence. The incident was a cornerstone in Kim's confidence that sport's ultimate appointment was within reach. As he explained years later:

The the Atlanta Olympics marked the end of my four-year term as Vice-president. I was heading the Television Committee, and busy back home being re-elected as KSC and KOC president in 1997 alongside my positions as president of WTF and GAISF. Election of the next IOC President was scheduled for 1997, Samaranch having completed his 12 years and then another four with approval of IOC Members. Those being mentioned now as main contenders for succession were me and Dick Pound. IOC Members from the third world in particular were backing me, on account of my experience hosting the Seoul Games, negotiating broadcasting contracts, my eight years as GAISF president, and my lead role with taekwondo. In February, IOC Legal Affairs Commission Member Keba M'Baye visited Seoul, explaining Samaranch had sent him to discuss 'a serious matter'. He travelled with me to Busan, where he told me that Samaranch wished to have a yet further four-year term as President, and was seeking my support: 'If you give Samaranch this opportunity (by not standing as candidate), and he then backs you in four years, there's no problem. Pound and other Members won't dare challenge him if you show your understanding.' Frankly, I did not have the power to oppose Samaranch; moreover, given our personal relationship, I was in no position to reject his request. Besides, I had my hands full at home trying to stop sports administration from falling apart during the IMF foreign exchange crisis. Samaranch's backing of me over two decades had indeed been total. When President Kim Young-sam had been busy negotiating for a host event at Busan, depending on support from South East Asia and Arab countries, I related our problems to Samaranch. Immediately he flew to South Korea. Imagine that – the IOC President venturing into a campaign for the Asian Games. I think everyone was astonished by the gesture. The vote was a lop-sided victory for Busan over Taiwan by 37 votes to 4. In my bid for the IOC Presidency, no non-Caucasian had ever before attempted in a century the position monopolised by Europeans and Americans. The position was the property of the major sports powers holding the majority of IOC appointments. It was into this fray that I ventured.

Compounding the confusing chemistry of this triangular contest was the clandestine manipulation of the retiring Samaranch, a President who had re-fashioned and modernised the IOC by his wilful though largely benevolent foresight. Both Kim and Pound knew first-hand of Samaranch's shrewd assessment of IOC Members' likely intentions, but none of the three contenders would have been privy, up to the day of voting, to Samaranch's final recommendation. That judgment, whether privately determined by Samaranch days or months beforehand, was evidently conveyed to trusted placemen only close to the event. Samaranch's priorities concerned the preservation of his legacy, which embraced geo-political stability within a non-political organisation. In his final analysis, possibly two of the three candidates might prove risky on that count. For all the exaggerated allegations of dictatorial government, Samaranch's actions were mostly to achieve change by consensus: to wait for the right moment to act in the IOC's interest. Thereby he mostly achieved what he wanted; retrospectively, that could be judged to have become disadvantageous to both Kim and Pound. The character of Samaranch was that off duty, and no longer wearing his presidential hat, he was the most unassuming of men, relaxed and without presumption. Back home in Barcelona, where he retreated from the IOC's Lausanne headquarters whenever possible, his favourite occupation was to have Sunday lunch with his sister. Off duty, he wore his importance inside his jacket.

Kim Un-yong's nature was not dissimilar to Samaranch's: wishing to act discreetly in collaboration with trusted friends, which was what forged their allegiance. Yet a problem for Kim was that while he, with his linguistic fluency, was of a gregarious nature among all nationalities, the majority of his Korean friends were more culturally insulated, and at international events tended to cling, limpet-like, to Kim's company. This gave some foreigners the misleading impression that Kim himself was insular, which stood to increase the cultural separation from Europe.

In my extensive travels to more than one hundred countries, Kim Un-yong was one of the most erudite internationalists I encountered. If he had a fault, it lay in his hope that everyone was as broad-minded as he; his cultural breadth spread from war-zone battlefield defiance to hands that could both caress the harmonies of Beethoven or smash wooden boards in taekwondo's formal display of aggression.

Manolo Romero, a perceptive close-range observer of the Lausanne regime, retains a broad, detached view of the election and the candidates' contrasting qualities:

Samaranch had been very much impressed with Kim's management of the Seoul Games, with his coordination of IFs, NOCs, stakeholders – he could detect that Kim would provide valuable support on the Executive Board, which would help keep IFs in line when taking charge of GAISF. It became difficult to evaluate the mood following Salt Lake, which probably damaged Kim – certainly didn't help him – yet he remained loyal to the President, loyal to the IOC, more so than Rogge, though I never saw Kim directly as favourite, as successor. As the election came nearer, it was perhaps evident that Rogge would be more effective. There is a big difference between 'capable' in the IOC and 'credible' (Kim the former). After Salt Lake, for a while we were going to the office not knowing if there would be tomorrow, who was the best man to save the IOC. By the time of the election, I believe Samaranch now considered Rogge was the best to protect his legacy.

Walter Troeger, a modest but wise Olympic operative as IOC sports director and later member of the Programme Commission, likewise holds mixed views: 'Kim was a capable possibility, yes, but Pound and Rogge in their way were maybe stronger candidates. Kim would have been an exceptional appointment. He opened minds in the IOC, to make the Olympic Movement truly global. He had intimate contacts in Africa as well as Asia which Anglo-Saxon Pound never had. Through Kim I knew Roh Tae-woo, initially Seoul's chief for the Games and subsequently Korea's President. When Samaranch contrived for Kim to replace Tommy Keller as GAISF president, Keller quipped, "Napoleon has returned!" Kim was effective in so many ways, assisting everyone, aware how hard it was to survive in the IOC maelstrom. He became persona non grata with Rogge (after the Pyeongchang dispute in 2003). Yet his influence remained high right through to the end, even after his eventual enforced resignation.'

Dick Pound was something different – his aggression intellectual rather than social, possessing what might be termed devouring energy. Equally or more ambitious than Kim, he had an intolerance of 'inferiors' that made him simultaneously commanding and vulnerable – at times his own worst enemy. His strength of self-conviction, as a Canadian Olympic swimmer and then lawyer, gave him intimidating authority; he labelled himself a 'cynical idealist' and operated on a simple basic principle: 'All you have to do is know a little more than everyone else on every agenda.... [I]f you write the first draft, you have control . . . and then you become indispensable.' All this he said in an interview with celebrated *Sports Illustrated* columnist Frank Deford, who added that Pound did not gladly suffer fools, 'even the ones who vote'. Pound would irretrievably learn this to his cost.

Of the three contenders hoping for, or needing, Samaranch's behind-the-scenes backing, the most uncontentious was Jacques Rogge, the unobstrusive Belgian orthopaedic surgeon, a three-time Olympian sailor and international rugby player, who held an influential conglomerate role as president of European Olympic Committees, granting him a numerically powerful voting cabal. Rogge's attraction for Samaranch would be that he was largely blemish-free: courteous, amiable, multi-lingual, the sort likely to have been made prefect at senior school, his being a private establishment prior to studying medicine at Ghent University. I travelled with him across politically unstable Central Asia in the wake of liberation from the Soviet Union in the 1990s as part of an IOC 'integration exercise'; his manner was essentially one of urbane conformity, of a medic's considered regulation rather than any extravagance, almost to the point of anonymity. He was unlikely to set an election campaign on fire, nor inadvertently to shoot himself in the foot in the most fraught contest in 105 years.

The first two of these – de Coubertin's contrived appointment of Dimitrios Vikelas, a Greek cosmopolitan and erudite businessman who would be acceptable to an equivocal Athens government, then to be succeeded after two years by de Coubertin himself – were unchallenged. Comte Henri de Baillet-Latour, a Belgian banker and obedient disciple who succeeded de Coubertin in 1925, sprang to the fore only because the senior Vice-president, Godefroy de Blonay of Switzerland – hitherto de Coubertin's trusted colleague – antagonised the founder by exercising too much authority in administration of the newly drafted Executive Board when de Coubertin became weary.

Comte de Baillet-Latour's death in the war-time year 1942 led to elderly Sigfrid Edstrom, Swedish founder of IAAF in 1912, taking the reins as senior Vice-president, confirmed unopposed as leader in 1946. Strident Chicago property millionaire Avery Brundage, an Olympian decathlete in 1912, was steered into place by Edstrom in 1952 and ended up lasting twenty demonstrative years until Munich's massacre-torn Games of 1972. Immediately prior to Brundage's inept handling of that crisis, soft-spoken Dublin company director Michael Killanin had been preferred by IOC Members as successor to another autocratic banker, Comte Jean de Beaumont of France, who was feared to be an elitist; the vote was 39-24 for Killanin. Brundage had observed, 'We need a leader, and Michael isn't.' A sociable compromiser, Killanin unavailingly attempted to harmonise rising self-interest among both International Federations and National Olympic Committees, each of them wishing to institute its own collective identity. Killanin was also confronted by successive boycotts at Montreal '76 and Moscow '80: suffering ill health, he retired without a four-year re-election. Into the breach stepped Samaranch, who had adroitly exploited his appointment as Spain's first-ever ambassador to the Soviet Union, enlisting Iron Curtain allegiance. He out-gunned his chief rival, Swiss lawyer Marc Hodler, by a vote of 44-21 in the first round; candidates James Worrall (Canada) and Willi Daume (West Germany) fell way adrift. Samaranch was to revolutionise a vulnerable organisation.

In April 2001, nine days ahead of the deadline for submission of candidacy, Kim Un-yong lodged his bid from the GAISF headquarters in Monte Carlo, three months ahead of the Session in Moscow where the vote would be taken. In an interview with leading news agencies, he stated, 'If I become President, I will lead the way in restoring Olympism, which has been tarnished by excessive commercialism. I will focus on youth education, which is the backbone of the Olympic ethic, and attempt to honour the philosophy of pursuing peace. This will require a universal leader with support from all five continents, a leader whose capabilities have been recognised. That is why I am a candidate.' Kim further stressed a range of objectives in an interview with Korean publication *JoongAng Ilbo*, elaborating on his intentions:

- That reform was about continual modernisation in all IOC fields, pursuing the campaign against doping, and harmonising international collaboration.

- To distribute financial support equally across continental associations and NOCs, ending Euro-centric benefits to expand support in developing countries.
- To ban Members' family scholarships overseas, entertainment and incidental inducements.
- To advance financial competence and improve Olympic competitions.

He reflected that in the Salt Lake aftermath 'I took a beating', adding that Samaranch now faced a difficult choice, but 'I hope he will remain neutral'. Over the years there have been a number of 'lost souls', racially denigrated heroes who engraved their fame on the Olympic map: Jim Thorpe, Jesse Owens, Sohn Kee-chung, Muhammad Ali, Tommy Smith and Cathy Freeman, to name a few. I am grateful to have known two who did not achieve fame or medals but are distinguished for their pursuit of Olympic ideals: John Moriarty, Aboriginal advisor to Australian governments during Olympic bids by Melbourne and Sydney, and Fekrou

Kim Un-yong's press conference in Monaco, 3 April 2001, home of GAISF headquarters, announcing his candidacy for IOC presidency

CHAPTER 5

Kidane, the erudite Ethiopian refugee who fled cultural infamy as opposed to physical destitution. Kidane was a background lynchpin during much of Samaranch's intercontinental negotiations for South Africa's restoration to the Olympic cradle. Like Francois Carrard – omniscient Director-General for more than a decade, though far from ever being a Samaranch 'groupie' – Kidane too questions the extent to which Samaranch may have backed Kim. While simultaneously holding negative views towards both Pound and Rogge, Kidane insists:

> As Samaranch's chief of staff, I knew what was going on in elections. Samaranch always used diplomatic language: Kim was his right-hand man, yet he would never say he was *not* supporting someone. But with all correspondence relayed through me, I remained unaware of any backing for Kim. But Kim complained, through his NOC, that Prince Albert, Denis Oswald and I were campaigning for Rogge! Later, when we met in Barcelona, he wouldn't speak to me. His country was in some political strife, and it was understandable that Europe would not accept him. Rogge, as president of EOC, had become Samaranch's natural choice.

Kidane perhaps is correct, yet from my personal awareness of Samaranch's complexity, I suspect that even an aide-de-camp could have misinterpreted Samaranch. Several others suggest this may have been so. Deeply experienced in Olympic machinations, they include John Boulter, distinguished British Olympic middle-distance competitor in the 1960s and global executive for Horst Dassler of Adidas, and Jean-Claude Schupp, secretary-general of GAISF and all but brother to Kim Un-yong. They were as intimate with the world of Samaranch as any who crossed his multiple paths.

Without identifying his exact evidence, Boulter is emphatic on Kim Un-yong's projected promotion as devised by Samaranch: 'The succession plan, once he had assessed the magnitude of Kim's capabilities in preparation and accomplishment of the Seoul Olympic Games, was to expand the IOC's global concept with Kim as his successor, and he to be followed by Thomas Bach, West German fencing team champion of 1976, whom he had elected in 1981 as one of the inaugural members of the Athletes' Commission. Of this plan, I have reason to be almost one hundred per cent certain. For Samaranch, Pound was never seriously in the running. Whatever the reason, Samaranch did not want him, and in all probability, though adroitly using Pound in many financial projects, that is why he appointed him as Salt Lake investigator – a hospital pass, the inevitable findings sure to offend many voters.'

However, Samaranch's intent was torpedoed by the deeply contro-versial disciplinary verdict against Kim by Pound's Commission. On the evidence of Boulter and Schupp, and whatever Samaranch's tactical log-ic, Samaranch did not finally and demonstrably pull the rug from under Kim until the evening before the vote in Moscow, irrespective of the ac-tual moment he privately took the decision. Boulter continues, 'Sama-ranch recognised that if the vote now went to Kim, and with a Winter Games scheduled a year away in hostile America, the IOC would never pull clear of the Salt Lake cloud. Cruel or not, there had to be somebody untarnished.' As Kim recalls:

> The situation in the IOC had changed in the wake of the Salt Lake scan-dal. Ten Members, most of them my supporters from the third world, were forced out, and around ten new Members from Europe replaced them. It was a sea change to the tune of twenty votes. On top of that, I was caught off guard by Samaranch, whom I had thought to be a solid ally. At an IOC meeting in Seoul in early 2001, ahead of the Session, I mentioned to reporters that we should do away with unnecessary committees in the IOC to reduce budget costs. Samaranch suspected I might be abandoning the Memorabilia Committee and challenged me

Kim Un-yong (left), Samaranch, Francois Carrard (IOC Director-General), Kevan Gosper, at the Executive Board Meeting, IOC Session, 1998, Carrard was equivocal on Kim's presidential prospects.

on this, and I responded merely that we should reorganize unnecessary committees, never anything about memorabilia. He requested a written statement of confirmation on this point. It was a very different climate than from before. In declaring my bid, I had outlined a platform including re-definition of Olympic ideology: cutting costs, covering IOC Members' expenses, preventing the IOC becoming too large, tempering commercialism, eradicating drugs, etc. In South Korea there was support from a few sports figures for me, but none at government level. I met with Samaranch in Lausanne ahead of the vote in Moscow, and he suggested, 'Why not bow out and serve as Vice-president?' I refused. He was now openly backing Rogge.

The unified, though separate, Boulter/Schupp recollection of events on the eve of the election is clear enough. At the conclusion of a banquet for several hundred people, the Executive Board left in a hurry for a scheduled meeting with Russian President Putin (elected one year previously). On his way out, Boulter overheard Thomas Bach distinctly telling close colleagues, 'Everything's changed.' Schupp, standing elsewhere and close to Samaranch's exit, echoes the sudden revelation: 'From a few feet away, I could well hear Samaranch as he grabbed the arm of Mario Vazquez (president of the Association of National Olympic Committees and vital vote-shaker), saying that the tactic was to switch the vote. Mario had been a supporter of Kim. Now he and Samaranch talked for several minutes, Samaranch instructing him in favour of Rogge. I'm sure. The fact is that Kim could still have won in Moscow but had made further vital mistakes. A shame, as his skill was in assisting individual people and not just sports, creating close relationships with IF leaders. He was aware of the partisan nature of all elections, having a slightly cynical view of life, of those who were corrupt. But if you had a problem, he would help, whatever it was.'

Depending on the extent of Samaranch's enduring power over the election – a majority of Members who now owed their status to him – it only required his prime cohorts Mario Vazquez Rana, Sheikh Ahmed of Kuwait, Keba M'Baye and possibly Thomas Bach, to switch 19 votes and determine the outcome as desired. Samaranch also had recourse to other subtle ways of manipulation.

Shortly after Kim had declared his candidacy in April, the Ethics Commission, headed by M'Baye and directed by Samaranch, had announced campaign regulations boasting wholly undemocratic conditions: IOC Members were prohibited from publicly expressing preference for any candidate; from visiting candidates; from travel expenditure and giving seminars or television interviews; and from manifesto publication. Did M'Baye have a hidden agenda? Having lost in all probability crucial supporting votes on account of Salt Lake expulsions, Kim, the Asian outsider, was further restricted; Samaranch's veiled promotion of Rogge was emphasised when the retiring President failed to keep an appointment in Seoul – of the IOC Cultural Commission embracing the

Olympic Memorabilia Collection of which he was chairman – but nonetheless managing to journey to India, Australia and elsewhere in the Far East.

It was not without reason that Samaranch acquired the nickname, among some, of 'Merlin the Magician'. Even those closest to him could never totally be sure of his intentions – often complex, often deferred over many months, his motives either personal or ulterior. Operationally at his elbow were Carrard, an astute legal brain in the IOC alongside Canadian maestro Pound, and Kidane, as already mentioned. Each dealt intimately day to day with the President's appointments, instructions and requests. Both are to a degree equivocal about Samaranch's inner conviction concerning the election of his successor, each wondering whether Samaranch at any point favoured Kim yet acknowledging the possibility. Carrard recalls:

Kim was frustrated, at times furious, with the Pound Commission during the Salt Lake enquiry. I knew nothing about the Green Card issue, though I felt there may have been a case, but never saw any papers (regarding Kim allegedly assisting his son). Samaranch had given Dick a very difficult job, and this opened the door onto Kim, but the Commission could not move because allegedly Samaranch instructed M'Baye to protect Kim under 'presumption of innocence'. Pound wanted to be harder on Kim (indeed it is known that Pound sought to expel Kim) than merely a severe warning. I'd been told for quite a while that Samaranch had once privately advised Dick (that he backed him as successor). Samaranch had been heard to say in 1988 that 'Dick's the best', but was known to want to expand Asian sport. Yet Dick, though so intelligent, was often agitated with colleagues. Privately, it could be detected that Samaranch was losing confidence in Dick. Frankly, I had no accurate idea regarding the strength of the Samaranch-Kim relationship. You could not ignore Kim's possible election, and I wouldn't have been surprised. Approaching the election, Kim was more and more around the office, engaging French and English support staff in case he was elected. Knowing how he had manoeuvred taekwondo into the Olympic Programme, he was not to be underestimated. But then Samaranch became afraid of Kim (and the adverse publicity) and switched to Rogge. Yes, there had been a groundswell promoting Kim's name, but you get used to rumours, often untrue and putting you off track. But Kim had been seen through increasingly rose-coloured glasses and was considered to be outstanding. We didn't know about the extent of his (political) relationships in Korea, which was 'another place' and very politically governed. I never felt totally comfortable with him. The night before the election I talked to Rogge, who seemed sure of victory, as if he knew the votes. We largely discussed the membership proposal for Adolf Ogi, the former Swiss President, which had been promised to him by Samaranch, but the Members elected Samaranch's son and rejected Ogi.

If the stage was not already hazardous for Kim, disadvantage magnified the day before election with his inadvertent self-inflicted wound. Approached by journalists intent on speculative prediction, Kim stepped into the minefield of the Ethics Commission's regulations: first by revealing, even if unofficially, an element of his manifesto; secondly, and worse, by the fact that it seemed to propose financial benefit to Members; and thirdly by his recommendation to reinstate Members' right to visit bidding host cities. He told his informal media audience, 'The Members with the authority to decide Olympic host cities cannot make the choice without first-hand evidence from visiting.... Members are honorary volunteers, so their domestic expenses at home, in representing the interests of the IOC for which purpose they are elected, should be reimbursed, for the cost of administering a small office.' This was not a major consideration for a Member from a larger developed nation, but courteous consideration for someone from, say, a Pacific or West Indies island. However, Kim's off-the-cuff remark, made while pressed by inquisitive journalists asking what he thought of a $50,000 per annum bursary, blew the lid. The news conflagration was instant, and it was swiftly relayed to the Ethics Commission; a formal protest was lodged just as swiftly by the Crown Prince of the Netherlands. An immediate, cynical question would be: who prompted Crown Prince William of Orange? The European anti-Kim undercurrent was in full flow, including non-voting Honorary Member King Constantine of Greece, yachting champion of 1960. Jean-Claude Schupp's recollection is that the financial subsidy was not merely a media suggestion but his own: 'The idea was sound, but the presentation was wrong; it was portrayed as corrupt, but in my view was not.'

Within an hour, Ethics Committee chairman M'Baye had posted a public warning on Kim; the tentacles of Samaranch's network had reached their target. M'Baye, of course, had his own wish to limit Kim's prospects, remembering his irregular request for his son's bank loan. Meanwhile, Francisco Elizalde, impartial scrutineer, remembers, 'I heard the platform of Kim's informal proposal, that it instantly became reality via the media. Then I heard of the royal complaint. I thought the response to the issue was out of proportion, ridiculous – though I have to say, I was never asked to vote by anyone in any particular way.' This comment encourages respect for Elizalde's role as a keen observer, especially within the existing mood of controversy surrounding the election days previously of Beijing as host for the Games of 2008, despite waves of human rights protest against China's domestic governance. Anita DeFrantz, America's outside challenger alongside Pal Schmitt of Hungary and only the second-ever presidential candidate in a contested election from outside Europe (the other having been James Worrall of Canada in 1980), gratuitously observed that Kim's proposal 'would be seen by the outside world as a bribe'. Yet within three years the Executive Board would grant to Members a bursary just as Kim had proposed.

If Kim had been emollient in 1997 towards Samaranch's private strategy – relayed by M'Baye – to continue as President for a fourth term, Pound had been quietly furious, opposing manipulation of the Charter's retirement age to accommodate Samaranch's wish. By casual calculation, it could be argued that by his adroit handling of the IOC's marketing and television rights commissions, Pound was more demonstrably leading the organisation forward than Samaranch – all the more so when he was appointed by Samaranch to head the Salt Lake investigation and then became first president of the inaugural WADA. In *Olympic Revolution*, my authorised biography of Samaranch, Pound's unmistakable authority in the hard cop/soft cop partnership with Samaranch was vividly apparent. 'He's used me to be the tough guy,' Pound reflected. 'Somebody had to be, and I didn't mind; it doesn't bother my nature. In that role, you have to play the character, because Samaranch doesn't send out people who can't pull the trigger. He himself can't say no and needs someone who can. He would ask me to try something out, test the reaction. He could then always retreat behind the excuse that I was impulsive. I didn't mind – we were pursuing the same objectives.' Michael Payne, Pound's partner in the marketing drive, quietly observed, 'Dick can be enigmatic – the only man I know who plays chess in three dimensions.'

Regarding his candidacy in 2001, Pound would write with hindsight in his *Inside the Olympics* what amounted to a defining forecast of his ultimate failure: 'Misgivings were not about my ability, since I knew more about every issue facing the IOC than any of the other candidates.... They related to what I would have to give up to do the job properly, . . . the inability to be independent rather than politically correct, . . . aware that I was not political by nature and had not spent much time cultivating Members, taking care of sponsorship and broadcasting rights rather than being charming to colleagues.... For a non-European to win was at best a long shot.... If you add my non-disposition towards schmoozing, the odds were not great.' Pound further castigated the Ethics Commission's travel limitations on campaigning, pointing out that only one IOC colleague was within 500 kilometres of his home in Montreal but that seventy Members were within similar radius of each other in Central Europe.

Pound knew from the outset that the arithmetic was stacked against him vis-à-vis Kim and Rogge, the latter riding high in estimation as chairman of Coordination Commissions for both Salt Lake '02 and Athens '04. Of the 118 Members present in Moscow (out of 121 total at the time), 57 were European as opposed to 11 from North America, the remainder being from Africa and Asia (17 each), Latin America (13) and Oceania (6). Even if Pound could exert Anglo-Saxon attraction within the Commonwealth, his task, post-Salt Lake adjudication by his Commission, was near impossible, without even a hint of approval from Samaranch via his policy loyalists: Mario Vazquez Rana, the Mexican media magnate whose personal wealth had kept afloat the Pan Am Games; Sheikh Ahmed of Kuwait, president of the Olympic Council of Asia; M'Baye; and, of growing importance, Thomas Bach.

In my forecast for *The Times* (London), I expected that if voting went to a final round between Kim and Rogge, Pound's support would switch decisively behind Rogge. Jon Tibbs, a detached strategic agency, was in no doubt. 'The IOC, at that stage, could not have withstood the cloud of suspicion that surrounded Kim's image (since Salt Lake),' he said. 'The organisation needed someone immune to accusation, an aura of stability. Rogge seemed the middle man, between Kim the ultimate manipulator, and outspoken Anglo-Saxon do-gooder Pound. Rogge was the compromise, impeccably mannered, attracting credibility as EOC president – ideal at that moment in time.' Australian Phil Coles and Dick Palmer from the UK echoed this view. 'Kim no longer had enough support; inevitably it was going to be Rogge,' Palmer said, adding that Pound 'had always been irascible, made a few enemies, so didn't have much chance. Kim was artful at picking up the pieces, and what he achieved to become a candidate was remarkable – but Rogge was going to win because by then Kim was plagued by rumours.'

The election of the eighth President was the last item on the agenda on 16 June, and in the first round Anita DeFrantz was predictably eliminated, her manifesto having been inadequate; I had been mocked by some IOC Members for having predicted, when she was elected in 1992 as the first woman Vice-president, that she might become a potential presidential candidate. In the second round, the voting figures were conclusive: Rogge 59, Kim 23, Pound 22, Schmitt 6. The scene of celebration depicted Rogge with a dignified smile of satisfaction, Pound with barely contained fury, and Kim departing the stage in profound dismay, incommunicado for the remainder of the Session (as he toured the sites of Moscow with his daughter Helen). Rogge's elevation was proclaimed at the ceremonial Column Hall where Samaranch's triumph had been announced 21 years earlier.

If Rogge's promotion had been expected by many, Pound's defeat in third place behind Kim was perceived by him as the ultimate insult, a rejection of his immense contribution to IOC financial equilibrium and modernisation. Yet perceptive Alex Gilady would quip: 'If Kim had been elected, the world would have turned against the IOC in five min-

Outgoing President Joan Antonio Samaranch with newly elected IOC President Jacques Rogge, Moscow 2001, Rogge having leap-frogged rivals Kim Un-yong (second) and Dick Pound (third)

CHAPTER 5

utes. If Pound had been elected, he in five minutes would have turned against the world.' An ardent supporter of Kim, Gilady further reflected that Kim Un-yong had become so powerful 'he thought he could go anywhere (even after Salt Lake)'.

Other friends of Kim were equally confused yet sympathetic. C K Wu from Taiwan thought that 'maybe he was a shade over-confident; he'd accumulated so many friends, dismissing the setback of his (Salt Lake) warning, instead weighing the qualities of the opposition. Infinitely courteous.' Nat Indrapana of Thailand, who died in August 2018, deeply lamented the defeat of Asia's talisman. 'I wasn't sure of his chances because of European solidarity,' he recalled. 'Kim Un-yong had given his loyalty to sports so spontaneously, telling everyone, "Ask me, and I'll do it!" There must have been affinity with him, considering his 23 votes. He had demonstrated such concern, not just for his country, but everyone in Asia, for his generous spread of knowledgeable coaching. He sent me as his representative to Vietnam and elsewhere: "Speak on my behalf, whatever you need, let me know."' Kim himself would reflect, 'An indignant Japanese reporter later said he had "never seen such a corrupt election" and suggested I should file a formal complaint. A UPI reporter called it a "sham election that the UN would have insisted be held again; it was like being forced to compete with your arms and legs tied." I had expected Samaranch to remain neutral, but he did all he could to back Rogge. I could not fathom why he had been so hostile, concluding that he was a Westerner and a pragmatist influenced by different interests. The former IOC Secretary-General Francoise Zweifel later said that Samaranch regretted his decision two weeks after the vote.'

Kim's energy and enthusiasm nonetheless remained indefatigable. Francisco Elizalde had asked him prior to the election whether he was anxious, whether he might fail. 'We'll see. I've never lost an election in my life,' Kim had replied. Elizalde himself has a particular equanimity, and for him it was no surprise that Kim had outperformed Pound, yet he was somehow shocked by Kim's apparent desolation in defeat by Rogge. 'The following day, my wife and I were on the same flight as Kim to Frankfurt,' he remembered. 'He and his wife approached us on the plane; he sits next to me, we nod to each other. I'm wondering, what can I say in sympathy? We take off . . . and he never utters a single word. We arrive, another nod, and off they went. He was so affected he couldn't speak, his expression so incredibly serious. I felt really uneasy, wanting to give condolence.'

The precise geometry of the strategy engaged by Samaranch to achieve Rogge's victory will never be known. On that final day, unending obeisance to Samaranch struck a disagreeable note: against subterranean but insufficient opposition, his son Juanito, a figure of only slender sporting association with modern pentathlon, was elected as a Member. Nepotism ruled – though son was perhaps unaware of father's lingering entrenched influence.

As a onetime would-be Olympian and for five decades a journalist at the heart of IOC affairs, I was as saddened by Pound's conduct in the aftermath of his third-place finish as he was himself incensed by the poignant wilful survival – and superiority against him – of Kim. I had witnessed over the years many moments, even at the end of a long evening, when Pound would still be on intellectual full throttle, debating ideological principles fundamental to Olympic survival: a disciple of de Coubertin, often engagingly humorous, yet betrayed by his unrestrained egotistical ambition – in adulthood, still the schoolboy hero. His ballooning pique, in defeat by the rival he had bureaucratically undermined, provoked him immediately to resign from both the Marketing Commission and WADA – a decision from which he would only relent at Rogge's request.

Eight days after the election, Pound addressed a damning letter to the bedrock sponsors essential to IOC's buoyancy. In a story run by informed commentator (and lawyer) Alan Abrahamson of the *Los Ange-*

les Times, Pound alleged that the election of Rogge over himself as IOC President demonstrated disregard for the chief sponsors and broadcasters! Pound expressed 'grave concern' for the future, urging the corporate backers to seek from Rogge 'early clear and unequivocal commitment' in the future partnership. Pound's resentment was evident – there was no doubt, he inferred, that Rogge was 'the personal choice of Samaranch' and that Vitaly Smirnov, warned in the Salt Lake scandal alongside Kim, 'had run unopposed for vice-presidency'. This was contentious, alongside exposure of his receipt of fees from the IOC for 'legal consultation'. Abrahamson asserted, 'He was the IOC's chief apologist until he was rejected as President. He is the one who never publicly uttered a word about the millions received for his service . . . while the rest of the Members served on a voluntary basis.' Was it not ironic that, having dented the ambition of Kim Un-yong, his sternest rival within IOC hierarchy, Pound himself should flounder at the prize-winning hurdle? His prejudice against Kim would resurface in his autobiographical *Inside the Olympics*, where he described feeling 'insulted by the fact that someone such as Kim, who had barely avoided expulsion from the IOC over the Salt Lake fiasco, had received more votes than I. This did little to increase my respect for the Members who seemed unable to differentiate our respective contributions to the Olympic Movement and the IOC.'

Dismayed but still resolute, Kim Un-yong needed to devise how to sustain his vision for South Korea's sporting prestige, his own now seriously reduced. Shortly after returning from Moscow, he was unexpectedly called to the Blue House by President Kim Dae-jung. The purpose proved to be not for commiseration but for additional demotion. With the upcoming Busan Asian Games likely to be overshadowed by FIFA's World Cup – South Korea and Japan serving as joint hosts – the President suggested Kim Un-yong should concentrate on his duties as National Assemblyman (a position he had thrust upon a reluctant Kim) and resign – not only as leader of the Busan event, but as KSC president as well. The unavoidable suspicion was that Kim Dae-jung already had in mind an alternative nominee for KSC, a close political associate. As ever, Kim Un-yong stood firm on course, telling the head of state in no uncertain terms that, while Busan could take care of itself after five years of preparations, the KSC still needed guidance prior to the imminent Olympic Winter Games at Salt Lake City. The Blue House supremo was politely advised: 'Never mind the remaining three-and-a-half years of my term as head of KSC – preparation for the Games will falter if I quit now. Leave the timing of my resignation up to me.' Stern stuff.

The following day, without public explanation, Kim Un-yong re-signed his Busan post to widespread, indignant criticism. Yet following that he was instructed by Blue House bureaucracy to publicly announce the date of his KSC resignation. He refused (on grounds that it would make him a 'lame duck'). Fate was continuing steadily to conspire against him.

Maintaining his status as Korea's most accomplished Olympic fig-urehead, Kim Un-yong duly attended Salt Lake's handsome Games in Utah's glorious setting. During a down-beat performance – slipping from ninth in the medals table at Nagano now to 15th – South Korea was involved in a judging dispute, in short track speed skating, which threatened to escalate into an embarrassing sulk by Korea's NOC with a boycott of the Closing Ceremony.

These Games had their fill of controversy. There had already been a spectacular dispute in pairs figure skating, the outcome a unique rais-ing of Canadians Jamie Sale and David Pelletier from silver to joint gold with the initially decreed Russian winners. Then came a four-man crash on the final bend of the men's short track 1,000-metre final. This was clearly but accidentally caused by South Korea's Ahn Hyun-soo, thereby robbing American favourite Apolo Anton Ohno of gold – won by the last man standing, Canadian Steve Bradbury, who prior to the crash had been lying a distant fifth and last! Spectators and commentators were furious that Australian referee Jim Hewish declined to order a re-run.

The nadir for South Korea came in the men's 1,500-metre short track final, where Kim Dong-sung, initially the winner, was noisily acclaimed on a victory lap. It was then announced that he had been disqualified for having supposedly obstructed Ohno, who was now elevated to gold, with Li Jiajun (China) and Marc Gagnon (Canada) the subsidiary medallists. Kim Dong-sung was judged to have 'cross-tracked', an evasive arm gesture by Ohno for supposed obstruction provoking the referee's judgement. Korea hired a Salt Lake lawyer to present their protest to the International Ski Federation (FIS) and threatened to boycott the Closing Ceremony. Fabio Carta of Italy, finishing fourth, told the Associated Press the disqualification was 'absurd'. Kim Dong-sung remained disqualified. Off-site the dispute boiled, and it was only placatory intervention by Kim Un-yong that averted the new IOC President Rogge being confronted with a major controversy – the enduring influence of Korea's 'Mr. Fix-it' on behalf of a supposed rival, under whose administration Kim Un-yong had retained his position on the IOC Television and Radio Commission.

From Salt Lake, Kim Un-yong returned home wondering how effectively his nation might emulate the splendour of Salt Lake's festival. He had against all odds achieved hosting of the Summer Games – why not now the Winter event, plans for which were already in train?

Scheduled only days after Salt Lake was a meeting of KSC, the last occasion at which he would preside, although he had warned no-one. After regular business, he declared his hand: the end of his reign as president of both KSC and the Korean Olympic Committee, as agreed upon with President Kim Dae-jung, notwithstanding the period of his unfinished term of office of three-and-a-half years. Interim appeals were made. Ahn Duk-ki, national equestrian president, and forty other sports leaders voted to refuse acceptance of his resignation, a campaign that lasted for many weeks. Kim Un-yong resisted; Lee Yeon-taek, backed by the ruling Millennium Democratic Party and serving as co-president of the Korea-Japan 2002 World Cup Organising Committee, was elected as his replacement. From here on, Kim Un-yong would focus on the hosting of Korea's first Olympic Winter Games.

CHAPTER 6

PYEONGCHANG REVERSAL

If your cousin buys land,
envy will assail you with bellyache.
Ancient Korean proverb

As a preface to the fall from grace and gross injustice that Kim Un-yong was to encounter in 2003–05, and as a means of understanding its magnitude, it is worth recording the publication in April 2005 of *Human Rights Features* by the United Nations Human Rights Commission – an organisation then, and to this day, not without its shadow of irony. The headline was a metaphoric left-hook at the Korean judiciary: 'Skewed judiciary undermines human rights'. This was followed by an upper-cut KO: 'Prosecution in South Korea exercises near complete control over the pre-trial and trial process'. Autocratic government and legitimacy – too often personified by both the Confucian yet supposedly democratic Korean parliament, with its subordinate judiciary, and by a symbiotic IOC – are never mutually compatible. Kim Un-yong was to be victim of both administrations. *Human Rights Features* stated:

> The South Korean prosecutorial system is in urgent need of reform. Judicial independence is being undermined by the predominance of the prosecution and the collusion between judges and prosecutors. Politicisation of the judiciary is rampant. There are shortfalls in evidentiary provisions and methodology, which also weakens the judicial process and denies justice to the defendant.
>
> The prosecution exercises almost *complete control* over the entire pre-trial and trial process, manifestly increasing the opportunity for bias, corruption and abuse of process. The *Public Prosecutor's Office Act* vests prosecutors with the 'duty and authority' to investigate crimes, in-

stitute and maintain public prosecutions, direct and supervise judicial police officers, and direct and supervise the execution of criminal judgment. Human rights petitions filed with the National Human Rights Commission of Korea revealed 'abuse of prosecutorial powers' was the most frequent complaint.

Judges strive never to return a not guilty verdict: the courts 'boast' a conviction rate of over 99 per cent. This is possibly attributable to the pre-supposition of the bench that if there is sufficient evidence for an indictment to be presented, there exists sufficient evidence for conviction. The result of this is that the defendant is effectively judged guilty upon indictment; the judgment by the court is mere rubber-stamp approval of what has already been determined by the prosecution. This is a violation of the United Nation's International Covenant on Civil Political Rights ratified by South Korea. It states in Article 14(1) that 'Everyone shall be entitled to a fair and public hearing by a competent, independent and impartial tribunal established by law'. Another by-product of this pre-ordained verdict is that defence counsel often does not bother with cross-examination.

A recent high-profile case in point is that of Un-yong Kim, the Vice-president of the International Olympic Committee and founder of the World Taekwondo Federation. Observers have described him as a 'prisoner of conscience', who is being scapegoated by South Korean politicians for Pyeongchang's failure to win the 2010 Winter Olympic Games bid in 2003. The Supreme Court concluded in its verdict on 14 January 2005: 'Since Mr. Kim failed to give convincing and rational explanation on why he drew the money and how he spent it, it can be *inferred* that he used the public money for personal purposes.'

The courts often exercise judicial restraint in their failure to interfere in matters regarding the Executive, or render a favourable judgment. Politicization of the judiciary, in the form of the grant of amnesties, pardons and stays of execution induced by political bias, only

Kim Un-yong at the Battle of Guman-ri (Gangwon-do) on June 4, 1951

serves to undermine the essence of judicial impartiality.... The practice
of initiating unfair prosecutions against political enemies of the ruling
party is also not uncommon.

The hand of fate repeatedly conspired against Kim Un-yong. After he was inaccurately impugned amid the Salt Lake scandal for allegedly aiding his adult son in a contrived application for a US green card based on employment at a telecommunications company with ties to Utah's Olympic bid campaign, and subsequently received a 'severe warning' from the Ad Hoc Enquiry Commission chaired by Dick Pound (a rival contender for the top IOC position) – a charge for which the Commission acknowledged it had no forensic proof, but merely suspicion – an echo of that issue surfaced in July 2003. With South Korea's campaign for Pyeongchang to host the Winter Olympic Games in full swing, Kim's son John was arrested by Interpol in Sofia, the Bulgarian capital, and faced extradition to the US on a charge of fraudulently obtaining a green card and repeatedly using the card to enter the US. This news from Sofia once more clouded Kim Un-yong's public image as he attempted to promote Pyeongchang's credibility internationally. The IOC enquiry had stated it was highly 'unlikely' Kim would not have known of the arrangement involving his son; the elder Kim asserted he did not know. John Kim was indicted in 1999 on the US criminal charge but had successfully sued David Simmons for defamation in a civil action in Seoul in 2000. In May 2003 he was arrested in Sofia, and spent several months in custody before the entire Salt Lake case was dismissed later that year.

Promoting Pyeongchang was no easy task for a relatively unknown, emerging Asian winter sports venue opposed by two established and acclaimed rivals from traditional continents, Salzburg and Vancouver. Kim's objective, as ever, was ulterior: not simply to host the Games, but thereby to promote the nation, its prestige and its tourist industry, just as successfully as had Seoul '88. Yet Kim instinctively knew it was a long-odds prospect *at the first attempt*. As he recalled in one of many later publications:

> Here was an opportunity for South Korea to make further strides, not only with its economy but with advancement in its lagging winter sports and use of the beautiful natural scenery to promote tourism. Since we had had such an easy time bringing international competitions to South Korea in the past, many people thought it would be not too difficult to bring the Winter Olympics here as well. But in comparison with our competitor cities in Europe and North America, we faced a much more difficult task bidding for the Winter Olympics than we did for the Summer. Consider how things were before 2003. We ranked toward the bottom in competitiveness for every winter sports event except for short track speed skating, and our competition and auxiliary infrastructure was rudimentary. We had no experience hosting winter

Kim Un-yong, three times decorated, at the battle of Geonbongsan Mountain's Hill 921 (Gangwon-do) in February 1952

sports international events, and we had difficulty finding competition staff and officials capable of managing the competitions. The country had only recently undergone a financial crisis requiring the IMF to intervene.

With the 2010 host city to be decided at the IOC Session in Prague, it was important to spread the word to many people about South Korea's bid. Even though a national winter sports festival was a domestic competition, I invited IOC Members, including Ivan Slavkov from Bulgaria, William Hybl of USA and Ukrainian Valeriy Borzov, and also invited Samaranch for a briefing. With both Pyeongchang and Muju (another potential candidate) completely unknown to the international community, my thought was simply to get their names out there in debate, and then aim seriously for 2014 rather than 2010.

Muju had been the first to express interest, confident after their hosting of the Universiade in 1997. Pyeongchang had not even applied for a winter bid when a document in the name of Prime Minister Lee Han-dong, granting Muju the right to apply, was presented before the Korean Olympic Committee. The prospect was undone by the foreign exchange crisis of 1998. In contrast, luck was on late-starter Pyeongchang's side, as it received full-scale support from the government and KOC, with me as chairman of its organising committee. As a primary grade officer during the Korean War, I had spent three years on the front lines of Pyeongchang's mountain regions. With its natural tourism endowments and a favourable environment for winter sports development, I believed it was possible to make the leap to become a world-class destination.

Emboldened by provincial success in having hosted the Asian Win-

Gerhard Heiberg, Norwegian IOC Member, IOC Evaluation Commission chair, with Gilbert Felli, Games executive director, at the closing evaluation press conference, Pyeongchang 2003 - a Winter bid spelling doom for Kim Un-yong.

ter Games, Gangwon-do's governor Kim Jin-sun had announced a Pyeong-chang bidding plan in January '99 and submitted it to the Ministry of Culture and Tourism and to the KOC in October 2000. Duly approved, the bid was submitted to the IOC in January 2003. With habitual courte-sy and up-beat analysis from the IOC's Evaluation Commission chaired by Norwegian Gerhard Heiberg, the Pyeongchang bid committee – in-ternationally ignorant – gained an inflated view of the town's capability, wholly unaware of the extent to which prospects were dependent on Kim Un-yong's global connections. He took every opportunity to introduce Kim Jin-sun and the campaign committee to IOC and IF officials vis-iting Seoul; he personally footed the bill for a delegation to attend, for familiarisation purposes, a GAISF conference in Colorado and an OCA meeting in Kuwait. As he recalled:

Many foreigners confused Pyongyang, capital of North Korea, with Pyeongchang; they knew about Pyongyang but had little knowledge of the latter. In contrast, Vancouver and Salzburg were already world-lead-ing cities in name recognition, natural environment, winter sports in-frastructure and accumulated competition experience. Pyeongchang's challenge would have to be based on our emergence as a new sports power, and recollection of the Seoul Games. Sometime before the Prague Session, I went to the Blue House to discuss the project with President Roh Moo-hyun. He had been advised by colleagues that he should attend the Session, and asked me what I thought. I told him: 'We're less prepared than the other cities, we don't have the resources and we are unlikely to win the vote this time. I think it would be a political burden on you if you attended the event and Pyeongchang lost.' I was telling him the truth as I saw it. Many times in the past, heads of state and even monarchs had attended Sessions – had met with IOC Members to campaign for their country's bid, given marvel-lous speeches, only to see the bids fail. That would not necessarily be a huge issue for other countries, but for South Korea it was delicate. In the end, Prime Minister Goh Kun attended the Session rather than President Roh Moo-hyun.

As the Session drew closer, I had the sense that the bidding committee was focusing too much on publicity at home and not enough on campaigning internationally for votes. I warned them again and again, but to no avail, my advice more or less falling on deaf ears. Indeed, I felt they were upset that I even suggested a more sensible course. Yet none of them knew anyone on the IOC. Arriving in Prague, only IOC Members were permitted on the top floor of the HQ Hotel. Campaign committees ate separately; you could not meet IOC Members with ease. On arrival I had been told that Samaranch, these days the Honorary President, wanted to see me. His view was that Pyeongchang was not going to beat either Vancouver or Salzburg, that we should focus on coming second, concentrate on a second bid four years later. As he said, 'If you are elected as Vice-president you'll be Senior Vice-president in four years' time, and Pyeongchang will have a clearer chance to win.' Other IOC Members gave me much the same opinion, but Samaranch was correct. It was a genuine perspective – we needed IOC sympathy to be in with a real chance.

Kim Jin-sun, the Gangwon-do governor, suggested that Kim Un-yong should give a speech during Pyeongchang's presentation, seeking Members' support 'in return for the sacrifice of abandoning your run for Vice-president'. Kim Un-yong knew such an approach would be invalid with the IOC, an ineffective strategy, and said so. This provoked Prime Minister Goh Kun to invite Kim Un-yong to breakfast to make the same proposal – notwithstanding that Samaranch had already spent an hour explaining to Goh precisely what he had advised Kim Un-yong. Pyeongchang's presentation nonetheless went with a swing, to a degree few outside Korea had perceived possible – but the outcome prompted unrestrained dismay and fury back home in Korea.

This mood was roused by voting in the first round, in which Pyeongchang remarkably led by eleven votes, 51 to Vancouver's 40, with Salzburg trailing at 26 and eliminated. In the second round the entire Salzburg votes transferred to Vancouver, which was elected by 56 votes to 53 – the Session widely astounded at Pyeongchang's unexpected success. Kim Un-yong recalls being roundly congratulated the following day while meeting NBC sports president Dick Ebersol, who told how Rogge, when making the announcement, had been stunned at the level of voting for Korea. The *Yomiuri Shimbun* in Japan reported that it was the influence of Kim Un-yong that took Pyeongchang so close, a view echoed by France's *Le Temps*.

Two days later came elections for the Executive Board, including the position of Vice-president. Kim had been equivocal about whether or not to stand in an attempt to regain that position, yet was prompted to do so in the light of his conversation with Samaranch and the author-

Post-election interview, Hilton Hotel, IOC Session Prague, July 2003, amid hostile Korean journalists

ity which that position would add to a second Pyeongchang campaign, plus the absence of He Zhenliang as contender (Kim Un-yong's previous Vice-presidency having been during the years 1992–96). In the event, he comfortably outperformed Gerhard Heiberg of Norway by 55 to 44.

Yet all was far from well. Back home, National Assembly member Kim Yong-hak of the Grand National (Hannara) Party, and a representative from Gangwon Province, claimed that Kim Un-yong had 'sabotaged the bid', alleging that Kim Un-yong had unconscionably refused to do as told by Prime Minister Goh Kun and sought preference for his votes as Vice-president. Kim Un-yong was also condemned by Governor Kim Jin-sun and another National Assembly member, Kim Hak-won, chair of the Pyeongchang Winter Olympic Bid Special Committee. At a rally in Pyeongchang, participants heaped abuse on Kim Un-yong, while a hundred buses were mobilised to transport provincial residents to Kim's neighbourhood in Seoul to burn effigies of this 'national traitor' ('mae-

Kim Yong-hak, a National Assemblyman from Gangwon-do and chairman of the Pyeongchang bid support special committee in 2003, roused the anti-Kim Un-yong campaign.

gukno' in Korean). As he reflected, 'After a lifetime of service to elevate South Korea's national stature, I was suddenly being branded a traitor. I could only laugh as I watched the news about the effigies. I thought, there is life in me yet, if I'm getting the same treatment as George W Bush.' More than that: a Special Committee from Pyeongchang's bid was formed in the National Assembly to launch attacks on Kim Un-yong for days on end.

The abuse was reported globally, including the *International Herald Tribune*, though there was sympathy in English-language publications even at home in Seoul. In the *Financial Times*, Andrew Ward reported on 10 July 2003: 'It is only a week since the South Korean city of Pyeongchang came within three votes of pulling off one of the biggest surprises in Olympic history. It was the rank outsider in the competition to win the right to host the 2010 Winter Games, but ran Vancouver, the eventual winner, closer than anybody imagined possible. That, it seems, is not the end of the story. The South Korean delegation has returned home and turned its fire on the country's most senior IOC Member, Kim Un-yong, elected an IOC Vice-president at the same meeting. Kim has been accused by members of the bid committee of secretly campaigning against Pyeongchang in order to secure his own election – supposedly aware that the IOC was unlikely to award both the Games and one of its senior executive positions to the same country at the same meeting. Korea's parliament is launching an investigation into the affair and Kim, already a controversial figure, has been vilified in the media as a traitor.' Comment from the IOC, aware of the issue raised in Korea, was that it would continue to monitor the situation.

Four days later, Samaranch, his loyalty to Kim Un-yong revived when he was no longer holding the IOC's reins and cold shouldered by an ungrateful Rogge, stated that in his opinion Kim's election was wholly unrelated to Pyeongchang's narrow defeat. 'Taking into account my experience as President, I think the election of a host city has nothing to do with the election of a Member to the Executive Board,' *the Korea Times* quoted him as saying. 'I really believe it makes no sense to suggest Dr. Kim had talked negatively about Pyeongchang with IOC Members. I rather think that thanks to his friendship with IOC Members, he personally gained a lot of votes for the city. My advice is to concentrate attention to the future and prepare a new bid.' The *Korea Times* also recorded Kim affirming his decision regarding the Vice-president election. 'I decided to run after Pyeongchang failed to make it. The decision was made after considering recommendations from some fellow Members of the IOC,' he had told media on arrival back at Incheon International Airport.

The furore at home continued throughout the autumn. On 26 October, Kim Un-yong filed a defamation suit against National Assembly member Kim Yong-hak and three officials of the Pyeongchang bidding committee Gong Ro-myung, Choi Man-lip and Choi Seung-ho, the four having claimed that Kim Un-yong had 'lobbied against Pyeongchang'.

Gangwon-do demonstrators burn Kim Un-yong effigies at the Hangang riverfront in Seoul, branding him a national traitor (maegungno) and calling for his death.

His claim for defamation ran to many thousands of dollars.

The torrent of abuse against him was unending, as he recalled: 'Day after day, witnesses claimed I had either actively sabotaged the bid or been too passive in my support. There was even a resolution in the National Assembly passed for my resignation from public offices, something with no legally binding force. Now that I had been designated as a scapegoat, I was unilaterally denounced. It was character assassination. I sued four people for defamation, but little progress had been made with the complaint when the prosecutors started to investigate me instead. (When subsequently in custody) Kim Yong-hak came to see me twice, pleading with me to drop the lawsuit; he needed to work as a lawyer but couldn't do so with a legal action hanging over him. Why, he asked, did I sue him "and not governor Kim Jin-sun? He was the top-ranking person in this." I replied that Kim Jin-sun would be needed if Pyeongchang was going to bid again for the 2014 Games. So I dropped the claim against him – and the rest of them too.'

While allegations against Kim Un-yong by the judiciary, by a free-for-all media roller coaster and, separately, by the IOC continued, a prime legal decision was reached in the United States on 5 December 2003 to conclude the case against Salt Lake City officials, which had been running for five years – a little late to have any bearing on IOC internal adjudication on the multiple Members expelled or, as with Kim Un-yong, officially 'warned'. The ruling may have been seen by some as questionable: the inducements given to IOC voters, whether or not reciprocated in a secret ballot, were improper, but the issue under US law was whether the officials charged, directors Tom Welch and David Johnson, were breaking a criminal as opposed to a moral code. As was reported on 6 December 2003 by the *New York Times*, Salt Lake's *Deseret Morning News* and media across the world, under the heading "*Acquittals End Bid Scandal That Dogged Winter Games*":

A Federal Judge on Friday acquitted leaders of Salt Lake City's Olympic bid, Thomas Welch and David Johnson, of charges that they illegally influenced international Olympic Committee Members for their votes. The Judge's action put an official end to the five-year-old bribery scandal that tainted the 2002 Winter Olympics. Judge David Sam, who had dismissed the case in 2001 before it came to trial, only to have it reinstated on appeal, granted the defendants' motion for acquittal without sending the case to the jury. He revealed that there was insufficient evidence to sustain a conviction on any of the 15 counts in the Federal indictment against Welch, 59, the former president of the Salt Lake Bid Committee, and Johnson, 45, the committee's vice-president.... Sam sharply criticised the government's case. He said that in his forty years of working in the criminal justice system, he had never seen a case so devoid of 'criminal intent or evil purpose'. He added that the evidence did not meet the legal standard for bribery and that his sense of justice was offended by the bringing of felony charges against Welch and Johnson while the rest of Utah enjoyed the fruits of their Olympic efforts.... Assistant Attorney General Christopher Wray issued a statement expressing disappointment and regret that Sam 'ruled before the jury could decide the case, leaving the government with no further opportunity to appeal'. The outcome might not have been different if the case had gone to the jury. Post-trial comments from five of the 14 jurors indicated uniform agreement with Sam's ruling. One juror, Mark Coombs, said of the government's case, 'I think the millions of dollars they [prosecutors] spent was totally a waste for something that should never have been brought to trial.'

When returning from an Executive Board meeting in Lausanne in early December 2003, Kim Un-yong had discovered that the World Taekwondo Federation was being investigated. For what? The IF received no government subsidy; his position was part-time, with no day-to-day authority. Accusations were, however, in flight. On 29 or 30 November 2003, a meeting had been called by Park Gwan-yong, speaker of the National Assembly, intervening to request withdrawal of Kim Un-yong's defamation charges against Kim Yong-hak and others.

On 9 December, prompted by National Assemblyman Kim Yong-hak, the prosecution (chaired by Suh Young-jae) raided Kim Un-yong's bank safe; the same day they broke into his apartment – past midnight, in his absence and without lawful witness – to seize private property and IOC documents and take photographs of personal belongings. It was transparent abuse of power under Article 4(2) of the Public Prosecutor's Office Act. Cash and foreign currencies were confiscated along with life savings. Execution of a search warrant of a private residence at night was illegal under the Korean Criminal Procedure Code (Articles 125 and 126) and the Constitution of the Republic of Korea (Articles 12, 13, 16–19, 23 and 29), as well as under the UN Universal Declaration of Human Rights (Articles 11, 12, 17 and 19) – to say nothing of the fact that he was then a member of the Legislature. Also unlawful under the Korean Criminal Procedure Code (Articles 116 and 198) was deliberate leaking to the media of false and damaging information, theories, hypotheses of bribery and embezzlement and photographs of family belongings, defaming the Kim family. Other abuses of prosecutorial power included 'threats and intimidation to World Taekwondo Federation staff to obtain false testimony; intimidation to hospital doctors to alter medical reports'.

On 9 January 2004, Kim was forced by the government to resign from the National Assembly along with his position as president of the World Taekwondo Federation, under allegations of embezzlement from the same WTF that he had founded and painstakingly developed for 30 years. He forlornly commented, 'My mistake is thirty years of voluntary service to the Olympics and to sport, to put my country on the world map. That is my mistake.' Investigators had been searching for allegations that he took bribes and kickbacks from former Olympic officials and taekwondo organisations. Unrelated financial and other irregularities had in recent weeks dogged taekwondo bases across the globe, with the US Olympic Committee planning a hearing in Chicago. Four days later, on 13 January, Kim was notified by the IOC Ethics Commission that President Jacques Rogge had submitted the Korean public prosecutor's accusations being reported by the media, 'some of which could constitute violation of IOC ethics'. Rules of Procedure, Point 5, concerned 'tarnishing reputation of Olympic Movement; election of President'; Point 3 stated, 'no assistance, financial, material or in kind, may be given to candidates'. Kim's response was invited.

Had he so wished, Kim could have replied that over three decades he had contributed, from personal family funds, to the promotion of the Olympic Movement on multiple fronts, including creation of WTF and Kukkiwon in the midst of the Middle East Oil Crisis – a sum totalling more than a million dollars! There had allegedly been a well-wisher donation to his election campaign in 2001, of which he was unaware until the election was over. Kim Un-yong's generosity in his tireless promotion of sport could have been compared at times to that of founder Pierre de Coubertin. Because government subsidies to the Korean Sports Council were minimal, he had increased the pension for Olympic medal-winners, frozen since the 1980s, to $10,000, $5,000 and $3,000 for gold, silver and bronze medallists, respectively, funded by his personal allowances as President of the Korean Olympic Committee. To a foundation created for African children denied the simplest of sporting facilities – started in Senegal in a simple attempt to generate playgrounds in twenty venues around Africa – Kim had donated $3,000 from personal funds (namely the travel expenses he had carried while visiting a football field in Senegal) as the Africa Olympic Foundation attempted to get off the ground. The IOC had not provided support, so Kim had individually raised $230,000 from a personal campaign. In tribute to his generosity, he had been named chairman of the Foundation.

On 23 January, Kim Un-yong received the following message from Paquerette Zappelli, special representative of the IOC Ethics Commission: 'The Commission, having deliberated in accordance with Point 9 of Part B of its Rules, recommends that the Executive Board, pursuant to Paragraph 4 of Rule 25.1.1 of the Olympic Charter, provisionally deprive you of all rights, prerogatives and functions deriving from membership of the IOC throughout the enquiry.'

The specifics of the Commission, in two instances founded on demonstrable untruths, began: '*According to sections of the media*, the public prosecutor of the Republic of Korea has established that Mr. Kim paid, or promised to pay, a sum of money to Mr. Ung Chang (IOC Member of DPRK) in order to enable teams of DPRK and the Republic of Korea to march behind the same flag, both in Sydney 2000 and at the Busan Asian Games in 2003, and to encourage the unification of these two teams for the forthcoming Olympic Games in Athens 2004; and, *according to sections of the media,* the Public Prosecutor of the Republic of Korea has established that a sum of money was paid to Mr. Kim to support his candidature campaign for the IOC Presidency in 2001. The Public Prosecutor appears to be accusing Mr. Kim both of accepting donations in return for his help in selecting certain taekwondo athletes and of misappropriating funds to the World Taekwondo Federation by Korean companies which were allegedly transferred outside the Republic of Korea. The accusations . . . also appear to concern origin of foreign currency discovered during searches carried out at Mr. Kim's office and home'. On 23 January, Kim Un-yong received the formal confirmation of the provisional suspension of all his rights.

These actions beggared belief. Here was the International Olympic Committee, triggered by the Korean judiciary – prematurely convicting someone on the basis of nothing more than media allegations, which, as would in turn be demonstrated, were dependent on inaccurate testimony by supposed witnesses. Was not the action taken by IOC, unprecedented in its presumptuousness and timing, in itself unethical and improper? This quasi-legal document, engendered by Commission 'rapporteur' Robert Badinter – former president of the French Constitutional Court – was provocative in its 'conviction by media'. The IOC, not without genuine legitimate cause, was intent on re-establishing its ethical image, yet was it not a shade hasty in inflicting a suspension under Charter Rule 25.2.1.1 which is discretionary, not mandatory? Morality in law applies both ways. The IOC's Executive had voted in a telephone conference to 'provisionally deprive' Kim, aged 72, 'of all the rights, prerogatives and functions deriving from his IOC membership'. The move raised the possibility that he could be expelled.

One hammer blow upon Kim Un-yong followed another. On 27 January, before he had even been charged or indicted and while he was undergoing further medical tests at Severance Hospital for declining health, public prosecution officials swept into the ward while he was having lunch, with his wife at his bedside, in order to remove him to prison. They intimidated Kim's doctors and hospital staff into altering medical records so his condition would be considered healthy enough for his removal; he would then face 15 hours of consecutive interrogation during which his lawyers were forbidden to be present, notwithstanding his age, now 73. He was confined to a draughty 3 metre by 3 metre cell, allowed only one five-minute visit per day from not more than three persons, with a stenographer on hand to record every word spoken for review by the prosecutorial authorities. His cell was without any furniture – not even a chair – and had a bucket for a latrine. Under such circumstances a proper defence was all but impossible. The telephones of friends and allies of Kim were tapped and their movements tailed by agents of the government prosecution. And this was someone yet to be charged.

In later publications, including *Challenge to the World*, Kim would write:

According to the indictment prepared by the public prosecutor Woo Byung-woo, they argued that seven years of pay and allowances for four employees – lunch money, telephone and fax usage charges, postal fees, seven years of newspaper subscriptions for my office as an IOC Member, cleaning expenses, and first aid medicine expenses – were 'misappropriated'/ embezzled because they came from the WTF. Based on accounting errors, they also characterised the $1.5 million in North Korean sports association support, and expenses for the invitation of seven IOC Members to the National Winter Sports Festival in Yongpyeong, as misappropriation. Costs for entertaining and accommodating IOC Members during official events hosted in Korea were characterised as misappropriation of public funds. Even though I was an IOC Member, president of an International Federation (WTF), and president of Kukkiwon, they claimed that this did not qualify as justification for these expenses.... Support funds as a National Assembly member and payments for four World Cup opening ceremony tickets I purchased at the IOC President's request, and 16 tickets to the US team's matches for the Eighth Army High School at their request – all considered 'misappropriation' (embezzlement).... Even expenses for a birthday party I didn't even know about (charged by secretary-general Lee Keum-hong)were included in the indictment's list of embezzlements.... Thanks to the cooperation of an irresponsible press that was painting me as unethical, I had to spend time in prison. The court sided with the prosecutor's arguments, as they usually do in Korea, helping them achieve their aim, regardless of truth and fairness.

WTF was an organisation that I built up from the ground as opposed to one that was supported by the government. It was steadily developing healthily, so the members were not worried about investigations. According to regulations, I was responsible for promotion and making it an official Olympic sport; I did not have an office at WTF, nor any decision-making authority. All matters were approved by its general assembly. Yet when I returned to Korea from abroad, the authorities had already investigated all my bank accounts and confiscated my and my family members' personal belongings, breaking down the apartment front door after midnight when they knew I was abroad, even confiscating IOC documents and then leaking fabricated stories about my personal life. Newspapers alleged that bundles of cash were found in my apartment, tens of thousands in foreign currency, a ring worth many thousands of dollars, that I was living a life of luxury on a par with Louis XIV. The media ran absurd, outrageous stunts, deceiving the public and my long-time colleagues in the sports field, portraying me as a greedy despot embezzling public funds. All my sacrifices and hard work were ignored, but they could not find any actual evidence to incriminate me. When I pleaded my innocence, the court and the prosecutors accused me of 'disgracing' the Korean judicial system, on grounds of an unprecedented number of petitions in support of me received from overseas. I was not given the opportunity to defend myself when on trial because I was not even allowed to get on the witness stand.

In the cosmopolitan world of the IOC, Kim Un-yong had come from an emerging but ancient Asian nation to transform personally over three decades into an international social entrepreneur *par excellence*. He had no equal besides Samaranch for engaging integration of ideas and objectives – hence the affinity between those two. Across multi-faceted fronts, Kim had forged trusted allegiances; inevitably there would be enemies as well as friends. The latter, whether social or administrative, were shocked by the vindictive domestic campaign now overwhelming him and his family. The rallying friends' distant support was no succour.

Gerhard Heiberg was one of the many. 'While I considered, as chairman of the Evaluation Commission, that Vancouver was the best of the bids, Kim Un-yong did not in any way damage the chances of Pyeongchang,' he reflected. 'On the contrary, he was constantly positive; I never heard a single word of doubt from him, and I certainly would have remembered – I had excellent cooperation with him throughout the campaign. It was not wrong that he was elected Vice-president. I sensed that issue was fair and square. I knew I was going to lose – he had been significant for a long time, close friends with Samaranch. I knew I would get onto the Executive Board at some stage for the first time, but now I went to congratulate Kim on the outcome. He was accepted so widely, and the IOC needed new blood from outside Europe.' Kim's reputation was easily spread across IFs and NOCs. Gian-Franco Kasper, a prominent president from international skiing, was emphatic about the election: 'Kim was never in any way negative about Pyeongchang, never critical, even if some of us were aware early on of the city's inexperience. Kim had been so authoritative with GAISF, making clear decisions on innovative ideas, approving or killing them almost instantly. I well remember a dinner for GAISF and NOCs in Seoul where he made a speech, proclaiming that dinner speeches were mostly better left brief, and promptly sat down, to general applause.'

Nat Indrapana of Thailand, one of Kim's closest allies, had cautiously questioned whether it was wise to have duplicated the bids for hosting and the Vice-presidency. He later reflected, 'We always used to say that the country should come first, but with what could he envisage in that situation; becoming Vice-president had to be advantageous (for the country). The subsequent abuse all but killed him, after he had given everything to his country and to the IOC.'

Manolo Romero viewed the same problem, recalling how at the Session of 1988 prior to the Seoul Games, Gunnar Ericsson of Sweden had simultaneously campaigned for the vice-presidency alongside the bid of Ostersund, who were regarded as favourites. Ericsson encountered criticism when Lillehammer from Norway were declared as outsider winners – to the visible surprise of Samaranch as he announced the name, and to the attendant King of Sweden. Romero recalled, 'During a coffee break in Prague before the Games election, I remember Kim remarking about his committee's campaign that "they don't know what they are doing". Not being in charge, Kim was blindsided some of the time; he felt he had lost control of the Korean campaign. When Rogge received the figures for the first-round vote, with Pyeongchang in the lead, he went pale at the prospect!'

John Boulter, the voluble Adidas executive, considered it to the disadvantage of Pyeongchang's campaign that Kim had become domestically side-lined in the nation's continuous political manoeuvres. 'Much of the bid was conducted at the political high level,' he explained, 'with Kim regarded as a parvenu by those at the top in Korea – he was seen as acceptable when useful, but could be disregarded, a similar situation to the one that had surrounded Tokyo's motivator for the Nagano Winter Games, Sol Yoshida, who tended to be socially disregarded by the top brass because he had an American wife. Yet the problem in Korea is that you cannot find one Korean who likes another Korean for very long!' Nobody was closer to Kim Un-yong than GAISF secretary-general Jean-Claude Schupp, who was all too aware of the false optimism for Pyeongchang existing at home. 'They should have made much more of their campaign in Prague, knowing that Salzburg was likely favourite and that Vancouver was experienced,' he said. 'There was inevitably a degree of empathy existing for those two. Yet the story of that election was really the internal one of Korean conduct. By that stage, Kim was not that popular at home, in the political arena, and one of the campaign team, Yoon Gang-ro (Rocky), stirred up trouble. I know that Kim privately acknowledged some awkward questions about Pyeongchang, that he knew their limitations and had his mind on a second bid.'

Ching Kuo Wu of Taipei, another close ally, to this day deplores the domestic antagonism in the wake of Pyeongchang's defeat. 'The whole country expected to win, irrationally,' he recalled. 'In the event, they made Kim the scapegoat. It was political revenge – appalling, that kind of humiliation, arresting him with his hands and neck tied; there could have been respectful procedure. With Kim's reputation, he created envy within the ruling party, who hated him because of his international fame. I was really shocked at the public brutality.' Equally shocked from a distance was the retired Walter Troeger, from Germany. 'I could not believe the accusations of sabotage against such a man as Kim Un-yong, who had made his nation so incredibly efficient on the sporting front, lifting them to global status,' he said.

Jon Tibbs, leader of an increasingly influential promotional agency, was just beginning to make an impact within the Olympic Movement. 'As a consultant, it was a revelation to discover how complex the IOC had become politically,' he recalled. 'I was sitting in a bar before the election and there was a media "sweep" on the winning city, and some were suggesting that Pyeongchang had a chance. That seemed astonishing, unless you recognised the work of Kim. I remember NBC remonstrating with Vancouver about how the contest could be so close – this was *their property* on the line! Outwardly, Kim always appeared calm; Pyeongchang had narrowly missed their chance in the first round. I'd discovered earlier that year, at a meeting for the Mediterranean Games, how generous was the nature of Kim, as he attended to anyone's enquiries.' Craig Reedie of Britain was equally observant: 'I never once heard Dr. Kim criticise the Pyeongchang bid – indeed, to the contrary, he was always fully supportive.'

A man of some scepticism at the best of times, Alex Gilady was of the opinion that Kim may have been resentful of not being in charge of Pyeongchang's campaign, never mind his continuing global initiatives. 'He was mumbling to me about the campaign's inefficiencies,' Gilady remembered. 'As for the Vice-presidency, an underlying problem was that he was not Rogge's cup of tea, and Rogge being ambitious to "clean" the IOC following the Salt Lake fiasco. Kim was a mover and shaker, but

Rogge was disapproving. Yes, Kim won the Vice-presidency, but I guess you have to realise when your emotional moment in sporting politics is coming to an end.' Francisco Elizalde's recollections are of sorrow. 'Among the IOC, we discussed the logic of whether or not you should go behind a city bid simultaneously for another project, but Kim Un-yong was always fair and square,' he said. 'The reaction in Korea was abhorrent, against a guy who had done so much for his country. I would not like to be victim of Korean judiciary, to be treated like dirt. I don't want to put down a country – we all nationally have our pros and cons – but Koreans are not exactly the most reasonable people if they feel they have been double-crossed. Kim was simply the fall guy – even up to eventually hosting the Games, Pyeongchang was not a wholly convincing candidate, but they did alright. What they did to Kim was unforgivable, but you cannot tell a nation they're a bunch of fools. They should have given Kim a break: a personality always doing his best, always accommodating, always addressing his correspondence "Dear My Friend". For the Korean government to deny him burial in the National Cemetery tarnishes its own image. There should instead be a monument for him.'

Lee Dong-sup is a prominent politician and distinguished performer and promoter of the nation's taekwondo obsession, operationally at the heart of a taekwondo club of more than 300 members within the National Assembly, which possesses its own training gymnasium facilitated by Lee. He is also repentant about what befell Kim Un-yong. 'There was something wrong with the penalties he received,' he said. 'He did not commit any wrongdoing; it was a political issue. For taekwondo he was the sport's hero. Merely a warning might have been suitable after the Pyeongchang controversy. The Korean Olympic Committee lost many opportunities because of his forcible removal; his imprisonment was legally false. His career had been immense, so many great achievements. He did so much for Korea and Korean sport.'

CHAPTER 7

—

SYMBIOTIC CONVERGENCE

Enchanted though I was in my early visits to South Korea by historic cultures and ancient oriental courtesies, I later became aware of a latent emotional undertone that can make a Korean male an alarming adversary when contemplating unexpected defeat. John Boulter and Francisco Elizalde have hinted at this national revengeful mood, something that I witnessed inadvertently first hand. Travelling to Augusta, Georgia, for that most appealing of all annual golf tournaments, I stopped off in Denver, Colorado, for the short track speed skating world championships – a Korean speciality, and coincidentally also one that year for the Calgary '88 Olympic demonstration champion from Britain, Wilf Dixon. A revelation involving Koreans was chilling.

In a semi-final, two Koreans – who shall remain nameless – were about to qualify comfortably for the final: an older multiple champion (the favourite) and an emerging teenager. On the last lap, the 'boy' needlessly attempted to overtake his leading compatriot, lost an edge, collided and crashed – and the pair were both eliminated. Journalistically curious, I went to follow the youngster out of the arena on his way back to an outside changing room. As he approached, the door half opened, and out stepped a middle-aged trainer. As if taking a rugby conversion-clearance 30 metres out, the trainer kicked the boy with full force in the testicles, turned on his heel, walked back into the dressing room and closed the door, leaving the boy semi-conscious on the concrete floor. Ashen-faced, I went to assist him to his feet. Here had been instant disciplinary brutality. The same indiscriminate moral totalitarianism was to be inflicted upon Kim Un-yong. My perception of Korea was radically revised: this remarkable nation, which had risen from the ash-heap of war to become one of the world's foremost industrial powers, had two faces. The 'land of the morning calm' hides a rogue streak.

On 2 February 2004, with Kim Un-yong prematurely imprisoned without charge by the Korean judiciary – and, in consequence, simultaneously suspended as IOC Member by the Ethics Commission – his elder daughter Helen, a British solicitor, addressed both IOC President Jacques Rogge and Ethics Commission chairman Keba M'Baye regarding the misapplication of Olympic Charter Rule 25.2.1.1, by which suspension is discretionary, not mandatory. Neither Rogge nor M'Baye replied. Rogge had not returned her previous phone calls. Helen Kim pointed out that the decision had been reached by a 'conference call' rather than a stipulated 'meeting' with 'written answers'; that the Ethics Commission's accusations were by their admission based on sections of the Korean media, not on facts of legal consequence; and that Dr. Kim was imprisoned while physically needing hospital treatment at the age of 73. On 20 January, Kim had written in faltering handwriting from hospital to respond to accusations that he had sacrificed the national interest by objecting to Pyeongchang's bid, and also, in 2002, by resisting the Korean boycott of the Salt Lake Winter Games closing ceremony after forfeiture of a gold medal. 'Huge media frenzy,' he protested, 'but I have never done anything to be ashamed of as an IOC Member in my life in my efforts for the Olympic Movement.' The IOC nonetheless remained seemingly unresponsive to specified legal procedure.

In February, Helen Kim began formulating a legal defence of Dr. Kim with British barrister Adam Lewis QC of Blackstone Chambers – the Ethics Commission having failed to provide details (Charter Rule 16.3.8) of how Dr. Kim had 'neglected or knowingly jeopardised the interests of the IOC'. Furthermore, prejudice in the Commission's decision of 4 February was evident in the allegation that Dr. Kim 'had expressed

Adam Lewis, QC, Blackstone Chambers (UK), planned Kim Un-yong's intended defence at IOC Session, Singapore, July 2005

regret at having sent letters to friends mentioning facts considered as unfounded and having damaged the image of the law in his country'. In fact, he had never made such comment; moreover, the suspension (23 January) prior to his arrest (27 January) and three weeks prior to his indictment (12 February) was, within the IOC Charter, a violation of the presumption of innocence without precedent in IOC history. The Ethics Commission failed to respond to Helen Kim's observations.

The IOC's symbiotic suspension thus added fuel and further 'evidence' to Korean judiciary's 'presumed guilt' – as had the equivocal Salt Lake penalty by IOC (Pound Commission) imposition of 'severe warning', notwithstanding the fact that all allegations by US authorities of son John's affairs were ultimately dismissed without charge by a US federal court. The 'severe warning' on Dr. Kim thereby had no legal standing or relevance to the Korean judiciary's perverse actions but would be repeatedly exploited by the Korean judiciary as well as the subsequent Ethics Commission proceedings.

Mid-February saw Kim Un-yong forced by public prosecutors to resign as president of WTF – his election as 'honorary president' conveniently being overlooked! The Minister of Culture and Tourism campaigned to replace Kim with the unconnected Choue Chung-won, a close associate of Moon Jae-in (then President Roh Moo-hyun's chief of staff, incumbent President since May 2017), which was in breach of WTF regulations: vice-president Bill Hybl, president of the US Olympic Committee, should have become interim WTF president, pending an election, but was opportunely bypassed by usurping, government-backed Choue.

On 6 April 2004, Seoul Central District Court held its opening consideration of the (unfounded) charges against Kim Un-yong:

- Alleged bribery in connection with taekwondo athletes' competition selection. Reality: the WTF president had no connection with this process.
- Financial assistance to North Korea. Reality: documented assistance given after North-South coordination for Sydney '00 Games (as well as 2002 Busan Asian Games) joint march had already begun with endorsement by the IOC and South Korean government.
- Staff salaries and expenses labelled 'embezzlement'. Reality: Ministry of Labour confirmed legality of salary payments to legal employees, and expenses related to legitimate visiting IOC Members.
- Alleged bribe by Lee Gwang-tae as election candidate for KOC membership. Reality: legitimate coincidental donations to the success of Busan Asian Games and the Olympic Council of Asia. Lee, then Busan Archery president, was nominated by the Busan Asian Games organising committee and elected through normal procedures, holding the position November 2000–July 2002.
- WTF's IOC allocations account opened in Monte Carlo (rather than in

Korea) labelled 'embezzlement'. Reality: justified commercial practice benefiting from favourable tax regime, as with many other IFs.

- Sponsorship/ contributions to WTF by Samsung and other corporates as supposed 'embezzlement'. Reality: exclusively used in sports promotion through IOC, GAISF and WTF; Kim Hyun-woo, former head of Adidas (Korea) and key prosecution witness, confirming he had given incorrect testimony under pressure from the prosecutors.

- In July/ August 2003, suspect allegations rampant at National Assembly's 2003 Pyeongchang Winter Olympic Bid Special Committee hearing. Reality: known political rivals of Kim Un-yong led by Choi Man-lip, asserting he had *heard* an IOC Member 'from North America' quoting Kim as saying 'Don't vote for Pyeongchang'; and that some IOC Members were chanting 'Kim Un-yong for Vice-president'. These were fabricated stories of apparent invention. The envy was transparent: Yoon Gang-ro (Rocky) from the Pyeongchang bid self-servingly suggested Kim Un-yong was 'assuming a position not as a Korean but as an international person', thereby 'interfering' with Pyeongchang's bid. Pyeongchang's provincial governor Kim Jin-sun claimed Kim Un-yong had been known to say that Pyeongchang 'can wait till 2014' – the truth being that Kim Un-yong's *expectation*, mentioned to some, was that Pyeongchang would probably *have to wait* for a second bid attempt. None acknowledged that Kim Un-yong did not determine to stand as Vice-president candidate until *after* Pyeongchang's defeat. Only Kang Seok-jae, bid delegation foreign press consultant, contradictorily and supportively asserted that he had heard no foreign press representative suggesting that Kim Un-yong hindered Pyeongchang's campaign.

- Public hearings of witnesses, without any form of cross examination, by Seoul Central District Court on 6, 12 and 26 April 2004 exposed instances of admitted hearsay and doubtful testimony. On 6 April Kim Hyun-woo, former president of Adidas and collegiate colleague of Kim Un-yong and a key prosecution witness, acknowledged that certain donations to Kim for sports projects had been from his own personal funds out of long-standing friendship, but admitted to providing false statements *when under duress* at the Public Prosecutor's Office for two whole days, during which time he was shown photos of valuables confiscated at Kim Un-yong's home. Suffering himself from Parkinson's disease and feeling ill, he had signed the witness statement without reviewing it properly – having been allowed just ten minutes to read 36 pages. Prosecutor Woo Byung-woo repeatedly accused defence lawyers of 'insulting' prosecutors for claiming Kim's innocence. On 12 April, Choi Man-lip, Pyeongchang bid vice-president, justified his allegation that Kim had 'obstructed the bid', claiming it was based upon 'what Richard Pound had told me'. Choi admitted that his IOC experience had been limited to 1980–92 and that he had not since attended IOC meetings, including the presidential election of 2001.

- Lee Kun-hee and Park Yong-sung, the two other IOC Members from South Korea, disloyally declined to appear before the court to testify on Kim's behalf, notwithstanding the attendant threat of a court fine.

With defamation of Kim Un-yong running wild in Korea, a petition to the Chief Justice from former WTF vice-president Lee Jong-woo was soberingly supportive:

About thirty years ago I was the very person who brought Kim Un-yong into taekwondo. I therefore present this petition to Your Honour with some sense of personal responsibility. In the early Seventies taekwondo was a wasteland, but Kim Un-yong has been the driving force making the present possible. The assessment that the prosperity which taekwondo has achieved, during the past thirty years, is much greater than any other sport has been able to achieve in a hundred years is also a consequence of Kim Un-yong's efforts.

However, the quest to globalise taekwondo has been full of tribulations, and Kim Un-yong was always standing in the front line. In the early 1970s, he built Kukkiwon by spending his own private assets. He also established foundations for the sport by unifying many contentious factions which were fighting one another until then, and started the arduous task of globalisation. Faced with a severe financial shortage and inadequate infrastructure, Kim Un-yong opened the way for overseas employment of thousands of taekwondo masters from Korea, creating an international foundation.

Additionally, he is the one who achieved the master plan to get taekwondo adopted as an official Olympic sport. It cannot be denied that without Kim's vision and insight, we could never have imagined the prestige which taekwondo enjoys today.

Propagation of taekwondo has exported Korean culture. Since the inception of our history, there has been nothing comparable to taekwondo's bringing international recognition to Korea. By enhancing

Lee Jong-woo, former vice-president of Kukkiwon (left), strongly protested against the incarceration of Kim Un-yong. With Uhm Woon-gyu, former Kukkiwon president.

national prestige, taekwondo has become a symbol of national glory – a result for which Kim Un-yong has made personal sacrifices throughout his life.... He has selflessly devoted his whole seventy years for the sport – someone who has given hopes and dreams to 50 million taekwondo men and women all over the world. I respectfully urge you to take appropriate care to deal with the circumstances with prudence and wisdom.

To no avail. On 3 June 2004, Kim Un-yong was sentenced to two-and-a-half years in prison, with a fine of $750,000 – a penalty upheld, with only five minutes' consideration, by Seoul's Appellate Court on 17 September 2004, which did reduce the sentence by six months. From there the issue moved to appeal in the Supreme Court. In dismissal of the appeal on 14 January 2005, the Supreme Court inexplicably and yet once more proclaimed:

Regarding Point 1, Reasons for Final Appeal: 'Since there is no material evidence indicating the use of money withdrawn from the official funds of WTF, Kukkiwon and GAISF, and since there has been no rational and satisfactory explanation of the reasons for withdrawal nor a breakdown of expenditure, it can be *inferred* that the Defendant, with the intention of illegally enriching himself, withdrew money . . . and spent it for personal reasons.... Even if the breakdown of the discretionary expenditure, which forms part of a single crime among the charges, *had not been specified in detail,* it is judged that this cannot be deemed to make the subject of the trial unclear for the Defendant in his defence.'

Reality: Kim Un-yong had sufficient private funds to have been subsidising the Olympic sport for three decades.

Regarding Point 2, Charge A, Korean Industries Support Fund: The Court ruled that the donation by Korean industries to WTF allegedly paid to the Defendant to support his candidature to the IOC President election was in fact paid to WTF to show cooperation in sports diplomacy for the globalisation of taekwondo. Further, it was ruled that the Defendant's son, Kim Jung-hoon (John), president of the Korean Canoe Federation, was not an employee of WTF, but was arrested in Bulgaria on suspicion of having obtained (illegally) US permanent residency. Therefore, it cannot be deemed the attorney fees spent in defending him fall under expenses for sports diplomacy in taekwondo globalisation.

Reality: To begin with, Kim Un-yong had no administrative access to WTF funds. It is more probable that Jung-hoon, a spendthrift always scrounging from family funds and exploiting WTF engagement for merchandising, may have 'borrowed' funds from WTF unbeknownst to his father through secretary-general Lee Keum-hong who held the organisation's purse strings.

Regarding Point 2, Charge B, Samsung Electronics Support Fund: The Court decided that the Defendant had used for personal purposes the Samsung Electronics fund donated to WTF and GAISF.

Reality: A presumption of guilt, Kim Un-yong having himself donated millions of dollars from private funds to create and develop Kukkiwon and WTF in difficult circumstances over decades.

Regarding Point 2, Charge C, Financial Aid to North Korea: A complicated charge dependant on evidence from a separate indictment involving four other witnesses concerning North Korean expenditure.

Reality: False testimony by prejudiced witnesses. In a letter widely published in newspapers, North Korean IOC Member Chang Ung all but admitted Kim's version of events.

Regarding evidential admissibility of suspect examination ('prosecution protocol') prepared by the Prosecution: Criminal Procedure Code stipulates that 'a written report containing the results of a verification prepared by the Prosecution or the Judicial Police *can be admitted as evidence* where the truth of such documents had been established.'

Reality: Korean criminal law is in conflict with human rights conventions (including the UN Universal Declaration of Human Rights and the International Covenant on Civil and Political Rights) and fundamental principles of natural justice.

Shortly after the Supreme Court rendered its decision, Kim's family received perplexing information from a highly reliable source close to the Judiciary. It indicated that Chief Justice Choi Jong-young's judicial clerk, who was tasked with preparing the Supreme Court decision, had written a 'not guilty' verdict, exonerating the defendant. The clerk was then asked by Justice Choi to prepare a 'guilty' verdict, saying that he wished 'to compare'. Justice Choi then ignored the original 'not guilty' verdict.

A demonstrably sick Kim Un-yong, needing eye surgery and suffering other ailments, was thus left forlorn, his jail conditions inhumane. He could only lament, 'At every ruling, the judge had claimed that he would take into consideration I had many political enemies, but this did not seem to happen. Despite my age, I was refused bail or probation. Before the arrest, pictures of confiscated materials from my house were broadcast on national TV. While I was working for UN headquarters in New York in 1965, I had bought a 3-carat diamond ring for my wife costing $3,000. This was transformed by the media into a ring "worth several hundred thousand dollars". It was one of the items returned after I was released, but my wife, disgusted by the treatment I had received, no longer wanted to wear it, and we sold it for about $5,000. When I had been elected as a member of the National Assembly, Yongin University President Kim Jung-haeng congratulated me by giving me a badge of 18-carat gold – customary for National Assembly members. This small golden badge, according to the media, was worth "millions". I could only smile bitterly at the notion of such an imaginary badge that would be too heavy to wear and probably rip off your shirt. In addition, it had been reported that I had millions in cash at home, but with the scent of money it would have been inadvisable to keep such cash in the house. I believe the media were referring to my mother's certificate of deposits, my family's life savings. The gold that was confiscated was from my grandmother's collection of gifts from family and friends over numerous occasions.'

An informed coverage of the protracted Kim Un-yong story was maintained by the best of all sports agencies, Karl-Heinz Huba's English-language German website *Sport Intern*. In the wake of the Supreme Court's rejection of the appeal, *Sport Intern* reflected:

> With the IOC Vice-president having returned to jail, the guardians of Olympic ethics will not hesitate to ask for Dr. Kim to be expelled from the ranks of the IOC. Too many (adversaries) have been waiting for too long to get rid of the controversial yet still highly respected sports leader. It would hardly matter to them that Dr. Kim is probably the victim of a political intrigue. Whether guilty or victim, due to the 'zero tolerance' credo of the IOC President, the Executive Board will most likely enter proceedings for Dr. Kim's expulsion by the IOC Session in Singapore in July (2005). This requires a two-thirds majority, and some members of the Olympic family doubt if the IOC leadership will be able to achieve this. After all, Dr. Kim was elected Vice-president with

no fewer than 55 votes in the summer of 2003 in Prague, despite the fact that even then a lot of nasty remarks were being made about his tricky campaigning. 'Kim's Army' has of course shrunk during the past few years, but there are still many who remember and are grateful for the many gestures and support that Dr. Kim bestowed on them over the course of many years. For this reason, some believe that a request for Dr. Kim's expulsion could very well turn into a debacle.

Yet there are those who would advise Dr. Kim to cut his losses. During the past three months, following his eye operation, he was almost a free man and aroused the impression in many telephone conversations that his old aggressiveness was back. Being put to jail, he will of course no longer be able to argue or manoeuvre in his usual manner. To resign his IOC Membership would certainly be an elegant gesture (author: *under coercion?*). Dr. Kim has yet to make an announcement concerning what he is planning to do about his official sports posts. In the meantime, Korea's sports leaders have realised that Dr. Kim may still be useful should Pyeongchang decide on a new bid. Only a few days before the court verdict, the local newspaper *Gangwon Province Citizen* reported that there was talk of settling the Korean dispute with the IOC vice-president, suggesting, 'Political circles and the Korean Olympic Committee are thinking that the two parties should reconcile, whatever the circumstances.' At the last meeting of KOC, it was said that Pyeongchang has to 'hold out its hand to Kim Un-yong', the speaker of the ruling Uri party suggesting 'reconciling with Kim in consideration of his influence within the IOC, even if ill sentiments still remain'.

Kim Un-yong's statement in full, dated 14 January 2005, had read:

In the hours before the decision by the Supreme Court regarding my appeal, I reached the following conclusions, whatever the outcome: I affirm my innocence of all charges. While I mean no disrespect to the Justices who had no role in bringing these allegations, the charges were baseless and politically motivated, directly related to the Pyeongchang controversy. I also affirm that none of what has happened during this past year has shaken my love for Korea, or my commitment to serving its interests in global diplomacy and peace on the peninsula through leadership in sports administration. My principal concerns at this time regard the well-being of my immediate family. The physical health of my wife, as well as my own, has been severely impaired by my ordeal, and my daughters and son have suffered considerable mental anguish. I am extremely grateful for the thousands of petitions sent to Korean authorities on my behalf by friends and associates, as well as other concerned observers, over the past year. They came from all corners of the globe. Many were from current and former Members of the IOC, including former President Samaranch. Their expressions of confidence in my honesty and integrity mean a great deal to me. I will assess the outcome of today's proceedings at a later date.

Simultaneously, the symbiotic IOC announced that the Supreme Court's ruling would be taken into account by the Ethics Commission as part of its own ongoing investigation into Kim Un-yong. It would be up to the Ethics Commission to make any recommendation to the Executive Board, its next meeting being 10–11 February, though it was uncertain whether the case of Kim Un-yong would be handled then or at a later date.

Fearing the worst, and in preparation for further possible penalties imposed by the Executive Board, Helen Kim composed a statement delivered to the Executive Board on 31 January 2005. The essential points of her categorised items were as follows:

- Kim Un-yong did not receive financial or other assistance when a candidate for the IOC Presidency, contrary to Point 3 of Part III of Ethics Code Provisions. Against the inadequacies of the South Korean justice system, it was not possible for the Commission to rely on the validity of his conviction. The charge that Dr. Kim received direct or indirect assistance in the presidential election was unfounded, and indeed the Supreme Court's decision *did not conclude* that Dr. Kim received such assistance, and decided that no sum of money was paid to Dr. Kim to support his campaign.

- The inadequacy of the South Korean judicial process in protection of human rights, including the right to a fair trial before an independent and impartial tribunal, currently remained.

- In Korea, it is still the rule that defendants are imprisoned during prosecutorial investigations; coerced confessions are admitted as evidence; and the right to counsel is subject to many limitations at the prosecutor's discretion, leading to violation of human rights.

- Regarding the 'controversy over evidentiary admissibility of prosecutor's interrogation protocol', it is an act of transferring the prosecutor's burden of proof of guilt to the defendant, and hence is against the principle of presumption of innocence provided under the Constitution.

- In South Korea, there is no right to bail; Dr. Kim's application for hospital treatment was rejected by the prosecutor despite strong medical recommendations citing risk of blindness.

- Judge Kim Byung-un, who ruled on the case, had not once ruled in favour of a defendant during his 19 years on the bench.

- Prosecutors obtained a composite of inherently unreliable allegations from those who were known political enemies of Dr. Kim and from disgruntled former employees or rivals with personal aspirations, and even bullied testimonies from others who feared prosecution themselves if they did not collaborate with prosecutors. At least two witnesses had subsequently stated that they were coerced by the prosecutors to give false testimony, while several material witnesses for the defence, including IOC Members Lee Kun-hee and Park Yong-sung, had disloyally ignored summonses and refused to appear in court to give evidence in support of Dr. Kim at the risk of being fined $500.

- The fact of the conviction could not be relied upon to establish that Dr. Kim had in fact acted in a way likely to tarnish the reputation of the Olympic Movement, the conviction being an unsafe and unsatisfactory basis for the Ethics Commission to determine the high standard applied by the IOC.

- The Korean conviction could not be regarded as likely to tarnish the reputation of the Olympic Movement, in the light of the dozens of protests against the judiciary received from IOC Members and many International Federation presidents.

- The IOC's decision provisionally to suspend Dr. Kim even before he was charged in Korea added fuel to the Korean judiciary's 'presumed guilt' – thereby inciting the prosecution. Both trial and appeal proceedings contained allegations of guilt buttressed by statements that 'even the IOC is aware of his guilt', thus providing prosecutors with supposed further 'evidence'.

Sadly, and it must be supposed inevitably, the presentation by Counsel Adam Lewis QC and Helen Kim before the IOC Ethics Commission on 4 February 2005 made no impact. The ultimate axe of the

IOC descended on 5 April 2005 with the letter to Kim Un-yong – pointedly addressed 'Mr.' rather than 'Dr.' – by director-general Urs Lacotte:

> The President of the IOC Jacques Rogge has instructed me to advise you that the IOC disagrees with the contents of letters sent to him and to the special representative of the IOC's Ethics Commission on February 14, 2005, and March 11, 2005, and that the IOC's position concerning the proposal of your expulsion from the IOC is the following:
>
> ① The proposal of expulsion has been unanimously decided by the Executive Board on February 10, 2005, following recommendations contained in the decision of February 4, 2005 of the Ethics Commission. The contents of these documents which have been communicated to you by the IOC President on February 10, 2005, describe the charges against you. These are based on the fact that *by Decision of September 17, 2004, of the Seoul High Court, you have been declared guilty,* in particular of embezzlement and acts of corruption, and that your appeal against such Decision *was dismissed on January 14, 2005, by the Supreme Court of the Republic of Korea.*
>
> ② As to your right to be heard, the IOC hereby recalls that the right within the framework of a procedure of exclusion from an association cannot be compared to the right to be heard in any form of judicial, administrative or disciplinary procedure. The Association determines itself the modalities of exercise of the right to be heard.... As far as the Session (*at which a vote would be taken*) is concerned your right to be heard will be exercised as follows: you are offered the possibility to file in any event a written submission to state your position. The IOC has been advised that you intend to avail yourself of the possibility to appear personally in front of the Session. If for any reason you would not appear in person, the possibility to file the above-mentioned written

submission shall constitute the opportunity for you to exercise your right to be heard.

③ If you decide to make use of the possibility to file a written submission, this should be addressed to the President of the IOC and received by him by May 15, 2005.

④ Your case to be considered by the Session on July 7, 2005, in Singapore. You will be offered the possibility to address the Session for a period of twenty minutes.

Thus was the symbiotic relationship between the Korean judiciary and the International Olympic Committee irretrievably entrenched: the allegations of each in turn encouraged by the other and relied upon as the basis for further allegations. Never mind any human rights consideration – Kim Un-yong was effectively doomed. What was he to do next in the face of such injustice? Inevitably, his thoughts were confused. 'I had remained in detention, with bail refused, for over a year,' he recalled. 'I had been scheduled for probation in May 2005. The review procedures were complete and I had been awaiting my release. One day, Kim Jung-kil came to see me ostensibly to greet me having become the new president of the Korean Olympic Committee. I asked him to do something so that I would be free before the IOC Congress in Singapore. He proposed to "bring it up with President Roh" and took his leave. But there was no further word after that; all I heard was that he had gone to the World Taekwondo Championships in Madrid. One of the weeklies published an interview quoting him as saying how it would be "a hindrance to Pyeong-chang's Winter Olympics bid" (*i.e., their second bid, scheduled for 2007*) if I did not resign from my seat as IOC Vice-president. The Blue House chief of staff Kim Woo-sik also came to see me several times in prison. He was a fellow Yonsei University alumnus who had chaired my support association as a National Assembly member. He told me there were rumours that IOC Members were alarmed at what I might reveal if I went to Singapore. I laughed it off. There existed a thinly veiled anxiety in this rumour: Ethics Commission chair M'Baye fearful of exposure?

Kim Jung-kil and Kim Woo-sik again came to visit Kim Un-yong, Kim Jung-kil now demanding a letter of resignation from the IOC. Kim Un-yong responded:

As a letter of resignation written in prison would be seen internationally as a sign of coercive government pressure, I said I would resign honourably as a free man once I had been released in late May. 'This won't do,' they told me, and demanded an official resignation right now, so I composed a letter in English proposing my resignation as requested. But the following day I was visited in prison by Blue House secretary Yoon Hu-duk. The date on my resignation had been June 15. The Blue House wanted it dated in May. The prison director stamped a new letter for May 15, and I sent it to my family asking them to send it directly to the IOC. The family was informed by Blue House that day that the letter should be dated May 9, so I now wrote a third letter from prison complying with that request. Yet my troubles were not yet over, my scheduled release in May was cancelled, with the Blue House saying that I should only be released after the IOC accepted my resignation, and I remained in prison for another month, my release only coming on June 30. There had apparently been debate at the IOC on whether my resignation had been voluntary or coerced, and thereby invalid, but they nonetheless accepted it at face value. It was not until a year later, in May 2006, that the KOC mailed me a letter from Rogge announcing that my resignation had been accepted. Who held onto it for a year? Since being elected an IOC Member in 1986, I had spent 19 years working as Vice-president and Executive Board Member to elevate the Republic of Korea's stature. Now I had been forced to resign my seat in disgrace.

In his position of acute ill health while abominably confined to a bleak prison cell, Kim Un-yong had little option but to yield, under pressure, and submit his resignation. Helen Kim vainly pleaded with the IOC for her father to be allowed to defend himself at the Session in Singapore in person; IOC's Charter Regulation required that a postponement of his case was allowed if he was unavoidably prevented from attending (as by imprisonment!). Natural justice. The question remains to this day: what was the level of collaboration between Blue House and the IOC in 'arranging' Kim Un-yong's resignation, which would obviate the possible defeat of the IOC's move to expel him by an IOC vote?

There were two crucial meetings prior to Kim Un-yong's 'resignation': Kim Jung-kil's meeting with Rogge on 15 April 2005 in Lausanne, and Rogge's visit to President Roh Moo-hyun at the Blue House shortly

KOC president Kim Jung-kil with IOC President Jacques Rogge, during visit to Seoul, October 2005. A close associate of Korean President Roh Moo-hyun, Kim Jung-kil led the national condemnation of Kim Un-yong

prior to the resignation. Stirring the controversy was an intended article in the May issue of *Monthly JoongAng* – suddenly censored at the last moment – mentioning an alleged deal between the Blue House and IOC. (Two days before, at the World Taekwondo Championship in Madrid on 13 April, Kim Jung-kil had stated publicly that Kim Un-yong 'should disappear as soon as possible for the benefit of the country'.) As reported on 23 June by *Media Today, Dong-A Ilbo, Segye Ilbo* and GamesBids. com, and by Mike Weisbart for *The Korea Times* on 26 January, the alleged tripartite deal was as follows: in return for forcing Kim Un-yong's resignation – and thereby avoiding a Singapore general vote by the IOC Members – the IOC would guarantee three things: maintenance of taekwondo on the Olympic Programme (scheduled to be debated at Singapore alongside other sports); election of Kim Jung-kil as IOC Member in place of Kim Un-yong; and promised support for Pyeongchang's renewed Winter Games bid. These notions are barely credible; more of that in a moment.

Aware of *Monthly JoongAng's* imminent exposé, Blue House staff met the magazine's editor on 16 May to block publication. This was refused. The following day an executive of Samsung, a major sponsor of the magazine, met with the editor and publisher Kim Jin-yong and demanded cancellation; 40,000 copies of the magazine were pulped and the reporters, as well as Kim Jin-yong and the magazine's CEO Lee Chang-kyu, resigned.

There are several possible interpretations of the controversy, besides, the immediate vigorous denial by the IOC's media director Giselle Davies and Rogge's later direct personal denial when asked by the author. All the issues may certainly have been debated by Kim Jung-kil during his Lausanne visit, but even a wilful IOC President cannot promise, preempt or pre-estimate decisions or attitudes of IOC Members at a Session. Equally, Rogge, driven by recommendations of the M'Baye-led Ethics Commission and by his own principled 'zero-tolerance' attitude post-

Salt Lake, would have accepted Blue House collaboration in Kim Un-yong's resignation. Yet all of this is hypothetical. The only known fact was that the resignation was coerced by the Blue House, despite the Blue House's denials. *Korea Times* columnist Weisbart claimed evidence that Kim Un-yong's genuine signature was missing from the 'third' resignation letter.

The observations of Karl-Heinz Huba in *Sport Intern* were, as ever, trenchant:

> Was Dr. Kim blackmailed or did he give up, so that he could finally get out of prison? Both are probably to some extent true. The ailing IOC vice-president was put under pressure by his country's government and finally accepted a deal after he was promised an early release from prison. In Seoul it is believed that he will be pardoned in August – a bitter end for what was once the most powerful man in Korean sports and one of the most influential figures in world sports. Kim's pugnacious daughter Helen has no doubts: her father was extorted to sign the letter with which he declared his resignation from the IOC. With this waiver, Kim is of course not only avoiding the IOC Session's vote on the Executive Board's 13 February motion to have him expelled. His resignation also prevents what may certainly still have been a defeat for the IOC President, who had vigorously pursued the proceedings against Kim with the guidance of M'Baye's Ethics Commission. More than just a few members of the Olympic family still believe that the IOC would not have been able to achieve the two-thirds majority necessary to expel Kim.
>
> Certain of having finally got rid of the unwanted vice-president, Jacques Rogge hurried to announce that the Executive Board had accepted his resignation and withdrawn the motion for expulsion. A few of the events that preceded the announcement did, however, give a number

of people pause. Misgivings that the letter could be a forgery not only arose because it took the letter dated 9 May eleven days to travel from Seoul to Lausanne, but those who had visited Kim between 10 and 20 May were surprised to hear the news, because the IOC Vice-president had in no way indicated that he was planning to resign. The IOC maintained its silence until Jacques Rogge commented on the situation, while on a visit to London to attend the centenary celebration of the foundation of the British Olympic Association. It sounded self-satisfied when, according to the Associated Press, he remarked: 'It's always nice not to have to vote on the exclusion of a colleague. I still believe the Session would have taken the right decision had we had to vote. But if we don't have to vote, and if he has resigned, which is the proper thing to do, of course everyone is pleased.' There is much evidence that supports the widely held belief that Korean sports officials and political leaders put Kim under massive pressure before he resigned. Kim Jung-kil, who succeeded him as NOC and national sports confederation president, had conducted a veritable campaign. During interviews, he had repeatedly called on Dr. Kim to resign from his office, indicating that it would also be in the interest of Pyeongchang's bid for the 2014 Winter Games. 'I hope that he will not become an obstacle to national interests,' Kim Jung-kil was quoted as saying.

Rogge's zero-tolerance campaign to uphold the IOC's reputation was on the one hand admirably legitimate – but with regard to Kim Un-yong it could not appear anything other than presumptive, in the IOC's failure to observe the Charter's concern for natural justice. The reflection of a close colleague, both in Olympic competition and in IOC administration, is revealing. Paul Henderson, a Canadian businessman who energetically led Toronto's bid campaign for the centenary Games and had rivalled Rogge on the water before becoming president of sailing's IF, knew the eighth IOC President intimately:

The way Jacques acted with Kim was the way he acted with everyone – if you stood up to him on any issue, for him you became irrelevant. He somehow believed he was also president of Olympic sailing, so he deleted keel boats from the Olympics.

Henderson had resisted: keel boats were an essential discipline for Paralympic sailors. But Rogge had his way, and the discipline was excluded. When Henderson retired as president of World Sailing, Rogge refused him honorary IOC membership: the two of them never spoke again.

Until the moment of Kim Un-yong's resignation, preparation for his defence at the Singapore Session had been intense. Part of this would come from Lee Sang-soo, an attorney-at-law and National Assembly member for the Uri Party. Lee was a specialist in administrative self-government, an executive director for the Association for People's Cooperative between South and North Korea and graduate of Chung-Ang University in Public Administration. A summary of Lee's proposed presentation to the Executive Board stated:

- Current President Roh Moo-hyun and four immediate predecessors have served jail time. Currently 46 national legislators are behind bars awaiting certain conviction. Whereas a conviction of a politician or business leader in the United States or Western Europe implies guilt, in South Korea it often means *justice was irrelevant.*
- Dr. Kim was vilified in public in 2002 when he took a principled stand at the IOC's request to prevent a South Korean boycott of the closing ceremony when a South Korean was denied a gold medal. Dr. Kim was branded a 'national traitor'.
- One of the organisers of Pyeongchang's Olympic bid in 2003 falsely accused of Dr. Kim of putting his re-election as Vice-president ahead of the bid, allegedly trading votes. Another organiser called for his im-

peachment.

- In November 2004, the *Kyunghyang Shinmun* newspaper reported that the name of the crime for which Dr. Kim was being imprisoned was actually the 'crime of impertinence'.

- Dr. Kim's conviction was vitiated by the absence of essential safeguards for the rights of defence and of the UN Human Rights Commission, the burden of proof being shifted to the defendant, and the Supreme Court applying presumption of guilt. Prosecution and conviction were 'unsafe'.

- With the prosecutor's restriction on the right to counsel, no lawyer was present during Dr. Kim's interrogations at the Public Prosecutor's Office.

- Witnesses were forced into giving false testimony against Dr. Kim, while witnesses on his behalf were intimidated and many did not testify, despite summonses. On 8 March 2004, former Adidas president Kim Hyun-woo testified that the prosecution protocol was false and he had given his testimony under duress.

- Prosecutors' witnesses were known political enemies of Dr. Kim, or disgruntled former employees, jealous associates or rivals with personal aspirations; while their testimony was inherently self-serving and unreliable, it was nevertheless admitted as indisputable evidence *with-*

Lee Sang-soo, Woosung Law Offices
- Korean lawyer pleading Kim Un-yong's defence

out cross-examination.

The summary of the prime defence argument scheduled to be presented to the Session, coordinated between Counsel Adam Lewis QC and Helen Kim, was as follows:

- Dr. Kim stands convicted of having embezzled funds from the World Taekwondo Federation and Kukkiwon, when these were organisations which he himself had established and funded with many millions of dollars of his own money. Funds paid by those organisations were applied in the interest of sport, including assistance to North Korea and the Olympafrica Foundation. Dr. Kim is being imputed with criminal liability more appropriately belonging to other officials.
- Conviction was politically motivated in the aftermath of Pyeongchang's failed bid for the Winter Games, critics ignoring the fact that registration of candidacy for IOC vice-presidency took place only after voting on the 2010 Winter Games had already taken place and Pyeongchang had lost.
- In the Supreme Court's rejection of appeal against conviction, it applied a presumption of guilt instead of presumption of innocence, ignoring the fact there was no proof that Dr. Kim had diverted funds for personal profit, it being presumed in the absence of evidenced explanation that he had done so.
- The IOC Ethics Commission and Executive Board based the proposal of expulsion on one proposition alone: that the fact of Dr. Kim's conviction constitutes action by him which 'seriously tarnished the reputation of the Olympic Movement'. Yet the IOC had no jurisdiction to question the validity of a conviction by a court of state, whatever the circumstances of conviction; and the IOC took no independent enquiry into whether Dr. Kim jeopardised the interests of the IOC, but relied solely on the fact of conviction, despite the fact that the Ethics

Commission had decided on 22 January 2004 that there should be an enquiry, the Commission refusing to appoint an independent expert on the Korean judicial system to investigate and advise on the reliability of conviction.

- The IOC Ethics Commission recalls that it is not within their jurisdiction to assess the validity of judicial decisions made by a country's legal authorities. The Commission held, without it being necessary to appoint an expert as requested by Dr. Kim's representatives, that the actions of Dr. Kim are contrary to the ethical principles of the IOC Charter, the Commission rejecting the allegation by Dr. Kim that there had been a breach of the implementing provisions of the IOC Code.

- It is a legitimate question for all IOC Members to ask whether it would be right or fair that a Member should be allowed to become a political scapegoat because his country fails to win its bid for an Olympic Games. A related question is, 'How is it that the IOC under its current leadership, among other inexplicably callous conduct in this case, will not only suspend the IOC Member before any official charges have been brought but will even refuse to clarify its own expenses policy relating to IOC Members' routine activities on behalf of the IOC?'

- Conviction for embezzlement from sporting associations was based not on proof, but rather presumption that in the absence of a contrary evidenced explanation acceptable to the Korean courts, he 'must have done so'.

- Nowhere did the Supreme Court deal with the implausibility of the proposition that a very wealthy man, who had invested massive amounts of his own money in various Korean sports associations, and who was a prominent contributor to the Olympic Movement, would then have set about embezzling money from those associations. Dr. Kim did not need money, and stood to lose a great deal if he acted unlawfully.

- The allegation that Dr. Kim ignored a 'severe warning' in 1999 at the time of the Salt Lake City case was groundless. The warning related to the actions of Dr. Kim's adult son's business affairs, and the US courts subsequently ruled that there had not been any improper actions even by the son. It is counter-intuitive to suppose that a man in Dr. Kim's position would ignore that warning and act unlawfully when there was no reason or need for him to do so.

- Prosecutors' submissions stood as 'evidence', a current Korean practice which is expected to be overturned by the Judiciary Reform Committee in line with international standards. The IOC Ethics Commission wrongly discounted Dr. Kim's contention that his trial was vitiated in this way by suggesting that he had not himself complained in Korea that his trial was unfair. Given his public position and the political sensitivities, Dr. Kim was not in position to criticise the Korean judiciary, and certainly never said that he received a fair trial as alleged by the IOC Commission. He never uttered the quotes attributed to him.

- The fact of the Korean conviction is insufficient to establish that Dr. Kim *actually* acted in a way likely to tarnish the reputation of the Olympic Movement . . . so it is not possible for the Session to rely on the validity of conviction by the South Korean court.

- The proposition of the IOC Ethics Commission, namely that it is not for it to question a conviction obtained in the courts of another state, is an abdication of function. To follow such a course would be for the Commission, and the Session, to abandon the task entrusted to them by the Rules.

- Where the validity of a conviction has been thrown in doubt by the political circumstances in which it was obtained, the IOC Executive Board has (previously, except in Dr.Kim's case) not in fact applied the general rule of enquiry, and has on the contrary disregarded a dubious imprisonment, conviction or investigation.

- Lee Kun-hee, chairman of the Samsung Group and an Olympic sponsor, was convicted of bribing two former Korean Presidents for government contracts and given a two-year suspended prison sentence in 1996. No steps were taken to suspend or expel him from the IOC.

- The Ethics Commission and the Executive Board ought to have conducted an enquiry, including if necessary using an independent expert to assist them. Under Rule 22 of the Olympic Charter, the Ethics Commission is charged with defining and updating a framework of ethical principles. It investigates complaints raised in relation to non-respect of such principles.

- When conducting an enquiry as a result of a complaint or denunciation, the Commission may conduct investigations in the field or send one of its members delegated by the Commission to shed light on the case in question.

- Although the Ethics Commission appointed Mr. Badinter as rapporteur and stated that it had decided 'to launch an enquiry', there was in fact no investigation or enquiry at all. There was only reliance on the Korean conviction. Mr. Badinter was only present via telephone conference.

- If the Ethics Commission had been, as it could only have been on the evidence, in doubt of the validity of the Korean conviction, it ought to have acceded to Dr. Kim's request, and appointed an independent expert.

- The IOC Ethics Commission and Executive Board pre-judged the issue by suspending Dr. Kim on 23 January 2004 before he had even been charged in Korea, which was not until 13 February, thereby adding fuel to the Korean campaign against him.

- In the event that Dr. Kim is not permitted by the Korean regime to attend the Singapore Session, he requests the Session to adjourn consideration until the next Session. Dr. Kim requested the Executive Board to agree to this course, but it refused to do so – wrongly, Dr. Kim having the right to be heard under Charter Rule 16.3.8.2. That right is internationally recognised, under Swiss law and under the European

Convention of Human Rights. Rule 16.3.8.2 provides that the right to be heard includes express entitlement to choose between appearing in person before the Session or putting in a defence in writing. Dr. Kim has chosen to exercise his right to appear in person, but he is detained in prison by the Korean regime. In these circumstances, the appropriate course for the IOC Executive Board, in order to protect Dr. Kim's right to be heard and express right to appear in person, would be to agree that if he were prevented from attending the Singapore Session, in consideration of the proposal that he be expelled, this should be adjourned until the next Session.

From these itemised details, a resulting if coincidental conclusion of symbiotic convergence by the respective organisations of the Korean judiciary and the International Olympic Committee is unavoidable. The Session in Singapore would surely have voted against expulsion of an innocent victim.

Celebration with Lee Kun-hee's election as IOC Member, 1996 – yet Lee failing to testify in court in support of Kim Un-yong

—

SQUANDERED ICON

Unmitigated judiciary's moral assassination within a supposed democracy is a bizarre phenomenon. In South Korea, six decades after colonial liberation, it was still standard practice – practice that befell an acclaimed national hero. Maybe that was partially Kim Un-yong's problem: he had become one of the most internationally celebrated personalities in his country, more at ease with global figureheads – even heads of state – than were current Korean political leaders. With Kim Un-yong and his immediate family emotionally crucified (including the career of accomplished pianist daughter Hae-jung), where was he to go after he was belatedly released from jail? Envy rose like mist from the political swamp; national pain could be exorcised in 2003 by placing blame upon Kim. To hell with human rights.

In June 2005, Mike Weisbart of the English-language *Korea Times* – a longtime resident of Korea and one of a minority of journalists able rationally to assess the Kim drama – perceptively held a mirror to Korea's face, under the headline 'Pyeongchang Olympic Bid [for 2014] in Jeopardy':

> It's called cutting off your nose to spite your face – when you hurt yourself in order to harm your enemy. In the case of Kim Un-yong, the now disgraced former vice-president of the IOC, member of the National Assembly and founder and long-time president of the World Taekwondo Federation – among a list of important titles through which he wielded tremendous influence on behalf of Korea in world sporting

circles – that is precisely what Korea has done to itself. In their effort to punish Kim, Koreans have brought about a remarkable loss of face for their nation in the eyes of the international community, and have dealt their hopes to host the 2014 Winter Olympics in Pyeongchang two potentially lethal blows.

Let me respond to the protests of over-generalisation. It is true that only a small group of powerful Koreans have persecuted Kim. Yet all the while there has been no outcry against their actions. The desire to have a scapegoat for the failed 2010 Olympic bid proved stronger than any public aspiration for a truthful and fair justice system. No one protested his incarceration; they simply believed the character assassination orchestrated by a rabid media, which eagerly lapped up the information fed to it by the political operatives of Kim's enemies. Even after some newspapers and a respected TV news documentary raised legitimate questions about the veracity of the 'evidence' against him and how it was procured, no one batted an eyelid. Since then, no one has protested his continued imprisonment, despite the fact that other men who were convicted of greater crimes have been set free on parole or given suspended sentences. Instead, the government's decision to treat differently, that is unjustly, a man once viewed as a hero, has been met with deafening silence by the public.

With Kim Un-yong effectively removed from public life, his Korean 'enemies' were able to manoeuvre to occupy his now eminently empty boots – most notably, his position as IOC Member. Leading this campaign in late 2005 – and totally failing to understand that such an appointment is not by national application but the prerogative of the IOC President and Members – was Kim Jung-kil, now president of the Korean Olympic Committee and duly notified by the IOC as a candidate under the recommendation of OCA president Sheikh Ahmed. This would be South Korea's third member, alongside Lee Kun-hee and Park Yong-sung (both also with past convictions and clouded domestic reputations).

South Korea's loss of sports diplomacy, of strategic credibility, became embarrassingly apparent in early 2006 at the IOC Session immediately prior to Turin's Winter Olympic Games. Besides harbouring ambition for a second winter bid by Pyeongchang, the Koreans were campaigning for the southern city of Busan – Kim Jung-kil's home town – to host the IOC Session of 2009. Blissfully ignorant of IOC protocol, the KOC's committee blithely ignored regulations by inappropriately lobbying IOC Members in Turin prior to the vote – and was thereby confronted by a Ethics Commission reprimand, missing the final ballot in which Copenhagen was elected. An ugly Korean internal post-mortem ensued. With IOC Members Lee and Park sidelined by domestic controversy, and Kim Un-yong's influence redundant, Pyeongchang's new expectations for 2014 were diminishing.

Subsequently, Kim Un-yong discussed Korea's international standing with Samaranch, now honorary IOC President. With that former mood of allegiance, Samaranch reflected, 'You made the Seoul Olympics a success and negotiated taekwondo's acceptance in the Programme.... Those objectives were achieved only because of you. You're the one who brought South Korean sports into the spotlight. I cannot understand why the nation attacked you the way they did. Yet in every field Korea attacks the No. 1 – you in sport, Lee Kun-hee (of Samsung) in business. It makes no sense.' A comment by *Agence France Presse*, quoting two anonymous IOC Members, touched another nerve; it claimed that successful city bids by Daegu and Incheon for the respective World Athletics Championships of 2011 and the Asian Games of 2014 inevitably impeded the prospects for intercontinental voting support for Pyeongchang – potentially granting a privileged Korean calendar. The article considered it almost unthinkable that a global vote in Guatemala in July would favour another Korean host over Salzburg or Sochi. Chang Ung, North Korean IOC Member, observed that he 'could not understand how a country bidding for the Olympics keeps shooting themselves in the foot', and suggested that Kim Un-yong's continuing influence from the fringe should be exploited – a view apparently echoed by both Thomas Bach of Germany and Singapore's Ser Miang Ng. In his publication *Challenge to the World*, Kim Un-yong reflected:

Before Governor Kim Jin-sun of Gangwon-do left for Guatemala, I suggested to him that he focus less on the 'showmanship' and more on winning votes. I don't know if my words had any impact. Before he left, I was told that Pyeongchang had 'secured' 49 votes. I laughed and told a friend, 'If they said fifty, you should see it as thirty'; such reports are always inflated. It's tough meeting with IOC Members; they don't normally let on whether you have their vote. When Governor Kim said Samaranch was backing Sochi, I told him it was important to meet Samaranch, who apparently then advised him to 'get full-scale support from Samsung'. Others visited Samaranch, but what do you expect from people who don't understand the strategy of negotiating, who hover around the periphery while ignoring the centre, putting on a show and attempting to gain concessions for themselves, people who credit themselves with every success and blame someone else for every failure? Samaranch asked me if I was a going to Guatemala. I wasn't sure. He suggested that if the bid failed again, 'they'll just blame you; I wouldn't come'. He thought it possible, he said. 'The law is a double-edged sword – instead of working to win votes, South Koreans pride themselves on their proposal explanations and the media assessment reports, and think that's enough. They start planning their victory celebration to claim credit for winning, and all of this without the knowledge of what the rival countries are up to.'

In the event, Pyeongchang won 36 votes in the first round, 15 fewer than the 51 at Prague; then, with Salzburg eliminated, they lost to Sochi by 47 to 51. Victory for Sochi hinged on several factors, as I reported for the *Daily Telegraph*:

Almost three out of four members of the IOC, trustees of Olympic ideals, preferred the wealth of Russia rather than Salzburg's potential packed-house festival. By an electoral twist, the second-preference votes of support for Salzburg, eliminated in the first round, enabled Sochi to leap-frog Pyeongchang – a fate suffered by the South Koreans for the second time, as in Vancouver four years before – and a host elected virtually without roads and rail to the mountain arena, with every venue and mountain centre yet to be built, and which has never yet staged an alpine ski competition. The IOC was swayed by the guaranteed government support from President Putin, in a bid involving a regional development programme of many billions of dollars. There were several sub-plots militating against the Koreans: heavy investment in Incheon's Asian Games hosting victory over Delhi alienating valuable Asian support; Tokyo's bidding for the summer Games of 2016 meaning that Japan opposed Korea and the risk of Asian 'congestion'; China, intending to campaign for Winter Olympics, likewise opposed to an intervening Asian winter host; Samaranch exercising clandestine influence on Russia's behalf; and at least two IOC Members opposed to Pyeongchang on account of the harsh imprisonment of Kim Un-yong.

The correspondent from Korea's *JoongAng Ilbo* was in no doubt about the determining factor lying behind Pyeongchang's loss: 'From around the bid committee a saying is circulating with self-irony that "four years ago we lost because Kim Un-yong was there, and this time we lost because he was not." It continued that in sports diplomacy a major figure was needed such as Kim Un-yong "because lobbying can only be effective when there is international friendship capable of trust". This time Korean citizens expected as a matter of course that Pyeongchang would happen, because it received praise from the Evaluation Commission that visited in February, and the sense of loss is even greater in the circumstances. No one has come to fill the void left by Kim Un-yong. In their obsession with inflicting damage and destruction on him, no one had devised any alternatives.'

Kim Un-yong's own judgment of Pyeongchang's second failure was one of dejected sympathy for a Korean public wantonly misled by a conceited campaign committee. 'This was the result of our unwillingness to believe that Rogge, Samaranch, China, Japan, the US and Europe were backing Sochi,' he said. 'It is in the nature of the IOC to compliment or flatter all candidate cities. They tell them all how 'everything is great', how the evaluation shows them to have capability, encouraging them to go ahead. In the end, the bid committee deceived the South Korean public and wasted money on a big charade. They even told President Roh Moo-hyun that it was going to succeed and encouraged him to go to Guatemala City. They inspired big dreams among the public, encouraging hope for united local development, an opportunity to venture out into the world, for the development of Gangwon-do, for Pyeongchang to become a global winter mecca – and then they let them down. People were asking overseas who is going to be the scapegoat for this second failure, but unlike Prague, this time the president himself had personally led the bidding efforts.... Sports diplomacy requires big players; lobbying only works when you are close to and trusted by the IOC Members. In many online messages, the content was effectively, "This is what we get for condemning our own candidate for the IOC presidency, for destroying South Korea's own sports world heavyweight."'

The extremity of legal abuse to which Kim Un-yong was subjected – a truly bizarre judicial charade of snakes-and-ladders, with convictions by the million and, on annual days of public celebration, pardons equally by the million granted by the President – displays a political theatre of the absurd. It continues to this day, fifteen years on from Kim Un-yong's brutal arrest – a moment seized upon by the IOC to exact their particular symbiotic 'justice' on an innocent man: part-guilty by birth, in the perverse European perspective, for being a 'dodgy' Asian. Whoever dealt Kim Un-yong his cards, his hand held several jokers among his many aces. And nothing has yet changed: at nationwide local elections in May 2018, over 40 per cent of National Assembly by-election candidates from at least two provinces had previous convictions. Among 970 candidates in one province for metropolitan council posts, 421 had convictions! In his 2012 thesis *Monopoly of Justice* at the University of Kent (UK), Choe Dae-hyun stated, 'The South Korea Criminal Justice System is described as "prosecutorial justice". Most investigations and prosecutorial power are exercised only by prosecutors.' That seemingly was acceptable by the reckoning of the IOC's Ethics Commission of 2004, unconcerned that on the night of 26 January 2004 Dr. Kim Sung-soon and colleagues at Seoul's Severance Hospital, while treating a severely sick Kim Un-yong, were threatened and intimidated by state prosecutors to alter their medical reports, thereby denying the 73-year-old IOC Vice-president adequate medical treatment. Should not the IOC have had pause for thought, at least instructing the Ethics Commission to institute an enquiry under IOC Charter regulations?

Not excused from the dictatorial judiciary are Korean Presidents. In April 2004, President Roh Moo-hyun was himself impeached by the National Assembly (although the impeachment was to be overruled by the Constitutional Court). As reported by Asia's *Wall Street Journal* in New York, 'Korea's contentious liberal democracy allows an illiberal Confucian zero-sum political culture that elevates naked power above the rule of law'; the impeachment, it said, illustrated 'the propensity of East Asian political elites to disregard the law'. In August 2004, Seoul's *Newsis* asked, 'Korean Public Prosecution: for whose sake do they wield such power?' In the article, it noted, 'The Public Prosecutor has complete monopoly over all the power and conduct of investigations and indictments, unprecedented elsewhere in the world.' On 19 October 2004, Seoul's *Yonhap News* published a report titled 'Criticism Against Surveillance on Pretext of Collection of Criminal Data.' The article read, 'On October 19 there was controversy during the annual national audit of the Supreme Public Prosecutor's Office by the National Assembly's Legislative and Judiciary Committee, due to suggestions that the Public Prosecutors are not only conducting surveillance activities outside the boundaries of collection of criminal data/ information, but also preoccupied with obtaining information with even such deceptive means as falsification of identity/ impersonation.' Kim Un-yong could confirm this.

Yet lo and behold: the following year, on the 60th anniversary of liberation from Japan, President Roh Moo-hyun – his impeachment shelved – pardoned 4,200,000 so-called criminals. Yes, 4,200,000 – everything from traffic violations upwards. For the Korea edition of the- an American lawyer at Seoul's Aurora law firm observed, 'So much of what is a civil matter in the UK or US is a crime in South Korea. If your company goes bankrupt, you are a criminal. If you harass a competitor, you can be prosecuted.' Or if you happen to lose an international sports election!

Gerald Koenig, past director-member of the US Olympic Committee and secretary-general of IOC's Association of Recognised International Sports Federations (ARISF), addressed a six-point supplication on 17 April 2004 to Kim Byung-un, Senior Judge of Seoul Central District Court:

> Your honour: Re. the matter of Dr. Kim Un-yong. It is with the deepest respect for equitable principles of justice that I presume to forward this unsolicited correspondence in the above matter. On that basis, if it is not contrary to your procedural and ethical rules, I ask that the following remarks be included as part of the record. I am attorney, licenced to practice law in the State of Wisconsin, USA. I received my Juris Doctor

Degree from the University of Wisconsin Law School in 1964. I practiced law for 19 years.... Although my impressions are offered without an in-depth knowledge of either the lengthy investigative statements or the testimony to date, I have examined what I believe to be accurate summaries of the proceedings. On that basis I have the following comments:

① I believe it would be reasonable and equitable to take judicial notice of the fact that the world of international politics is rife with jealousy and no-holds-barred competition for personal recognition.

② I believe it would also be reasonable and equitable to take judicial notice of the fact that international sports federations are faced with the 'labours of Hercules' in their never-ending search for the financial and human resources needed to do the best possible job of preparing their athletes for successful worldwide competition.

③ I believe it would also be reasonable and equitable to take judicial notice of the fact that no single person, no matter how high-ranking they may be in the international pyramid, has anything more than personal opinion when it comes to evaluating the circumstances that may have led to a particular result in matters such as the selection of venues or the election to offices.

④ In my experience with allegations of bribery, the exchange of money does not take place in a way that a paper record becomes available for later examination by others. Yet in this matter, based on the information available, it appears there was *no attempt to hide* any financial transaction. It also appears there are differing 'opinions' about the intent of the financial transactions, but all of those opinions seem to be questionable since they are offered by those who are political enemies, disgruntled former employees, jealous associates or competitors with personal aspirations.

⑤ In evaluating the testimony in any criminal charge, the question of 'reasonable doubt' permeates the overall analysis. And when accusations are not backed by motive, the benefit of doubt is usually accorded to the accused. In this case, it is difficult to imagine Dr. Kim had a motive for personal financial gain because the amount in question is literally *trivial in relation to his personal assets.*

⑥ So, given the indisputable fact that Dr. Kim is a man who had devoted his entire career to the advancement of sport and has earned the respect and admiration of thousands of key officials in the global arena, it seems virtually inconceivable that he would risk the diminution of his reputation for, to him, such inconsequential amounts of money.

In closing: I hope you will not mind a reference to the Salt Lake City bribery case here in the US. As I am sure you are aware, Judge Sam acquitted the defendants of each and every count of the indictment brought by the US Government. You may not be aware that, in doing so, Judge Sam made the following statement: 'In my forty years' experience with the criminal justice system, as a defence and prosecuting attorney, and as a Utah State Judge and a United States District Court Judge, I have never seen a criminal case brought to trial that was so devoid of mens rea or criminal intent or evil purpose.' Thank you for this opportunity to offer what I consider to be unbiased insights. I wish you well in your deliberation.

Gerald Koenig.

On 26 April 2004, Sara Bond, a UK solicitor, politely queried three judges – Choi Jong-young (Chief Judge), Kang Byung-sup (Chief Judge) and Kim Byung-un (Senior Judge) on the Seoul Central District Court – on four points of order and trial conduct: imprisonment, prior to charge, of a sick man denied bail; seizure of private funds and property; incredulousness of alleged misappropriation of funds by a man of considerable personal assets who had founded and given generously to the WTF; and legitimate use of foreign bank accounts for WTF funds utilising foreign tax benefit, a common practice for international federations.

In May 2008, the *Ilyo Shinmun* newspaper suggested that following the recent replacement of President Roh Moo-hyun, there was government consideration for Kim Un-yong's restoration within Korea's sporting regime, for the benefit of international relations for taekwondo and in the wake of Pyeongchang's second Winter Games hosting defeat. Similar 'reinstatement' had been accorded by French President Jacques Chirac to IOC Member Guy Drut. Equivocation by the IOC regarding errant Korean Members, Park Yong-sung and Lee Kun-hee, had been in sharp contrast to instant denunciation and suspension of Kim Un-yong. Park, the chairman of Doosan Heavy Industries, was indicted in October 2005 but not arrested or detained: the IOC's suspension, without any threatened expulsion, came only in March 2006, the suspension being extended by a mere six months upon Park's domestic conviction. Park was reinstated by Roh Moo-hyun 'in the national interest' in February 2007. Lee, the internationally prominent chairman of TOP sponsors Samsung, was convicted in 1995 – for alleged bribery of two Presidents for government contracts – with a two-year suspended prison sentence.... without IOC suspension or referral to the Ethics Commission. Lee evaded IOC attention by temporarily living overseas and bypassing Session attendance, and likely Ethics Commission pursuit, to survive a second indictment/ conviction in 2008 for tax evasion.

Kim Un-yong, on the other hand, was mercilessly hounded when immediately imprisoned before charges by public prosecutors Woo Byung-woo and Chae DongWook, Chae working in team with Chief Prosecutor Suh Young-Jae. He was simultaneously forced to abandon his defamation lawsuits against the four Pyeongchang bidding committee leaders leading the accusations against him, including Gong Ro-myung, the Minister of Foreign Affairs and Pyeongchang bidding committee chairman. Notable past disciplinary lenience by the IOC concerned

General Lassana Palenfo of Ivory Coast, who was jailed on suspicion of involvement in a coup d'état but subsequently released; Mohamed Mzali of Tunisia, who was jailed under multiple charges but never suspended by the IOC and fled to live in exile in Paris, with the verdict eventually being overturned in 2002; and Major-General Francis Nyangweso of Uganda, who was temporarily imprisoned in the wake of Idi Amin's dictatorship without IOC suspension or enquiry.

The emotional harassment suffered by Kim Un-yong, simultaneously at the hands of the Korean Judiciary and the IOC Ethics Commission, extended to his enduring and loyal wife and daughters, each of them irreparably harmed emotionally by the continuous public onslaught – especially concert pianist and former child prodigy Hae-jung. Here was an artist of special talent, winner of multiple awards, acclaimed performer with celebrated orchestras in Germany, Italy, Switzerland, Japan, the USA, the UK and the USSR. Hae-jung's father was naturally as indulgent in promotion of her success as possible. As his friend and admirer over three decades, the author would in hindsight say he was perhaps too benevolent in exploiting his many connections to help her gain performance appointments at concerts associated with Olympic events. Transparent envy of his own fame was thus inexorably extended among foreign observers and critics onto Hae-jung. Juan Antonio Samaranch, as IOC President, was close enough to advise caution by father Kim – yet Samaranch himself conspicuously indulged in nepotism, controversially currying favour among Members for IOC election of his son upon his own retirement in 2001. Hae-jung's devotion and gratitude for her father's encouragement made his humiliation all the more devastating for her, as she would later recall:

My father never insisted that I choose a career as a pianist. He believed that it is not for the parent to interfere with or determine the future path of his children, but instead to give them courage and strength through love and trust once they have made their own choice. My father said that he spotted my talent as a pianist when I was four years old. He saw how I had the ear to play any kind of music I heard on the television or audio media, and started giving me private lessons in earnest from when I was six years old. Thereafter, I studied at the Yewon School in Seoul and the Juilliard School of Music in New York, and henceforth have travelled along the path of music.

Among an array of reviews, a critic for the *St. Louis Post Dispatch* (1994) wrote: "The St. Louis Symphony's featured artist was Hae-jung Kim, a Korean-born, American-trained pianist who is new to the scene but who is surely destined for a brilliant future. Her phrasing was dramatic and her range of tone-colours seemed enormous. Like every note that rang from the orchestra, every note she played fit beautifully into an exquisite pattern, even the spaces between the notes spoke with rare eloquence." A piece in *The Age* (Melbourne, Australia) titled "*Cleansed and enthralled by sounds of Beethoven*" (August 1990) had praised Hae-jung Kim who "gave a very lovely account of this concerto (Beethoven Piano Concerto No. 1), finished when Beethoven was 28." According to the *News Record* (Greensboro, NC), "Intermission was followed by a virtually flawless performance of Mendelssohn's Piano Concerto No.1 in G minor and it is easy to see how she has so quickly established an active international career at such an early age. Her playing was filled with energy and bravura in the outer movements and in the more expressive passages of the opening Allegro. The audience received her with enormous enthusiasm, which was altogether appropriate for so polished a performance." The *Morgenpost* wrote: "With the entry of the green-clad beauty from Korea, the evening's sensations began. Hae-jung Kim mastered the most famous of all piano concerto solo parts (Tchaikovsky Piano Concerto No. 1) with a virtuosity which united phenomenal power, elegance and sensitivity. Her playing blended so beautifully with the orchestra that this all-time favourite blossomed with delighted freshness, simply carrying the audience along with it."

In April 2007, momentum in Korea was gathering behind the campaign for a restoration of Kim Un-yong's status and a presidential pardon. The publication *Taekwondo Shinmun* carried a piece titled 'Vigorous Demands for Pardon and Restoration of Rights for Kim Un-yong.' It read, 'Kukkiwon plans to submit some seven thousand petitions to the government this month. Public opinion that the WTF founder and former president Kim Un-yong should be pardoned and his rights restored for the sake of furthering national interests in the international sports stage as well as restoring his damaged reputation at an individual level is recently spreading throughout the entire taekwondo world.... Supporters have made efforts from many angles in order that he may be pardoned. However, they have been continually frustrated, as Dr. Kim has been excluded from the special pardonees' list at every available opportunity. In February 2007, even on the occasion of the fourth anniversary of President Roh Moo-hyun's inauguration, the Blue House resolutely carried out special pardons but excluded Kim Un-yong from the final list. As the circumstances developed, former WTF president's supporters were outraged, especially when former Doosan chairman Park Yong-sung was allowed actively to return and recover his IOC Member status by being pardoned following convictions on embezzlement, false accounting and other criminal charges. General public opinion has also started growing. People have pointed to the inequalities relating to pardon and restoration of rights... Lee Geun-chang, Kukkiwon's chief of Project Co-ordination, revealed in April that we will be submitting to the government petitions signed by over 7,000 persons, including not only more than one thousand overseas Korean coaches but also city and provincial taekwondo officers and frontline practitioners.'

Finally the day and the document arrived – on 12 August 2008, midway through Beijing's Olympic Games:

Minister of Justice Certificate of Pardon/ Reinstatement of Rights: Kim Un-yong. National ID: 310319-1047616. Name of crime: Act on the Aggravated Punishment etc. of Specific Economic Crimes (Embezzlement). Sentence: Two years imprisonment. In respect of the above person, this Certificate of Pardon/ Reinstatement of Rights is issued in accordance with the Presidential Order under the provisions of the Pardon Act, Title 5, Article 1, Clause 5.

Seoul Yeongdeungpo-gu Police. Criminal Records Check Report. To Kim Un-yong. Re. Criminal Records Check Report. Subject of Search: Kim Un-yong, criminal records, verification of contents. Result of search: No applicable record.

The announcement arrived on National Liberation Day: a pardon and reinstatement from newly inaugurated President Lee Myung-bak. Congratulations poured in from around the world, and Kim Un-yong received an immediate congratulatory visit from Samaranch, who was likewise attending China's Olympic Games. 'I heard the good news and came to see you,' said Samaranch, somewhat lamely adding, 'I'm so sorry the IOC did not use its influence at the time because it was a political case.'

Recovery from imprisonment was itself a tortuous process, as Kim Un-yong recalled:

'After being released in 2005, I arrived home a free man, yet relieved of all my positions and responsibilities. First order of business was to restore my damaged health. Since my younger days, I had practised sports, including running, sumo wrestling, karate and taekwondo. I had been skilled enough to compete as a representative player and was still confident in my strength. It was this basic fitness that had allowed me to travel around the world as an IOC Member and president of five institutions and member of various committees. Yet after walking away from all this, confined in prison, my body and spirit were in tatters. I needed to see various doctors: of ophthalmology, cardiology, orthopaedic surgery, urology and dentistry. For over seventy years I had never been hospitalised; now, all at once, these conditions had caught up with me.

'Normally in cases like this, I would have travelled to the US to get my mind and body in order. Now I decided instead to go to neighbouring Japan, specifically as a visiting professor at Keio University, a sister institution of my alma mater Yonsei. Keio provided all amenities, including a small apartment and research office. For the first time in ages, I had time to sit back and read. I met the university president Yuichiro Anzai, who expressed that it was an honour to have a former IOC vice-president at the school. I considered that my time at Keio would

Reunion with past advocates, IOC honorary president Juan Antonio Samaranch (centre) and ANOC president Mario Vasquez Rana, at the Beijing Olympics 2008, celebrating Kim's Korean Presidential Pardon

CHAPTER 8

be a good opportunity to study how Japan had achieved its modernisation, how it developed into an economic power in the wake of World War II defeat, and what kind of relationship South Korea should now form with its close yet all-too-distant neighbour.'

'I was in Beijing for the Olympics when I received the news of my special reinstatement with the pardon from President Lee Myung-bak. Congratulatory messages arrived from Yoido Full Gospel Church pastor David Yonggi Cho, Korean Women's Basketball League president Kim Won-gil, Hannara Party policy chairman Yim Tae-hee, and many overseas taekwondo masters.'

Some leopards' spots remained unchanged, as Karl-Heinz Huba's *Sport Intern* reported:

Just how stubborn and inflexible the IOC President is was demonstrated once again in December within the context of SportAccord's gathering in Seoul. As the Korean Olympic Committee invited its former president, Dr. Kim Un-yong, not only to its own reception but also to the traditional dinner of ACNO (Association of NOCs), Dr. Rogge did everything in his power to prevent Kim's presence. ACNO President Mario Vazquez Rana made himself the bailiff of the IOC President, and sent two messages to Kim with the recommendation that 'in view of the cool relations between the two of them', it would be better that he did not attend the two functions. Kim adopted a diplomatic approach and complied with the wish, in the interest of a return to normal relations with the Korean sports leadership. There, they have accepted in the meantime that the former IOC Vice-president, humiliated by the IOC leadership, could be useful on an international level. Kim maintained his distance from the events, but did not fail to take the opportunity to invite some of his former IOC colleagues to a private dinner. Among his guests were Ser Miang Ng from Singapore and former Member

Paul Henderson, past president of the World Sailing. Francoise Zweifel, former IOC Secretary-General, was also present.

Although Pyeongchang would succeed with a third bid in 2011 for the Winter Games of 2018 – at the expense of supposed favourite Munich-Garmisch – the effects of the loss of Kim Un-yong's international influence on Korean sport would take years to become fully apparent. Entitling himself 'IOC Vice-president (Retired)' in his correspondence, he remained on the touchline, an esteemed figure and point of reference for IOC colleagues and anyone seeking advice. Yet Korean international *presence* remained transparently diminished, even if Chung Mong-joon, the prominent Hyundai industrialist, was a significant figure in FIFA. (The author was once more a 'silent' consultant for South Korea's bid in 2010 for World Cups 2018 and 2022.) The expectation of each successive Olympic Games was becoming more and more demanding in economic, diplomatic and technical terms. In the twelve years of Rogge's presidency, the IOC did little more than mark time, blinkered from foretelling the future during an era when Kim Un-yong's wisdom might have been formative. In his *The Greatest Olympics*, Kim had reflected:

Although I understood the strong will and desire on the part of Olympic family members to do their best for participating delegations, I thought the demands of the Olympic family were becoming bigger and bigger and, for 1988, were almost beyond the capabilities of our Olympic Organising Committee. That is the price of success. I instructed all of my bureaus to do their best concerning four principles: according to the Olympic Charter, on past precedent, on our capabilities and on our willpower. 'Do your best according to these four principles, but never do anything beyond them if anybody threatens,' I told my committee. 'When we are asked for help, we just do our best.' If anybody threatened us, we would not do more than whatever was prescribed in the

Charter. I was concerned with demands growing beyond the Charter obligations, or at the whim of some individuals concerned about future Games. Prior to important political changes in Eastern Europe, the Seoul Games were the last integral participation of the Soviet Union and the German Democratic Republic in the Olympic Games, and the medal distribution at the top was extremely close: USSR 132, GDR 102, USA 101 and, to the surprise of many, South Korea in fourth place with 33, ahead of West Germany and Hungary.

Before and after his vengeful imprisonment, Kim Un-yong was ever at anyone's call or assistance from anywhere on any continent. Witness a letter from African IOC Member Youssoupha Ndiaye, minister of sport from Senegal, shortly after the 2003 Session in Prague which had triggered Kim's catastrophe:

Dear friend, I am glad to renew my warm and friendly congratulations for your election as Vice-president of the IOC. This election is highly deserved. You have worked a lot for development of the IOC and promotion of the Olympic Movement. May I urgently ask that you advise me if it is possible to find in Korea a provider of the electronic notice-board for a football stadium. I would like to provide the major venue in Senegal, the Leopold Sedar Senghor stadium, with a high-tech electronic board with video images. If this is available, please do tell me the cost. Always in our field of cooperation, may I also ask you whether it is possible to provide Senegal a modern room for our young sportsmen practising taekwondo and other indoor events. I know I can rely on your kind comprehension. Best regards dear friend, Youssoupha.

If Kim Un-yong was denied power in his eighth decade – what might he have done in his seventh as IOC President? – moments of lingering honour still arrived. In November 2015, KSOC president Kim Jung-haeng presented a plaque from the Sports Hero Hall of Fame, which proclaimed, 'Despite difficult and challenging circumstances, with deep devotion you have contributed greatly to the development of our country's sports through your exceptional leadership in the international sports and taekwondo fields. Accordingly, upholding the united wishes of sports men and women, we have elected you as a Sports Hero of the Republic of Korea for its Hall of Fame, and hereby dedicate this plaque to you.'

By the time of his 86th birthday, Kim Un-yong was sadly contemplating a decline in South Korea's international sporting status, its prestige in Asia surrendered to prime rivals Japan and China in the respective wrestling, badminton and judo world championships of 2017; in the last, it had failed to win a single gold, compared with Japan's seven. Worse was the probability of being out-performed at Tokyo 2020 – as at Rio 2016, with a medal count of 9-3-9 against Japan's 12-8-21. Furthermore, Ser Miang Ng observed, 'Karate being included at Tokyo could be a threat against taekwondo in 2024/ 2028 – a serious question.' John Boulter identifies the arithmetic of election-voting influence which Pyeongchang had lacked in 2011 (Lee Kun-hee having resigned), yet had benefitted tangentially from the support of OCA President Sheikh Ahmed.... whose backing Europe's Thomas Bach would need in his election campaign two years later. 'Yes, Bach publicly backed Munich,' Boulter recalled. 'But what did Sheikh Ahmed want? Every IOC President is jockeying with different seats of power. Bach had his game to play; he needed the allegiance of Asian power. Could he have had in mind the North/ South Korean collaboration? In 2011, he prospectively required the personal backing of Ahmad in 2013.'

But for his cruel judicial incarceration, Kim Un-yong's ninth decade would have seen him occupying advisory roles as *eminence grise*, and this he nonetheless now was: consultant for Incheon's 2014 Asian Games and the Gwangju Universiade of 2015; lifetime honorary president of the Korean Taekwondo Association and Kukkiwon; advisor to the Korean Sports Council; and honouree in Yonsei University's naming of its Sports Science Complex, 'Kim Un-yong Hall'. A permanent enshrinement of his cultural contribution to the nation came with his 2016 founding of the Kimunyong Sport Committee (KUYSC), with its inaugural 2017 Kimunyong Cup International Open Taekwondo Championships on 28 October-1 November 2017 attended by 3,000 global athletes and officials. By way of welcoming this celebration, Kim wrote:

> I have dedicated the last forty years of my life to the Olympic Movement, to Korean sports development and to taekwondo, in my capacity as IOC Vice-president, KOC president and founding president of Kukkiwon and the World Taekwondo Federation. After military service during the Korean War, I served in Washington, London, and with the UN as a diplomat. Through the use of sports diplomacy, I global-

With wife Dong-sook, daughter Hae-jung and son-in-law Oh Chang-hee at the ceremony launching the Kimunyong Sport Committee, November 2016. Hae-jung's musical talent was a lost jewel

ised the Korean martial arts sport taekwondo in record time and made it an Olympic Sport at the IOC Congress in 1994.... The Kimunyong Sport Committee (KUYSC) will work to promote the Olympic Movement, to support Korean sports and diplomacy and the globalisation of taekwondo. KUYSC will organise a leadership training programme and international seminars to meet new global challenges.... We will continue to organise the Grand Women's Sport Awards, held since the 1988 Games, to foster outstanding sportswomen. We will do our best to support all Korean sports to move another step forward with new vision.

In a lifetime in sport, the author has been moved by many scenes; among these will remain memories from Seoul in 2017, including children barely in their teens sharing mixed-gender bouts of exceptional action, the girls often emerging as the winners. This truly is an ideal educational sport. As Kim once astutely observed, 'The reason that our today is possible is due to the existence of our past.'

Poignantly for his exceptional yet latterly scarred life, Kim Un-yong died two weeks prior to the tournament's opening. Of the many obituaries, none was more sensitive than that of Mike Weisbart from the *Korea Times*:

Dr. Kim was Korea's leading light in the world of sports diplomacy. For four decades starting in the Seventies you would be hard pressed to find a national-level sports administrator anywhere from around the globe who did not know him personally. Amazingly, he was still working into his eighties: still organising, still making his rounds, networking internationally and advising, helping Korea in his own quiet way as it prepares for the Olympic Games next year. It was inordinately sad that he was not with us this past weekend as the curtain rose on the inaugural taekwondo tournament bearing his name. I spoke with him a few months ago and his voice was buzzing with excitement about the cup, a creation he brought to life at a time when it is harder than ever to raise funds for amateur sports.

His spirit was with us, and you could see it in the eyes of the young athletes warming up for the competition outside the stadium under a bright autumn sky. This is what he did throughout his life: bringing people from around the world together in the spirit of sports and peaceful competition. And he did it so well. The opening ceremony hit all the right Olympic notes, from the beautiful opening performance by the Hanyang University dancers and musicians to the grand entry of athletes behind their countries' flags. Singapore's IOC Member Ser Miang Ng summed up: 'While we grieve after Kim's loss, we must celebrate his life and his many contributions to society, to his country, and to the world.' Equally sad is that he will not be with us in a hundred days when the flame is finally lit in Pyeongchang. He surely would have taken a place of honour because, it can be said with no exaggeration, no one did more than Dr. Kim to bring the 1988 Seoul Games to fruition or to advance the cause of taekwondo, both as a national sport and an Olympic discipline. It was Dr. Kim who, in 1974, rolled the dice on a bid for the 1978 world shooting championships. Korea defeated heavily favoured Mexico for its first opportunity to play host for an international event. It was Dr. Kim who, in 1981, drove the efforts behind the winning bid for the 1988 Olympics, stealing what was supposed to be a sure thing for Nagoya. This was no mean feat. Remember, Korea was still economically in the dark, did not have diplomatic relations with half of the UN – not to mention Olympic boycotts being traded between the democratic world and the Soviet sphere. Korea managed something incredible, putting on an amazing Olympics: the largest, most technically advanced Games to date, that placed Seoul on the map and truly made this great country proud.

Dr. Kim poured heart and soul into his work, all of it done on behalf of this great country. Let's remember this national hero and use his legacy of achievements to inspire others to follow in his footsteps.

Kim Un-yong's reach had long encompassed the sporting globe, as related by Dr. Ken Min, Professor Emeritus of Physical Education and Director of International Martial Arts Research at the University of California, Berkeley, USA:

Dr. Kim was an internationally respected leader who focused the world's attention on Asia, especially Korea's culture and economy. His brilliant accomplishment as the president of WTF spearheaded the development of taekwondo as an Olympic sport. WTF was organised in 1973, became an Olympic sport within 23 years in 1996 following demonstration programmes in the Seoul and Barcelona Games. This was progress unparalleled to any other amateur sports movement in the world. He was the motivator for Asian amateur sports leaders, in an environment of Western dominance in the Olympic Movement.... It is an honour to document my professional association with Dr. Kim, a diligent individual whose goal was to advance Korea as an important and viable nation in the Olympic Movement. I met him through the first WTF championship in 1973, when I participated as US team manager. We worked closely to solidify taekwondo as a US Amateur Athletic Union official sport. I initiated contact with him, on behalf of the AAU president, to organise an official visit to Korea as part of our effort to create an affiliation between the two countries through taekwondo and other sports.... I was fortunate to serve under Dr. Kim's initiative and leadership as national chairman of the newly formed AAU taekwondo committee, and during this time we organised the third WTF championships, after the first two in Korea. He was so dedicated to making our event a success that he visited just about all of the fifty States in America, to which I accompanied him... With Dr. Kim,

I visited the USA representative of PASO (the Pan American Sports Organisation), an influential but anti-taekwondo and pro-karate individual who happened to be a law school professor in San Francisco. Dr. Kim decided we should convince him, with patience and persistence, of taekwondo's value to the Pan Am Games – with PASO finally recognising the sport on their official programme.... Inspiring dedication and commitment, the pinnacle of Dr. Kim's success was the acceptance of taekwondo on the Olympic Programme at the centennial Congress in 1994, where I was privileged to speak on Sports and Politics as a representative of WTF. It is a pleasure to write on Dr. Kim's career in this memorial of an heroic figure.

No truer devotion can exist than that between parent and child, and a perfect relationship shines through in this paean of love from daughter Helen in her foreword to a biography of her father published by the Kukkiwon Research Institute of Taekwondo:

Despite many adversities and even political persecution that must have tested his will and commitment to the limit, my father held steadfast and true to his beliefs. When his dream of a diplomatic career was interrupted, he channelled his skills and talents into diplomacy through sport, and achieved miracles of creating many things out of nothing for Korea and Korean sports over the next fifty years. A great man. To me personally, however, he was truly the best father a girl could ever wish for in every respect, and my absolute best friend. What I miss most about him is his gentle kindness, self-deprecating sense of humour, generosity of spirit and absolute trustworthiness. He believed that girls as well as boys should be encouraged to pursue their dreams, and was unsparing in his support for my desire and efforts to gain the education and training for a career in international law. Despite his demanding schedule involving constant world travel, he took a close interest in my life in the UK, and delighted in opportunities to meet and get to know my friends.... We had the most interesting conversations about the world and how we could make it better. He was deeply caring. Words cannot fully describe what a very interesting and wonderful human being he was.

Raised during the Japanese occupation, 1931–45, he witnessed how bleak life is for an occupied people, and experienced the jubilation of national liberation in 1945. He keenly understood the importance of national independence and was deeply patriotic. He had great hopes for the future, both for himself and his country, when Korea gained independence, and entered the Political Science and Diplomacy department at Yonsei University in 1949. Very early on, his dream had been to become a diplomat. However, that dream had to be put on hold as he joined the army to defend his country when Communist North Korea invaded in 1950. He was twice decorated during the war as a national defence hero. My father very much took after his father, Kim Do-hak, who died young in 1936. It was not easy growing up without a father, and life must have been difficult for his mother, Lee Gyung-yi, at a time when the status of women was very low in Korea and the country was occupied by Japan. I often wondered whether the experience of losing his father helped shape my father's extraordinary sense of responsibility, family values and love and devotion to his family. Much of his life coincided with pivotal periods in the history of Korea: the end of monarchy, the occupation, the Second World War, national liberation, the North-South divide, the Korean War, rapid economic development under President Park Chung-hee, the military government under President Chun Doo-hwan after Park's assassination, and the road to democratisation…

Generosity in time, care and personal finance was the essence of Kim Un-yong's working life, as revealed by former Korean Sports Council secretary-general Bae Soon-hak:

> My first impression of Kim Un-yong was that he seemed rather West-
> ern in bearing, natural and mild-mannered, and that this carried over
> into his working style. Perhaps this had to do with his duties in inter-
> national sport, as IOC Member and president of GAISF and WTF. Yet
> except where they involved major policy decisions, in most domes-
> tic matters he would accept the opinions of working-level staffers and
> work would proceed very smoothly. When we were deciding the HQ
> staff for the Olympics or Asian Games athletic teams, he would rarely
> revise the list of officials and never gave orders. At the same time, he
> also observed the rule that all authority granted came with responsi-
> bility.... Kim Un-yong showed much care and concern for employees,
> especially the lower-ranking ones. As many know, the KSOC president
> is a part-time, honorary position with no pay, his only compensation
> a monthly allowance for external activity. This was far from enough to
> cover meetings and dinners with members of around sixty sports asso-
> ciations. Yet in the more than nine years that he served as the longest
> president in KSOC history, Dr. Kim never spent a penny of his month-
> ly allowance, saving it to donate to the union at the end of the year to
> be shared among the non-management employees.
>
> Whenever he visited the Korea National Traning Centre in Taer-
> eung, he would stop at the cafeteria to visit the kitchen and offer words
> of encouragement and financial gifts to the staff, saying, 'It's thanks to
> your care that our national athletes achieve such good results interna-
> tionally.' To the employees he was the greatest of presidents. Dr. Kim
> also returned the entire subsidy of 100 million won per year given by
> the government to Korean IOC Members.... Another achievement was
> the opening in 2000 of a sports museum, possibly inspired by his expe-
> rience in joining forces with Juan Antonio Samaranch to open an IOC
> museum in 1994 for the IOC's 100th anniversary. For the Korean mu-

seum, Dr. Kim raised seven million dollars. At the time of its opening, I retired as general-secretary and became the museum's director. Sadly, it would be closed down eventually for financial interests, and its contents would be banished to a corner of the Taereung Skating Centre.

To succeed Kim Un-yong as president of WTF was to try to occupy the boots of an elephant. Choue Chung-won is one who tried. He was fulsome in his tribute on Dr. Kim's passing:

All my efforts for taekwondo are based on the solid foundation of Dr. Kim's earlier achievements. He was the founding father of Olympic taekwondo. Everyone in global taekwondo today benefits from the structures he created; every taekwondo player today who dreams of Olympic glory owes Dr. Kim a debt of gratitude. I know all members of our world family join me in expressing condolences to Dr. Kim's wife and children. His passing was a sad day for our world family, but while the man has departed, his legacy lives on.

This was echoed at a memorial service on the first anniversary of Kim Un-yong's passing by Choi Chang-shin, president of the Korean Taekwondo Association:

Kim Un-yong is the man who took on the task of laying the stepping stones that have enabled taekwondo to take a great leap in the world and widely spread its wings. We owe him a debt of gratitude for raising the stature of the sport in the international world and for his landmark achievement in creating great things out of nothing.

On the occasion of the second Kimunyong Cup International Open International Taekwondo Championships on 11–15 August 2018, the author interviewed Lee Kee-heung, president of KSOC, who was mag-

Lee Kee-heung, Korean Sport & Olympic Committee president, pays extensive tribute to Kim Un-yong's transformation of Korea's modern history

nanimous in his memory of Korea's sporting icon:

> As a representative of sports in Korea, Dr. Kim is remembered for his unique affinity with others and his networking skills, which greatly enhanced the diplomatic status of Korean sport. In particular, his efforts and dedication to globalise the sport of taekwondo, both at home and abroad, in a difficult environment will be remembered for ever. He was known for being an international sports leader who focused on cooperation and harmony rather than through confrontation, had a great passion to develop sports in Korea and did his best to achieve his dreams and goals till the very end. During the Opening Ceremony of Sydney's Olympic Games, he showed the world how world peace could be promoted through Olympic values and ideals when South and North Korea marched together as one. The hosting of the Seoul Olympic Games had been a challenge for Korea to make its entrance into the international community. During the bidding process, Korea faced a financial crisis, with fears that the bid might be cancelled – but eventually we became the host country with Dr. Kim's persistence, staging the safest and largest Games thus far in Olympic history, free of terrorist

Lee Si-jong, World Martial Arts president and Chungcheongbuk-do governor, acclaims Kim Un-yong as "Prince of Sport"

attacks and with anticipation of all countries from both Eastern and Western Blocs. The Eastern Bloc was shocked to see the progress of Korea when aired on television – the Games representing a turning point in establishing Korea's presence in the international world.

Prior to the Seoul Games, the key words related to the image of Korea were 'war, starvation and poverty', but the Games transformed the image of Korea, providing a great opportunity to enhance our international diplomatic capability. Following the Seoul Games, Dr. Kim contributed greatly to the diplomatic efforts of Korea in the international arena, especially in diplomatic relations with Poland, Hungary, what was then Czechoslovakia and other Eastern European countries. When Dr. Kim became an IOC Member in 1987, he specifically learnt the Russian language in order to negotiate with the Soviet Union's IOC Members, more effectively creating a good impression to persuade them to participate. Had Dr. Kim been elected as IOC President in 2001, being the first Asian to contend for the position, I believe he would have helped Asian sports to rise to world-class standards. I also think that he would have tried to make the NOCs and regional federations in the continents of Asia and Africa more harmonious and as strong as the European continent's within the IOC.

In the first bid by Pyeongchang for the Winter Games, the citizens of Korea had a strong desire to become hosts, and it was regrettable that the Pyeongchang bidding committee and the media created a negative image (regarding Dr. Kim) on the issue of defeat. Dr. Kim was an outstanding leader who accomplished many remarkable goals, holding a strong influence among fellow IOC Members. Had he remained IOC Vice-president after being elected in 2003, I think that Korean sport could have achieved much more. The absence now of the networks and sports diplomacy in international sports which he had acquired over the past thirty years is indeed regrettable. Dr. Kim contributed greatly to the globalisation of taekwondo during a difficult era, managing to make it an official Olympic sport. I believe that the taekwondo family,

IOC Vice-president and WTF president Kim Un-yong with IOC President Samaranch awaiting a taekwon-do medal ceremony, the first time as Olympic event, Sydney 2000

being aware of his achievements, will take into serious consideration a variety of ways to honour him posthumously in the near future.

The contemporary taekwondo arena has no finer exponent and advocate than middle-aged parliamentary member Lee Dong-sup, ninth *dan* exponent and initiator of the 300-member National Assembly club, which boasts its own in-house gymnasium. Lee is a demonstrative symbol of excellence bearing Kim Un-yong's banner of commitment. His tribute to the WTF founder is heartfelt:

> Kim Un-yong was a hero to sport; he had a gift from God. Taekwondo is an Olympic worldwide sport because he made it so. He developed and unified the sport; following the Seoul Olympic Games, South Korea could diplomatically be an advanced country. No one other than Dr. Kim, with his six foreign languages, could have achieved this. Had Dr. Kim become the first Asian President of the IOC in 2001, with his experience in the military, in diplomatic service and as aide at the Blue House during the Cold War era, he could have led Korean sport everywhere in the world. A genuine hero.

Taekwondo is just one of a prolific array of martial arts, most particularly across Asia. The president of the World Martial Arts Commission (WMC) is Lee Si-jong, also governor of Chungcheongbuk-do. He elaborately identifies the debt owed to Kim Un-yong – in Korea, in Asia and globally. Speaking with the author prior to the second Kimunyong Cup Open International Taekwondo Championships in August 2018, Mr. Lee reflected:

> Kim Un-yong could be termed 'the President of Sports'. He unified the world of taekwondo; nobody is able to live up to his name in Korea. He was an icon of dialogue – you could detect that at his funeral; he cannot

be omitted from history. With his presidency of GAISF, their collaboration was inseparable from our development strategy. In WMC, he recognised the educational need for discipline among young people, for the moral elements of mind and body. For expansion in Africa and Latin America, our main path remains through GAISF; the system is already in place. For continental global development, we need internationally celebrated performers, and that is why I campaign with prominent sports leaders at major multiple events such as the Asian Games.

An objective of this biography has been to attempt to portray the extraordinary breadth of contribution to Korean and world sport by Kim Un-yong, someone who is genuinely recognised internationally. Yet the imposed diminution, illogical and illegal, from two sources had caused intolerable pain to an entire family. It would be the ultimate recompense for Dr. Kim, and especially for his ailing widow, were the IOC to initiate a retraction of past symbiotic allegations and penalties and posthumously reinstate his Honorary Membership, erasing the forced resignation of 2005. This would grant historic honour upon an Olympic administrative icon. I believe that Thomas Bach, the current IOC President, is such a man of integrity, repeatedly having recognised Kim Un-yong's rare personal status, as in his gesture at Sydney's Olympic Games of 2000.

Kim Young-ho, a talented fencer in foil, had reached the final with a string of victories. His German opponent now was the favourite for the gold medal, and Thomas Bach had been pre-assigned to present the medals. Bach and Kim Un-yong were seated side by side to watch the contest. Bach spontaneously told Kim Un-yong, 'I'll make the presentation if our man wins, but if it's your South Korean, I'll pass the honour to you.' Kim Un-yong asked whether such an alternative protocol was in order; Bach confirmed it. Kim privately wondered whether Bach was in fact confident of a German victory, yet when Kim Young-ho took his chance, the podium staged a prized South Korean duet of two Olympic heroes. Bach's gesture epitomised de Coubertin's ineradicable Olympic ethic. Upon Kim Un-yong's death in 2017, Bach's consideration was echoed with his immediate letter: 'Dear family of Dr. Kim, It is with great sadness that I learned of the death of Dr. Kim Un-yong,' it read. 'Please accept my most sincere personal condolences. Words cannot be of consolation, especially when his passing happened so suddenly. My thoughts are with you and your family at this difficult time. With deepest sympathy, Thomas Bach.' A warm response from an authoritative leader, reliably entrusted to promote Olympian morale.

While the modern democracy of South Korea was being liberated from colonialism in mid-20th century and developed at astonishing pace to establish its status at the forefront of an at times fragile global equilibrium, it had become a responsibility to observe certain civic institutional principles. One of these is the recognition, establishment and upholding of acknowledged human rights. In the life, and death, of Dr. Kim Unyong, this principle has conspicuously not been observed. A country involved, willingly or unavoidably, in the global political balance of power should be identifiable for its fundamental moral goodwill. The wanton, bureaucratic abuse of an individual national hero, however proportionally insignificant he might be in the passing torrent of international affairs, is an irreconcilable blight upon the national conscience. Dr. Kim deserved, and deserves, better.

This consideration refers, most recently, to the decision by Korea's National Cemetery Management Division (Ministry of Patriots and Veterans' Affairs) to reject Dr. Kim's burial at the National Cemetery. This defies the sense of honour in which Dr. Kim is held not merely by millions of Korean compatriots, but around the globe – by countless sports administrators in dozens of countries who witnessed, over five decades, Dr. Kim's dedicated gifts, emotional and functional, to world and Olympic sport. This due recognition was wretchedly compromised: firstly by unsubstantiated allegations by the IOC of impropriety in the Salt Lake City bidding campaign, and subsequently by the IOC's symbiotic acceptance and constitutionally irregular condemnation for alleged criminal charges and imprisonment by a vengeful Korean judiciary, which had inflicted political reprisals. The time has come posthumously to erase the continuing social denials of an Olympic icon. For this to happen, aspects of his imprisonment in 2004, and the reaction of the IOC Ethics Commission – headed by a Senegalese lawyer who had sought financial advancement for his son through his Olympic connections – need belated acknowledgement in order to emphasise the inconsistency of the National Cemetery's decision.

The provocation for the IOC's symbiotic move to expel Dr. Kim from the IOC in 2005 – or, as already explained, the Blue House leverage on an imprisoned sick man to obtain his 'voluntary resignation' – was that, by the politically driven Korean allegations regarding Dr. Kim's conduct, he had in theory breached IOC ethics. Yet if that were so, why would more than fifty IOC Members and International Federation presidents have expressly protested in defence of Dr. Kim, either to South Korea's president or the chief justice – or to both, as did retired honorary IOC President Samaranch? The protests cited the erroneous 'evidence' that Dr. Kim had 'obstructed' Pyeongchang's Winter Games bid of

Thomas Bach, reforming IOC President, German Olympic fencing champion, heralds a totemic colleague and hero

2003 – whereas its exceptional near-success in a first attempt was almost exclusively due to Dr. Kim's international diplomacy, while its narrow second-round defeat was in no way attributable to his candidacy for re-election as vice-president two days later. Before considering the National Cemetery controversy, aspects of some of the defensive letters and protests over Dr. Kim's post-election imprisonment should be recalled:

Dr. Thomas Bach (IOC, Germany, subsequently elected President in 2013) to a Korean complainant: 'The results of the two IOC elections in Prague were a great success for Korea. The number of votes for Pyeongchang was unexpectedly high and is a great encouragement for future candidatures, and I would like to congratulate Pyeongchang and Korea for this remarkable success. The two elections are not related to each other. I am convinced that IOC Members are looking separately at the election of an Olympic host city and of a Vice-president. This you can also see from the fact that Richard Pound of Canada was running for IOC President at the same Session, in 2001, when Toronto was a candidate for the Olympic Games of 2008.'

Professor Vasily Mikheev (Russian Academy of Sciences, Carnegie Endowment for International Peace, USA) to Hon. Kim Byung-un (Senior Judge, Seoul Central District Court): 'This letter is a final call for justice, democracy and respect to the son of Korea who contributed a lot to strengthening Korean positions in the world.... who is in line with Kim Dae-jung, Nobel Prize winner and former State President. It is difficult to over-estimate Dr. Kim's contribution to the success of the Seoul Olympics and normalisation of Russian-Korean ties.... Under a very difficult situation, Dr. Kim's influence and diplomatic wisdom played a decisive role in pushing Moscow to participate in the Seoul Olympics.... His political activity finally led to the first ever Russia-Korea Summit between Presidents Gorbachev and Roh Tae-woo that put an end to Korea's global isolation during Cold War times.'

Nat Indrapana (IOC, Thailand) to Kim Un-yong: 'I was interviewed by TV in Bangkok in July 2003, the reporter concentrating on the Pyeongchang bid and vice-president election, asking about your personal activities to enhance Pyeongchang's bid. I told him you were daily the first one in the IOC breakfast room to meet fellow Members, to assure them the excellent quality of Pyeongchang's bid, and that I saw and heard you lobbying other IOC Members.... I told the interviewer that the overwhelming support for your Vice-president election manifested that your vision and experience is highly needed by the Executive Board. When asked if you should have withdrawn from the election to aid Pyeongchang, I said that this would have damaged the bid, losing IOC trust and respect for you.'

Don Porter (USA, President of International Softball) to Judge Lee Ho-won (Seoul Court of Appeal): 'Having known and worked with Dr. Kim for over 25 years, I am writing this letter as testimony to his devotion to his country, to his family and to the many millions who wish to have opportunity to play sport around the world. Dr. Kim and I served in the military at the same time, in 1951–52, helping to defend South Korea from the invasion of North Korea.... Post-war years saw Dr. Kim and I sharing the development of sport to bring opportunities to young people all over the world. His creation of the World Games in 1982 brought over sixty-five countries together in sixteen different sports. His involvement is a matter of record, providing not only citizens of South Korea but untold millions elsewhere to have sport as part of their lives – his passion not limited to the Olympics, but to schoolyards worldwide.'

Shunichiro Okano (IOC, Japan) to the Korean judiciary: 'Observing Dr. Kim's accomplishments over many years, I have deep anxiety regarding the fact that, having contributed so much to the Olympic Movement, he has been arrested by Korean prosecutorial authorities.... The success of the Seoul Games was the result of concerted efforts by the Korean people and by Dr. Kim…personally carrying the precious role of communicating the voice of Asia to the world. In his selfless efforts in a wide range of roles, it was due to Dr. Kim that the organisation and competitiveness of National Olympic Committees in Asia were strengthened – that as a result of his efforts, South and North Korean athletes marched together under the flag of the Korean peninsula at Sydney's Olympic Games.... I request the Korean judiciary to exercise maximum indulgence – considering Dr. Kim's key role in representing Asia in the international sports community.'

Francis Nyangweso (IOC, Uganda) to Judge Lee Ho-won (Seoul Court of Appeal above.): 'Kim Un-yong was outstandingly different from sports administrators from Asia – boldly approaching African delegates to support Seoul's bid for the Olympic Games, South Korea having approached many problems diplomatically for the UN during the Cold War. He managed to win the hosting of the most sentimental and humorous Games, which opened up the world. From that time, he brought changes throughout the world and the Olympic Movement, and Africa will remember him in the struggle against Apartheid through his generous contribution to the OlympAfrica Foundation.'

Henry Hsu, OBE (IOC, Taipei) to Hon. Kim Byung-un, Senior Judge, Seoul Central District Court: 'Many of us are astonished by the harsh prison sentence recently imposed on Dr. Kim. Anyone involved in international sport can tell you how he contributed to Korea and Koreans over several decades… His colleagues will vouch for him as an honest, hard-working, kind and generous person… We cannot express how

Hsu Henry (Heng), OBE, late, constitutionally precise Taiwan IOC Member waived a banner for Kim Un-yong's historic fame

deeply it violates our sense of justice to see Dr. Kim persecuted in this manner.'

Dr. Julio Cesar Maglione (IOC, Uruguay) to Kim Un-yong: 'I want to clearly express that the only thing you asked of me, during the enterprises prior to the election of the candidate city for the 2010 Winter Games, was to vote for Pyeongchang – never to vote for you. I know that this same thing you asked of many friends of mine in the IOC. I am sympathetic for you as someone who really loves his country.'

Jean-Claude Killy (IOC, France, triple gold medallist) to Kim Un-yong: 'Your candidacy to the IOC Executive Board had, in my opinion, no negative effect on the voting for the 2010 Winter Games. The result for Pyeongchang (in defeat) is terrific, and I hope this city will come back and try again.'

Kevan Gosper (IOC, Australia) to Kim Un-yong: 'Re. the false allegations that Pyeongchang's bid failure was linked with your Vice-presidency success: This is entirely untrue; these are separate and unrelated issues. On many occasions you spoke positively about Pyeongchang's bid, and it is disappointing that people forget your contribution to the advancement of sport in your country, throughout the Asian region and internationally.'

Ivan Dibos (IOC, Peru) to Dr. Kim Un-yong: 'Congratulations on your election as Vice-president. With your knowledge, capacity, wisdom and other attributes, you will benefit the Olympic Movement. Those believing your candidature damaged the possibilities for Pyeong-chang should have thought instead that the high number of votes they achieved was due to the fact that IOC Members recognise you as some-one valuable for IOC organisation and for the Olympic Movement. Pyeongchang should be proud of the high level of voting they achieved, as Korea is not known widely for winter sports.... Talking to the Korean Ambassador, he agreed that Pyeongchang's voting was recognition of the support given to you as IOC Member, and Pyeongchang should be proud of its success."

Phillip Coles (IOC, Australia) to Kim Un-yong: 'The accusations against you are ridiculous, when it was clear you were lobbying your IOC colleagues to support Pyeongchang. Many IOC Members believe Pyeongchang received so many votes due to your influence. I am sad-dened your countrymen do not appreciate the respect and friendship which you have in the IOC, and this attack on your integrity will not be well received by your colleagues.'

In the wake of Dr. Kim's belated and absolute presidential pardon and reinstatement in 2008 – which included total statutory erasure of his police criminal conviction – and his continuing invaluable advice and diplomatic service to international projects over the next nine years, it could be supposed his monumental status was now without blemish. But no: iniquity still lurked. A hero's grave was apparently barred to him.

According to the Policy Division chief Kang Min-seon, the adherence to regulations by the National Cemetery Management Division/ Ministry of Patriots and Veterans' Affairs would purportedly be in breach of their own constitution, viz. Article 5-4-3 of the Act on the Establishment and Management of National Cemeteries, which excludes acceptance of those convicted under the Act on Aggravated Punishment of Specific Economic Crimes (Embezzlement). Dr. Kim's pardon had conferred a clean slate on a national hero and benefactor. Again, the critical protests flowed:

Ching Kuo Wu (IOC, Taipei) to President Moon Jae-in, February 2018: 'As a young man of nineteen, Dr. Kim Un-yong served as an infantry officer, helping defend his beloved country during the Korean War. In subsequent years of national reconstruction, he served as diplomat in the USA, the United Nations and the United Kingdom, then as first secretary to the Prime Minister and deputy director at the Blue House. He founded Kukkiwon and the World Taekwondo Federation when taekwondo was virtually unknown outside Korea, yet successfully globalised the Korean national sport. As Vice-president of the IOC and president of the Korean Olympic Committee, Dr. Kim was a tremendously effective leader to help to shape the history of modern Korean sports…bringing prestige and honour to Korea…. Moreover, he orchestrated the historical joint march of South and North Korean athletes under the single flag of the Korean peninsula at the Sydney Olympic Games of 2000…. I have recently learned with dismay that he has been denied burial at the National Cemetery by officials on the grounds of the domestic controversy involving the Pyeongchang bid for the Winter Games in 2003. This is most deplorable. Dear President Moon Jae-in, I respectfully request that you recognise Dr. Kim Un-yong's lifelong service and contributions to Korea and grant his burial at the National Cemetery.'

Fumio Ogura (left), director of international relations, Tokyo 2020 organising committee, receiving HRH Sultan Azlan Shah Award, 2018. Ogura seeks honour of Kim Un-yong's delayed National Cemetery burial

Fumio Ogura (Deputy Executive Director, International Relations, 2020 Tokyo Organising Committee) to President Moon Jae-in, February 2018: 'As Vice-president and Executive Board Member of the IOC and president of the Korean Olympic Committee and Korean Sports Council, Dr. Kim Un-yong was an effective leader who helped shape the history of modern Korean sports and was instrumental in successful hosting of the Asian Games 1986, Seoul Olympic Games 1988, Winter Universiade 1997 and Korea-Japan World Cup 2002, bringing prestige and honour to Korea.... He has made enormous contributions to the development of Korea and Korean sports, and for both the male and female athletes who proudly represent Korea. As his colleague in the Olympic Movement and international sport and someone familiar with his achievements, I would have expected that he would be interred at the National Cemetry.... I respectfully request that you recognise Dr. Kim's lifelong service and contributions to Korea and grant his burial at the National Cemetery.'

David Hamilton (General Manager, United Taekwondo Association, Cincinnati, USA) to Kang Min-seon (National Cemetery Management Division, Ministry of Patriots and Veterans' Affairs), August 2018: 'Thank you for your letter of June 2018, in which you state that Dr. Kim was denied interment in the National Cemetery because he was sentenced to two years in prison as set out in the "Act on the Aggravated Punishment" etc. There appears to be a contradiction with the position that you have taken." These indicate that Dr. Kim's criminal record was expunged and that he received a Certificate of Pardon/ Reinstatement of Rights. This was issued in accordance with the Presidential Order under the provisions of the Pardon Act, Title 5, Article 1, Clause 5. If you could provide an explanation based on this information, it would be appreciated.'

Samih Moudallal (IOC, Syria) to President Moon Jae-in, March 2018: 'As international sport leader and IOC Member, it is a duty to highlight how much Dr. Kim Un-yong was important to his nation and to international sprot.... In 1994, Dr. Kim's dedicated efforts over the preceding thirty years brought about the official adoption of taekwondo as an Olympic sport for provisional inclusion in the 2000 Sydney Games, at which he orchestrated the historic joint march of South and North Korean athletes under a single flag. Dr. Kim made enormous contributions to the development of Korea and Korean sports. He spread taekwondo into my country, and I well remember how much he supported us through frequent training programmes arranged in Korea, also sending skilled coaches to furnish many taekwondo arenas throughout Syria.... I have learned with dismay that he has been denied burial at the National Cemetery on the grounds of domestic controversy. I respectfully request that you recognise Dr. Kim's lifelong service and contributions to Korea and grant his burial at the National Cemetery.'

Don Porter (USA, President, International Softball) to Kang Min-seon, April 2018: 'I am aghast at the reason that Dr. Kim was turned down for being interred at the National Cemetery, in the light of his exemplary record over five decades; I note the reason was that Dr. Kim was imprisoned for two years for alleged misappropriation of funds. Most people know that this was a political set-up supported by rivals of Dr. Kim. It would seem that his great service, sacrifice and remarkable accomplishments over many years would be sufficient to overlook a wrongful conviction that was politically motivated. The 37,000 Americans who lost their lives in the Korean War, alongside Dr. Kim and I, would be rising in their graves to protest this unfairness.'

John Coates (IOC, Australia) to Kang Min-seon, May 2018: 'We are well aware that Dr. Kim was unjustly victimised for political purposes when Pyeongchang failed in 2003 in its first bid for the Winter Games. Dr. Kim is a national and international sports hero as well as a decorated veteran of the Korean War. It seems to me that his great service, sacrifice and remarkable accomplishments over many years would be enough to overlook a wrongful conviction that was politically motivated and subsequently annulled.'

Manolo Romero (President, International Sports Broadcasting) to Kang Min-seon, April 2018: 'Dr. Kim was unjustly victimised for political purposes when Pyeongchang failed in 2003 to win its first bid for the Winter Olympics. Dr. Kim is a national and international sports hero as well as a decorated veteran of the Korean War.'

Sakis Pragalos (President, World Taekwondo Europe) to Kang Min-seon, April 2018: 'Thank you for your letter dated March 2018 regarding my letter to President Moon Jae-in appealing for his assistance in connection with the burial of Dr. Kim at the National Cemetery. We are well aware that Dr. Kim was unjustly victimised for political purposes, though a national and international sports hero. It seems to me that his great service and sacrifice over many years would be enough to overlook a wrongful conviction, politically motivated and subsequently annulled.'

It cannot but be hoped that current President Moon Jae-in will be overtaken by conscience, by belated acknowledgement of Dr. Kim Un-yong's incontrovertible status as Olympic icon: a genuine diplomatic statesman who individually conspired to alter the course of South Korean history in 1988 and onwards. He should rightly be granted a hero's burial in hallowed ground. It can be claimed, with justification, that no other emblematic sports leader across the world has made such specific impact on his or her nation's history as Kim Un-yong's creation of the Summer Olympic Games in Seoul – a hitherto anonymous city, reborn out of ashes only forty years before – and succeeded by his globalisation of the national sport of taekwondo within three decades. Hail the Romulus of modern South Korea, his honourable interment at the National Cemetery proclaimed by the undersigned (among countless others from around the world):

Grandmaster Ahn Kyong-won (USA), United Taekwondo Association, Cincinnati OH; Maria Borello, president, Guatemala Taekwondo Federation; Ali Suliman Ali Hussien, secretary-general, Sudanese Taekwondo Federation; Cesar Valentim Rodrigues (Austria), head coach, Wien Taekwondo Centre; Pascoal Nalanquite, secretary-general, Guinea-Bissau Taekwondo Federation; Phivos Christou, president, Cyprus Taekwondo Federation; Angelo Cito, president, Italian Taekwondo Federation; Dr. Narinder Batra, president, International Hockey Federation (FIH); Dr. Rafael Santonja Gómez, president, International Federation of Bodybuilding and

Fitness (IFBB); John Boulter (UK), former Adidas executive; Ollan Cassell (USA), vice-president, International Association of Athletics Federations (IAAF); Yosuke Fujiwara, member of Japanese Olympic Committee (JOC) Executive Board and IOC Radio and Television Commission; Paul Henderson (Canada), past IOC Member and president, World Sailing (ISF); Kirsan Ilyumzhinov, president, World Chess Federation; Nellie Kim (USSR/ Russia), Gymnastics Olympic champion/ vice-president, International Gymnastics Federation (FIG) and World Taekwondo (WT); Dr. Klaus Schormann (Germany), president, International Modern Pentathlon Union (UIPM); Artur Chmielarz, president, Polish Taekwondo Federation; Lee Sang-chul, US Taekwondo Committee (USTC) president; Dr. Ken Min (USA), University of Berkeley, CA; Grandmaster Kim Chan-yong (USA), Oriental Moodo Association, Cerritos, CA; Victor Hugo Morales, president, Ecuador Taekwondo Federation; Pascal Nalanquite, Guinea-Bissau Taekwondo Federation; Kim Byung-il, senior counsel, Kim & Chang Law Firm; Professor Sohee Park (USA), Vanderbilt University, Nashville, TN; Dr. Valery Rukhledev, UN Committee on the Rights of Persons with Disabilities (OHCHR); Grandmaster Steven Shin (USA), Taekwondo Academy, Lynnwood, WA; Olegario Vazquez Rana (Mexico), president, International Shooting Sport Federation (ISSF); Fatima Al-Quaiti (UK), British solicitor; Dr. Mari Watanabe, M.D., PhD (USA), St. Louis, MO; The Hon. Christina Darell-Brown (UK).

An Olympic Life, Kevan Gosper, Allen & Unwin, 2000.

Behind the Olympic Rings, Geoffrey Miller, H O Zimman, US, 1976.

Challenge to the World, Kim Un-yong, Yonsei University Press, 2002 & 2008.

Five Rings over Korea, Richard Pound, Little Brown, 1994.

Future of the Olympic Games, Prof. John Lucas, Human Kinetics, US, 1992.

He Zhenliang – China's Olympic Dream, Liang Lijuan, Foreign Language Press, 2007.

I Say This to Japan, Chung Mong-Joon, Gimm-Young, Korea, 2002.

Inside the Olympics, Richard Pound, Wiley, Canada, 2004.

My Olympic Years, Michael Killanin, Secker & Warburg, 1983.

Official History of the Olympic Games and IOC, David Miller, Mainstream, 2012.

Olympic Factbook, Connors, Dupuis and Morgan, Visible Ink Press, 1992.

Olympic Politics, Christopher Hill, Manchester University Press, 1996.

Olympic Philosophy, Ed. Heather Reid/ Michael Austin, University Press Kent, 2012.

Olympic Revolution, David Miller, Pavilion, 1992.

Olympic Turnaround, Michael Payne, London Business Press, 2005.

Our Sporting Times, David Miller, Pavilion, 1996.

Sixty Olympic Years, Artur Takac, 2004.

The Big Man Who Embraced the World, Chung Tae-hwa, KSOC, 2018.

The Greatest Olympics, Kim Un-yong, YBM Sisayoungosa, 1989.

The Great Olympic Swindle, Andrew Jennings, Simon & Schuster, 2000.

The Olympic Century, Worlds Sports Research, LA, 2000.

The International Olympic Committee – One Hundred Years (Volume 1–3), IOC, 1996.

Thirty Years of the Olympics, Forty Years of Taekwondo, Kim Un-yong, *JoongAng Ilbo,*
    2008-2009.

Whitaker's Olympic Almanack, Stan Greenberg, A & C Black, 2003.

Deford, Frank

DeFrantz, Anita

Demarco, Roland

Dibos, Ivan

Disraeli, Benjamin

Donike, Manfred

Drut, Guy

Dyer, Geoff

E

Easton, James

Ebersol, Dick

Edstrom, Siegfried

Elizalde, Francisco

Ericsson, Gunnar

Essomba, Rene

Essomba, Sonia

Ewald, Manfred

F

Felli, Gilbert

Fifield, Anna

Fouly (General), Ahmed

Frank, Barry

Freeman, Cathy

Fuente. Antonio Garcia

Fujiwara, Yosuke

Fursler, Kurt

G

Gagnon, Marc

Ganga, Jean-Claude

Gilady, Alex

Glen-Haig (Dame), Mary

Gómez (Dr.), Rafael San-
tonja

Gong, Ro-myung

Gosper, Kevan

Griffith Joyner, Florence

H

Haggman, Pirjo

Hamilton, David

Hasan, Bob

Havelange, Joao

Heiberg, Gerhard

Helmick, Robert

Henderson, Paul

Henning, Harold

Henrika, Yushkevitch

Herzog, Maurice

He, Zhenliang

Hill, Christopher

Hinckley, Gordon

Hodler, Marc

Hong, Jae-ik

Hong, Sung-chon

Hsu, Henry

Huba, Karl-Heinz

Hurel, Pierre

Hussien Ali Suliman Ali

Hybl, William (Bill)

Igaya, Chiharu

Ilyumzhinov, Kirsan

Indrapana, Nat

J

Johansson, Lennart

Johnson, David (Davd)

Johnson, Derek

Johnson, Ben

Joklik, Frank

Jones, Roy

K

Kang, Byung-sup

Kang, Min-seon

Kang, Seok-jae

Keita, Lamine

Keller, Thomas (Tommy)

Kerdel, Cornelius Lambert
(Kees)

Khristov, Aleksandar

Kidane, Fekrou

Killanin (Lord), Michel

Killy, Jean-Claude

Kim, Byung-il

Kim, Chan-yong

Kim, Dae-jung

Kim, Do-hak

Kim, Dong-sung

Kim, Hae-jung

Kim, Hak-won

Kim, Hye-soo

Kim, Hyun-woo

Kim, Il-sung

Kim, Jin-sun

Kim, Jin-yong

Kim, Jong-ha

Kim, Jong-il

Kim, Jong-pil

Kim, Jung-haeng

Kim, Jung-heun

Kim, Jung-hoon (John)

Kim, Jung-kil

Kim, Ok-du

Kim, Sam-hoon

Kim, Seong-jo

Kim, Sung-soon

Kim, Taek-su

Kim, Won-gil

Kim, Woo-sik

Kim, Yong-hak

Kim, Yong-sik

Deflected academically from science studies at Cambridge University to sports journalism and thereby embraced by emergent South Korea's sporting impact, David Miller recognised the landmark international diplomacy on Olympic sport of Kim Un-yong, iconic Asian flag-bearer – his story told in this book. As a member of Britain's football training squad for the Melbourne Olympics in 1956, coached by Corinthian legend Norman Creek – though not ultimately making the team – David Miller is a survivor from an era when Olympians were predominantly amateur. Nevertheless, for many elite performers from major spectator sports wealthily funded by huge crowds, such as athletics, football and tennis, this nominally amateur status had long been a covert fiction ultimately regretted by modern Olympics founder Pierre De Coubertin himself. Elite athletes have to train, and someone has to fund the training: parents, schools, universities, governments, National Olympic Committees, sponsors, national lotteries. As the debate on professional athletes reached a crescendo in the Eighties, Miller, by then a Life Member of Corinthian-Casuals FC and formerly a member of Pegasus, the brief shooting star of Oxford and Cambridge that had twice won the Amateur Cup in front of Wembley crowds of 100,000, and a onetime moderate sprinter/hurdler at national championships and javelin thrower for the famed Achilles club, lectured passionately at the International Olympic Academy in the interest of professionalism, though conscious of the current threat of doping.

Over six decades as journalist and author, Miller attended for the *Daily/Sunday Telegraph, Daily Express* and *The Times* of London twenty-four Summer and Winter Olympic Games; fourteen World Cup football finals; fifty-two Wimbledon tournaments; sixty-two FA Cup Finals; and countless world events in Rugby Union, Rugby League, Tour de France, rowing, boxing, skiing, skating, hockey, and anything from snooker to gliding to America's Cup yachting. From 1970, he published four consecutive histories of World Cup football tournaments (including an English edition covering the West Germany World Cup in 1974) and biographies of Matt Busby, Stanley Matthews, Sebastian Coe and Juan Antonio Samaranch (translated into eight languages). Commissioned by Samaranch, he has been compiling the *Official History of the Olympic Games and IOC*, updated every four years and digitally available in 2019 including coverage of the Rio 2016 and PyeongChang 2018 Games – all these in addition to official IOC publications of the individual Games of Seoul, Albertville, Lillehammer, Atlanta and Nagano.

Motivated by sport's fundamental principle of social and cultural integration, by the Olympic microcosm of life's challenges – success, failure, friendship, education, integration, and human rights – Kim Un-yong's ultimate Olympic contribution lay in his concept of global harmony across continents, that the very existence of mankind is a gift to be preserved. Miller's intimacy with Korean sport beckons his acclaim for this traduced Olympic icon: Kim Un-yong, an historic model not just for international harmony but our unified survival on planet earth.

Credits

Publisher	Kim Hyunggeun
Copy Editor	Colin A. Mouat
Proofreader	Anna Bloom
Designer	Lee Chanmi